THF...M

THE DAGENHAM MURDER

The brutal killing of PC George Clark, 1846

LINDA RHODES
LEE SHELDEN
KATHRYN ABNETT

The London Borough of
Barking & Dagenham

www.barking-dagenham.gov.uk

London Borough of Barking and Dagenham
Department of Education, Arts & Libraries

ISBN No. 0 900325 37 2

Designed by Good Impressions
020 8522 0499
www.goodimpressions.co.uk

CONTENTS

BLACK & WHITE ILLUSTRATIONS

COLOUR ILLUSTRATIONS - Between Pages 168 & 169

INTRODUCTION

'Here he lays!'

The two policemen dragged the farmyard pond but without result. They had endured another day of fruitless searching – the fourth – and their thoughts were turning towards a walk back to the station in Dagenham Village and the prospect of a beer or two in the Bull or the Rose and Crown before going on night patrol. It was the year 1846, and one of the hottest summers on record. Evening sunlight slanted across the yard of Thorntons Farm, Rush Green. The men were heaving the drag-pole out of the stagnant water when Elizabeth Page, the farmer's wife, approached and told them of a second, smaller pond nearby. 'My boys will take you to it if you wish', she said. Twelve year-old William and his brother needed no second bidding. They knew what the police were looking for – all the parish had heard the rumours by now – and were naturally in a state of high excitement. The lads bounded along the edge of a potato field, calling to the weary policemen Abia Butfoy and Thomas Kimpton to follow in their tracks. The line of moving figures cast long shadows across the parched and dusty earth of this flat Essex landscape.

Meanwhile, Sergeant William Parsons was combing the neighbouring field together with constables John Farnes and Jonas Stevens. Stevens moved slowly along, turning his aching head from side to side as he bent over the dry ground. The uniform he wore felt increasingly heavy and uncomfortable in the intense heat. Stevens's thoughts kept returning to the missing man, who had shared his lodgings in the police station for the past six weeks. He and George Clark were both just twenty years old.

His colleagues had hoped at first that Clark had gone absent without leave. He came from Bedfordshire, and they knew he was soon to marry a girl who lived near his home village. Was it possible that he might have decided, on the spur of the moment, to pay a visit to his bride-to-be Elizabeth rather than spend all night trudging along the lonely Eastbrookend beat? Yet the other policemen had to admit to themselves that conscientious, reliable Clark would have been the last person to desert his duty, whatever the temptations.

Stevens heard raised voices. 'Yes, that looks like his staff all right', one of the men in the next field was saying. A few moments later the air was ringing with screams from the Page boys. Stevens stood up, hardly able to breathe, his heart gripped with fear. 'Here he lays!' yelled Butfoy. Stevens shakily followed Parsons and Farnes towards the spot. They clambered through a gap in the blackthorn hedge into a cornfield belonging to neighbouring farmer James Parfey Collier. The wheat was high, almost ripe, and swayed gently before them in a shimmering golden haze, embedded with starry jewel-bright cornflowers. As he stumbled along the rough path at the edge of the field, Stevens became aware of a strong, vile smell. Feelings of nausea rose within him. He stopped, hands on his knees, and struggled to take some deep breaths in the thick throbbing air. After a few moments he forced himself to press on towards the scene. The sight that met him there destroyed what was left of his self-control. 'Oh God!' he gasped. The ground seemed to give a lurch, the agitated voices of the others faded away, and he dropped unconscious alongside his room-mate amongst the standing corn.

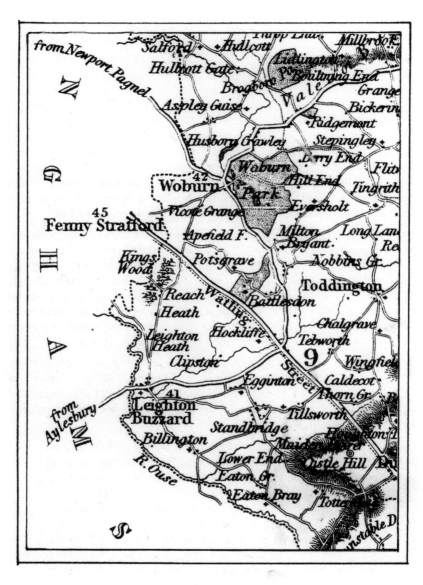

Map of part of Bedfordshire, showing Battlesden and surrounding areas, 1834

CHAPTER 1

'The first duty of a Constable'

George Clark came into the world on 2nd June 1826 in the Bedfordshire village of Battlesden, and was baptized there at the church of St Peter & All Saints on 25th June. He was the first child of James Clark and Charlotte Ashpole, who had married at Battlesden two years previously. George's ancestors on both sides were agricultural labourers. The Clarks were rooted in the nearby village of Milton Bryant, while the Ashpoles hailed from Crafton, a hamlet of Wing in Buckinghamshire. In 1829, when George was three, he was joined by a sister named Mary Ann. Unfortunately, the baby died the following year. This was an era of high infant mortality, but nevertheless a tragedy for the Clark family. When George was six another daughter, Ann, was born. The youngest child, Mary, arrived in 1840.

Battlesden is a small isolated village, about two miles from Woburn and close to the Roman Road of Watling Street, which is now the A5. In 1841 the population of the parish was 179, falling to 160 ten years later. Although small, it was renowned far and wide for its delicious cream cheese. According to the 1847 Kelly's Directory, Battlesden had six farmers, but no tradesmen or shopkeepers of any kind. The largest house, an Elizabethan mansion described by Kelly's as 'a noble seat, commanding a fine view of the surrounding country', was occupied by the Page-Turner family.

The Clarks, on the other hand, had to make do with a two-room cottage. These homes were vividly described by Charles J. Kilby, a native of Battlesden born in the mid-19th century. Kilby began work on the land at the age of eight, not unusual in those days before schooling became compulsory. He tells us that in Battlesden:

> ...there were five groups of cottages, twenty all told in what was known as the village...the men of those cottages were all employed by the farmers and the 'Big House'. The cottages had two rooms, one up and one down. They all had large open fire-places and chimneys up which it was said you could drive a wagon and horses...the rent was a shilling a week...Any man who was dismissed or for reasons of his own left work on the farm, had also to leave the cottage. There was much overcrowding, and to my own knowledge several families of nine children were brought up in these two-roomed cottages.[1]

Baptism of George Clark, 1826 (third entry)

The interior of Battlesden church. Watercolour by George Shepherd, 1819

The Clarks, like most Victorian working-class families, left no letters, diaries, photographs or wills to help us gain an insight into their lives. There isn't even a description of George Clark's appearance. However we can be sure that he, like Charles Kilby, would have received only a very basic education, perhaps at a Sunday school or a Dame School. When the 18 year-old Queen Victoria came to the throne in June 1837, George had recently celebrated his eleventh birthday, and was probably already working alongside his father as an agricultural labourer. The principal Battlesden farmers were George Armstrong and John Welch, and it is likely that James Clark and his son worked for both men at different times. George would have spent long, exhausting days toiling in the fields in all weathers. According to Charles Kilby, the monotony of this labour was relieved once a year by the Harvest Home celebrations. He writes that when the final load of corn was being taken on the cart from the field to the stackyard, the youngest farm boys would ride on top singing:

> Hickley, Hockley, Harvest Home,
> Three plum puddings are better than one.
> We want some beer and can't get none.
> Hickley, Hockley, Harvest Home.

Kilby also describes the scene at the Harvest Home supper. The feast consisted of a boiled round of beef and legs of pork, with beer and plum puddings. The joints were carved by the farmer, with the farmer's wife acting as waitress. We can imagine the farm workers ranged elbow to elbow around the long tables, making the most of this rare feast.

As George approached adulthood, living conditions for families such as the Clarks grew steadily worse. The mid-1840s saw several years of failed potato harvests. There was no absolute famine in England as was occurring in Ireland, but nevertheless people faced much hardship. Newspapers urged readers to turn instead to beetroot. It was claimed to be 'a cheap and salubrious substitute for the now failing and diseased potato…If these roots were as universally cultivated in England for human food as they are on the continent of Europe, and baked and sold as cheap as they might easily be, many a poor person would now have a hearty and good meal who is now often obliged to go without one'.[2]

The other staple food, bread, was also in short supply on the tables of labouring families. Corn Laws were in force to protect the interests of Britain's farmers by levying high taxes on imported grain. This made a loaf of bread extremely expensive. Farm workers were finding it next to impossible to achieve a good standard of living for themselves and their families.

In 1851 Bedfordshire agricultural labourers were only paid eight shillings and eightpence per week, 43p in today's money.[3] Trade unions were illegal, and breach of contract by an employee was a criminal offence. Three Essex farm labourers – William Clark, William Watts and Jonathan Humphrey – were sentenced to six weeks in prison in 1858 for leaving their jobs at Navestock because they were unhappy with the wages of 12 shillings (60p) a week.[4]

Previous generations had been able to supplement their income by grazing animals, gathering fuel and growing food on common land, but this land had now been appropriated and enclosed by the large landowners, leaving labourers absolutely dependent on their meagre wages. It was practically unheard of for a labourer to become a farmer himself. Old Age pensions didn't exist at that time, and the prospect of the Woburn Workhouse loomed for elderly Battlesden villagers without sufficient savings or family support.

It's hardly surprising, then, that George Clark made up his mind to leave the rural poverty of Bedfordshire behind. On Monday 2nd June 1845, his nineteenth birthday, he was enrolled into the ranks of London's Metropolitan Police. His warrant number was 22098. Clark was far from alone in taking this step. In *Labouring life in the Victorian countryside*, Pamela Horn writes that 'many young country workers found the career of policeman an attractive alternative to labouring on the land, and both urban and rural police forces burgeoned in consequence'. Others took work in factories in the Midlands or North of England. Many landowners, including the Duke of Bedford at nearby Woburn Abbey, joined local Poor Law Commissioners and parish vestries in giving financial assistance to farm labourers who wished to emigrate. The most popular destinations were Canada, the United States and Australia.[5]

Another factor may have influenced George's decision to seek better prospects elsewhere. We know that a year later he was on the point of marrying a young lady named Elizabeth How. Perhaps they were already engaged at the time Clark left for London. Elizabeth was the same age as George, and lived in the nearby village of Eversholt. This was a considerably larger place than Battlesden. It had a population of around 900, including a wide range of tradesmen plus Woburn estate employees such as the Duke of Bedford's librarian. Eversholt has a very curious layout. It has many 'ends,' or clusters of houses, but no obvious centre. Elizabeth lived in the area known as Wit's End with her father John How, an agricultural labourer, stepmother Charlotte and several younger half-brothers and sisters. Her own mother, John How's first wife Mary Ann Bowyer, had died when Elizabeth was still an infant. Her father had remarried in 1830.

In response to his initial letter of application around April or May 1845, Clark would have received an invitation to undergo a medical, together with the following sheet headed *Metropolitan Police Qualifications:*

The following qualifications are indispensable, and no Candidate should attend for examination who does not possess them.

1st. To be under 30 years of age.

2nd. To stand clear 5 feet 7 inches, without his shoes.

3rd. To read and write.

4th. To be free from any bodily complaint, of a strong constitution, and generally intelligent, according to the judgement of the Chief Surgeon of the Police, by whom he will be examined.

Furthermore, it was decreed that men would not be enrolled if they had more than three children depending on them for support.

Clark may have travelled to London on the stagecoach which left Leighton Buzzard at seven o'clock every morning. It's more likely, though, that he chose to take the train. The London to Birmingham line had been completed in 1838, and it stopped at Leighton Buzzard. Clark would have arrived at London's Euston Station. On his way out he must have marvelled at Philip Hardwick's magnificent Doric archway, which stood 72 feet (22 metres) tall.

Clark headed for 4 Whitehall Place, a turning off the east side of Whitehall at its northern end. This may have been his first trip to the capital, and we can imagine him arriving early and spending some time exploring nearby Trafalgar Square. Nelson's Column had been erected there just two years before. The whole scene must have been full of interest for a young man from a small and isolated village like Battlesden.

When Clark reached his destination he would have seen a large building straddling two parallel side-streets, Whitehall Place and Great Scotland Yard. The Metropolitan Police Commissioners and their staff occupied the Whitehall Place side, while the Great Scotland Yard or 'Back Hall' entrance led to the headquarters of the A or Whitehall Division.

For sixteen years the two Commissioners, Sir Charles Rowan and Richard Mayne, had worked from Whitehall Place in setting up and supervising the policing of the whole of London except the City, which still to this day has its own police force. The Metropolitan Police had been the brainchild of Sir

A mid-Victorian view of Great Scotland Yard. The lamp on the left is above the original entrance to the headquarters of the Metropolitan Police. After George Clark's day, the police also used the buildings on the right-hand side of the picture

Robert Peel, in his capacity as Home Secretary in 1829, but Rowan and Mayne succeeded in putting the scheme into practice within a short space of time and overseeing every detail of its administration. Rowan, a bachelor, even had a flat above the Whitehall Place offices. The Commissioners were well supported by their Chief Clerk Charles Yardley, together with the Receiver, John Wray, whose job was to look after the financial affairs of the Force. Another vital member of the team was the Chief Surgeon of Police, John Fisher. As we have seen, he carried out a medical examination of every potential new recruit, including Clark.

The next part of the application procedure was quite straightforward. James Grant explained in his *Sketches in London* of 1838 that a candidate

…has only to present a petition to the commissioners, accompanied with a certificate as to good character from two respectable householders in the parish in which he resides…his name is put on the list of eligible candidates for the situation whenever a vacancy shall occur…The average time which an applicant has to wait, after his name has been inserted into the list of persons eligible to the office, is about eight weeks.

Clark offered references from Battlesden farmers George Armstrong and John Welch, plus his cousin William Markham, of Bexley in Kent.[7] His application was accepted, and back home in tiny Battlesden he awaited details of his appointment. When the letter eventually arrived, Clark learned that he had been placed in the K Division in London's East End. At this time the Metropolitan Force was divided into seventeen divisions. Clark was to live at the Divisional Station of K Division at Arbour Square in Stepney.

A police constable was paid three shillings a day, and worked seven days a week. *Provisional Instructions for the different ranks of the Police Force,* a manual written by Rowan and Mayne, stated that each man 'will devote the whole of his time and abilities to the Service' and always appear in uniform even when off-duty. Furthermore, 'A certain number, when so ordered by their Officers, must sleep in their clothes, to be in complete readiness when called on'. An applicant had to be prepared to work a nine-hour shift at night, plus shorter periods during the day.[8] Two-thirds of the entire force was on duty during the night, most of them patrolling alone in streets that were at best dimly-lit and at worst pitch black.[9]

Days off were allowed very rarely. The pay and conditions had been fixed back in 1829 by Robert Peel himself. Clark would have had no complaint, as it was probably three times as much as he was earning as an agricultural labourer. Yet London's skilled manual workers, such as carpenters, earned

An early 20th-century view of Arbour Square Police Station, where Clark spent the first year of his police career

around five shillings a day and enjoyed Sundays off. Some of Peel's colleagues pointed out at the time that he would be deterring good applicants. His friend J.W. Croker told him that 'Three shillings a day for men capable of even reading, to say nothing of understanding and executing the printed instructions seems wholly inadequate...You must by some means or other contrive to improve your scale'.[10] Peel replied that 'No doubt three shillings a day will not give me all the virtues under heaven, but I do not want them'. He claimed rather optimistically that a single man could pay for lodgings, food and other expenses out of a constable's wages and still be able to save ten shillings a week.

Having said goodbye to his parents, sisters, friends and possibly a tearful fiancée, Clark left for the metropolis. No doubt he was in many ways sorry to leave behind the village that had been his only home. But life in 1840s rural England could offer him little, and he now had an opportunity for better things.

Arbour Square police station, together with the neighbouring Thames Police Court, had been purpose-built just a few years before, on land obtained in 1841 on a 61-year lease from the Mercers' Company. It accommodated a large number of men in barrack-type quarters. The 1851 census gives us a good idea of its composition in Clark's day. It records 24 unmarried police officers living there, two of whom were sergeants. Most were in their mid-twenties. They came from far and wide, their birthplaces including Scotland, Ireland, Dorset, Somerset, Suffolk, Sussex, Devon, Norfolk and Berkshire. Clark would have slept with the other single men in a large dormitory on the upper floor. In 1851 there were also two constables with their wives and families in the building's married quarters. The kitchen, the mess room where the meals were served, and the laundry room were all in the basement. The washing facilities were very limited compared with what we are accustomed to in 21st century Britain. There was no hot running water, and the men had only hand-basins to wash in.

Some of them were obviously not too tidy. Commissioner Richard Mayne declared in September 1846 that 'the attention of the Superintendents is particularly directed to prevent the clothing and boots of the constables lying about in the Section Houses – and they will give directions that, after it has been used, it is to be properly cleaned, folded and put away in proper places, and be not left lying dirty, and in a state of disorder in the rooms'.

Clark's police training was meagre compared with that given to today's recruits. Clive Emsley writes:

Most nineteenth-century policemen received such training as they got on the job. The Metropolitan Police was probably the most advanced in the instruction of recruits, but instruction in the mid-nineteenth century lasted for only two weeks, largely concentrated on drill and sword exercise, with two afternoon lectures by a superintendent, and a considerable amount of legal material to learn by rote. Following this, the new constable patrolled with an experienced man for about a week; he was then moved to his division and sent out on his own.[11]

According to the *Official Encyclopaedia of Scotland Yard*, 'candidates were sworn in and attested at the end of their training'.[12] They also received instruction in foot drill at Wellington Barracks.[13] This was necessary because police constables had to line up on parade and be inspected by their Sergeant each time they went on duty. Other aspects of the routine were also of a military nature. Kit and clothing were inspected once a week, for example.

Clark, like other new recruits, was given a copy of the *Provisional Instructions,* and would have spent many hours studying it. The sixty-page manual contained a lot of information to commit to memory. It had been written, as we have seen, by Commissioners Mayne and Rowan in time for the launch of the Metropolitan Police in 1829. It listed the duties of the different ranks of officers – constables, sergeants, inspectors and superintendents – and also gave them a basic working knowledge of the law. Clark would have been reassured to read there that 'Every Police Constable in the Force may hope to rise by activity, intelligence, and good conduct, to the superior stations'. From the outset, there was a policy of promoting from the rank and file. This was in contrast to the Army and Navy, whose officers had to purchase their commissions and thus tended to come from the middle and upper classes.

The manual was backed up by a constant stream of directives from the Commissioners to be cascaded down the ranks. These survive in the Police Orders records at the National Archives, and make fascinating reading. In August 1846, for example, Mayne wrote: 'Complaints having been made to the Commissioners of some of the Police being in the habit of keeping pigs. The Commissioners direct that in future no individual belonging to the Police shall keep any, and those who now have them will take immediate steps to dispose of them'. He doesn't tell us why policemen and porkers made such a bad combination.

Clark's new neighbourhood, Stepney, had been a village within living memory, but the construction of the East India Docks to the east had led to rapid building development. Arbour Square was situated just north of the Commercial Road. The immediate area was highly respectable, and many of its elegant houses can still be seen today.

However, the policemen based there often had to venture into very dangerous districts. Only half a mile (800 metres) from the police station was the infamous Ratcliffe Highway, described by Charles Dickens in *Sketches by Boz* as 'that reservoir of dirt, drunkenness and drabs'. The road ran parallel to the Thames beside docks crowded with shipping and seamen from all corners of the world. Montagu Williams, writing in 1894 but describing Ratcliffe Highway as it had been much earlier in the century, says it was 'the scene of riots, debaucheries, robberies, and all conceivable deeds of darkness...the police themselves seldom ventured there save in twos and threes, and brutal assaults upon them were of frequent occurrence'.[14]   During Clark's time at Stepney, many suspects were hauled before the Thames Police Court accused of violence against the police. For example in July 1845 a seaman named John Davidson attacked a Constable Beale with a knife inside a police station and was eventually disarmed by Sergeant Waller using the flat of his cutlass.

The very name of the Ratcliffe Highway brought to mind a terrifying series of murders back in 1811. Seven people, including a three-month old baby, had been brutally killed in their own homes. The chief suspect, John Williams, hanged himself before he could be put on trial, and was buried with a stake through his heart at the junction of Commercial Road and Cannon Street Road. His skeleton was rediscovered in 1886 by workmen digging a trench for a gas company.

Most likely only experienced officers were despatched to notorious areas such as the Highway. George Clark is said to have been given a beat on the Mile End Road. This was north of Arbour Square, and a pleasant middle-class area. Looking at the 1851 census we can see that its inhabitants included many people of independent means. There were large families with servants and governesses. Other residents included clerks, especially in docks and banks, as well as customs officers, ship brokers, music teachers and commercial travellers. In addition there was a wide range of shopkeepers and tradesmen. That is not to say that Mile End was completely free of danger, however, as one of Clark's colleagues found out in the early hours of the morning of Boxing Day 1845. Constable James Parsons was patrolling Sidney Street, Mile End, when he was beaten unconscious by a glass-works labourer named William Smith.

A group of Metropolitan Police officers in early uniform

Clark would have been given a card with a description of the beat written on it and shown round the route, being introduced to all the prominent householders and tradesmen. Because of the high population density of the area, his beat would not have been a long one. A circuit would only have taken twenty minutes or so, even at the rather slow regulation pace of two and a half miles (4 kilometres) per hour. Clark had to familiarize himself with every detail of the area. As the *Provisional Instructions* manual put it:

> It is indispensably necessary, that he should make himself perfectly acquainted with all the parts of his beat or section, with the streets, thoroughfares, courts and houses. He will be expected to possess such a knowledge of the inhabitants of each house, as will enable him to recognize their persons. He will thus prevent mistakes, and enable himself to render assistance to the inhabitants when called for.

Clark would soon have become a very well-known figure in the area. As we have seen, he donned his uniform seven days a week. He wore a blue serge swallow-tail coat with brass buttons and a badge marked 'Metropolitan Police'.[15] He also had a blue great-coat, with a cape attached. The trousers were blue during the winter months, and there was the option of a white pair in summer which the officer had to pay for himself. Clark would also have worn a leather belt about 4 inches (10cm) wide.

Clark wouldn't have had the police helmet familiar to us today. This wasn't introduced until 1864. His headgear was a tall black top hat, made of beaver with a cane frame. It was topped with leather and strong enough for an officer to stand on if need be. The satirical magazine *Punch* commented in 1844 that 'the hat of the policeman has been compared to a chimney pot, wherefrom, however similar to it in shape and weight, it differs in the important particular of not allowing the heat and exhalations which ascend into it to escape'.[16]

Punch was also amused by the regulation footwear: 'policemen's boots are of two sizes only, the too small and the too large. The latter class are by far the most numerous; so that it is easy to judge a policeman by his foot, which seems about twice as big as anybody else's. These boots, or rather boats, presumably consist of leather, but they look as clumsy, awkward and inflexible, as if they were made of cast iron'.[17]

Adam Hart-Davis describes it as a 'curious uniform,' and goes on to say: 'Because they were servants of the people – after all, the people paid their wages – they wore tailcoats, like servants. But they often had to take control and tell people what to do; so they wore top hats for authority'.[18]

A humorous look at the size of police footwear from the pages of Punch, 1844

From the outset, it was ruled that every officer should be readily identifiable. 'Each man is conspicuously marked with the letter of his Division, and a number, corresponding with his name in the books, so that he can at all times be known to the public.' So on either side of the collar of his coat Clark bore the number K 313, made up of individual metal letters and numbers pushed through the cloth and screwed onto a plate at the back.[19] The high-standing collar itself measured 2 inches (only half the height of the original regulation collar of 1829, but no doubt still uncomfortable.) Underneath the collar Clark wore a leather stock. This was to safeguard him against the much-feared 'garrotters' who attacked their victims from behind and half-strangled them before rifling their pockets.

Clark was issued with a bulls-eye lantern to carry when on night patrol. This was an oil lamp and demanded frequent cleaning. If Clark needed to raise an alarm he didn't blow a whistle. These had been used experimentally earlier in the 1840s, but had not proved successful. Instead, he carried a wooden rattle.

When it was swung by the handle, its tongue revolved against a ratchet and made a loud clacking noise. This will be familiar to soccer fans of a generation ago who used to swing such rattles to encourage their teams from the terraces. By the 1880s whistle technology had improved and the rattle was then phased out.

The rattle could also be used as a weapon, of course, in addition to the two items supplied for this purpose. These were a truncheon (at that time usually referred to as a staff) and a cutlass, or curved sword. The truncheon was about 20 inches (51cm) long and made of a hard, heavy wood such as teak, ebony or lignum vitae. It was carried in a leather case attached to the belt, and was decorated with a painting of a crown, with the letters VR ('Victoria Regina') and MP ('Metropolitan Police'.) The cutlass was only carried by officers on night duty in certain unsafe areas, or when confronting rioters. It was to be used only as a last resort in self-defence. It had a 24-inch (61cm) blade within a black leather scabbard.

As Clark went around his beat his attention was not confined to watching for signs of criminal activity. He also had a number of mundane day-to-day tasks to deal with. One was to note the state of gas lamps and report to the Sergeant 'any that are dirty or extinguished'. Commissioner Rowan had also issued this directive in May 1840: 'Accidents frequently occur by persons stepping on pieces of orange peel carelessly thrown on the foot pavement, the constables on duty will be directed to move any orange peel which they notice there into the carriage way'. They also had to look out for defective drains and check that the footways and watercourses were clean and in good repair. Also, in those days before alarm clocks were widely owned, police were often asked to call people up in the morning. They were told, though, that unlike the old night-watchmen they weren't required to call the hour.

What was the major objective of the so-called New Police? Rowan and Mayne went to great lengths to stress that it was *not* the capture of criminals. 'The first duty of a Constable is always to prevent the commission of a crime'. He was to keep watch on known villains, his presence acting as a deterrent. 'Observing them whenever they are loitering about, and making it known that they are watched, so that they may be prevented committing crime or detected should they make the attempt'.[20]

As an advance on the old network of local lockups, Arbour Square station contained purpose-built cells. The 1851 census reveals a little band of prisoners there, under arrest and waiting to be taken up before the sitting magistrate at the adjacent Thames Police Court. Two were women, Ann Halpin, a 60 year-old servant from Ireland, and Ellen Smith, aged 24, listed as a prostitute from Barking. Three men also languished there that night. Most people held in the cells could blame alcohol for their plight. The *Daily News* commented in March 1846 that 'there is a column in the police-sheet, extending from the top of it to the very bottom, which is invariably full of names. It is headed *Drunk, and incapable of taking care of themselves.* Every morning this particular column is full, and sometimes – like the parties themselves, whose names it records – full to overflowing…'

If pub drinkers became too boisterous, the licensees could also get into trouble. Margaret Robinson, landlady of the Chequers in Dagenham, was prosecuted in 1847 after an instance of 'drunkenness and other disorderly conduct in her house, against the terms of the license'. The drinker causing the disturbance was also a woman.[21]

Clark would have been instructed to keep a special watch on pubs and beer houses. These hotbeds of local gossip were also places where criminals were likely to meet and do deals. Landlords had to abide by strict licensing regulations. They could not open before 4am in summer (6am in winter.) Town pubs had to close at eleven o'clock at night, rural ones an hour earlier. Landlords were frequently brought up before the magistrates for breach of these rules. At the Ilford Petty Sessions of 14th March 1840, for example, the police prosecuted William Wackett, who ran a beer-shop in Chadwell Heath, a hamlet in the northern part of the parish of Dagenham. He was convicted of selling beer outside the licensing hours, and was fined forty shillings (£2) plus costs. As this wasn't his first such offence, he was warned that if it happened again he might be disqualified from selling beer for two years.[22]

Another rule, dating back to 1642, was that no drinking should take place on the Sabbath during the time of divine service. A Dagenham policeman, James West, told the magistrates at the Ilford Petty Sessions that on Sunday 22nd November 1840, at the time of the afternoon service, he had found six people smoking and drinking in the tap room of a beer-house in Marks Gate, an area close to Chadwell Heath. The landlord, Henry Colegate, was fined forty shillings plus costs.

David Taylor writes that 'Peel could have had little doubt but that his new police would be used to bring both order and decorum to the streets of London as well as to fight crime'.[23] This objective is evidenced by a number of regulations which the general public tended to view as petty and unnecessary. For example, the police had to attempt to prevent traders, particularly fruit and fish sellers, from crying out their wares on Sundays. There was also a crackdown on street entertainers such as Punch and Judy men.

Noise pollution was as much a problem in Victorian times as in the present day. The police were advised that 'any one blowing any horn, or using any noisy instrument, in the streets, for the purpose of hawking, selling, or distributing any article whatsoever, may be apprehended'. They also had to stop 'music and other noises in the streets when persons are dangerously ill'.[24]

Police were also instructed to prevent children flying kites near horses, many accidents being caused in those days by horses taking fright and galloping off. Officers were also on the lookout for 'boys trundling hoops in the streets, parks or thoroughfares, where accidents or danger to passengers may be caused'. Today the police are often accused of concentrating on 'soft touch' cases such as minor motoring offences rather than tracking so-called 'real criminals'. The Victorian public grumbled in a similar way at what they saw as persecution of harmless street traders and children.

Youngsters on the watch for a policeman out to spoil their fun wouldn't have cried 'Look out, here comes the Old Bill', or 'There's a Copper heading this way'. These nicknames hadn't been invented in the 1840s. Instead, the police were known variously as Crushers, Blue Devils, Blue Drones, Raw Prawns, Peelers or Bobbies (the last two referring to Sir Robert Peel, who had founded the Metropolitan Police in 1829.)

The Police Orders also show that officers were regularly used for crowd control at public events. When Queen Victoria attended the House of Lords in July 1847, for example, almost 1500 men were drafted in from all divisions to line her route. In July 1845, during Clark's time at Arbour Square, a chimney caught alight in the house of a man named West in Polly Row, Blackwall. It caused a huge blaze, 'completely lighting up the river as far as Greenwich and Woolwich'. Eight homes were destroyed. Sightseers were drawn to the scene, and we are told that 'a strong muster of the K Division of police rendered essential service in keeping the great crowd out of the reach of danger'. It is possible that George Clark was one of the men who did duty there that night.

In the early days of 1846, Clark and the others at Arbour Square must have been surprised to see a fellow officer, Stephen Walker, put in the dock. Walker had been on duty as gaoler when a trouser-maker named Elizabeth Spencer was taken into custody charged with illegal pawning. The young woman alleged that Walker had then indecently assaulted her, but the magistrate dismissed the case.

A month later, a tragedy occurred at number 16 Arbour Square, very close to the police station. A man named Jeremiah Spence Stark killed his pregnant young wife Helen and then committed suicide by cutting his own throat. The

Daily News paints a vivid picture of the terrible scene. 'There was a pond of blood at the foot of the staircase, and the door, the tables, and the chairs were spattered and smeared with gore. The fender, fire-irons, and furniture were scattered about in every direction, and all things betokened a silent but terrible struggle'. Sergeant Frederick Shaw of the Detective Police placed officers in the house 'to preserve everything in the state in which the scene first presented itself…The only object which has been removed is the weapon with which the horrid deed has been committed, and that lies wrapped in a newspaper at the Arbour-square station house. It is a black-handled carving-knife, covered from the point to the hilt with thick clotted gore'.[25]

George Clark would most likely have seen this ghastly object. Perhaps he was even one of the officers at the murder scene. The description of the knife is a macabre foreshadowing of what was to occur in Dagenham just four and a half months later.

On 3rd February 1846, Clark was awarded a bonus of a shilling (5p) for good conduct. Many such gratuities were given for various reasons, for example a particularly good arrest. The Commissioners saw the potential conflict between this and their stated aim of 'preventing the commission of a crime'. The Police Orders of 18th November 1846 advises Superintendents 'to take great care that the rewards for the apprehension of thieves after an offence is committed shall not lead to the neglect of any measure of prevention of such a crime'.

On 20th February 1846 the news came through of the murder of Constable James Hastie. He had been attacked by several men during a street disturbance in Deptford, just across the Thames from Stepney. He was the twentieth Metropolitan Police officer to lose his life in the course of his duty, his death following close upon that of Constable Fitz Henry Parsons, who had fallen into a dry dock when patrolling the Woolwich Arsenal in a fog. Two more fatalities were to follow in that bleak year of 1846.

We learn something of George Clark's personality from statements made after his death. He was, it seems, very neat and tidy, and was not one of those who would have needed reminding to fold up and put away their clothes. He was also good at managing money. Even on the non-too generous wage of twenty-one shillings (£1.05) a week, Clark was in a position to lend some cash to a cousin. He may also have been rather absent-minded. While at Arbour Square he lost the key to the small deal box in which he kept his belongings, and broke open the lock before he left to demonstrate that he was only taking away what belonged to him. The *Bedfordshire Times* says Clark was 'known to be a person of extremely correct habits, and much respected in the force'. It also describes him as having 'inoffensive manners'.

Unfortunately there is no known photograph of George Clark. This image shows Charles Carpenter, who joined the Surrey Constabulary in 1856 aged 20 and served for three years

Surely Clark was eager to take in some of the sights of London during his limited spare time. Perhaps he was one of those who flocked to the Egyptian Hall in Piccadilly and paid a shilling (5p) each to see the world-famous General Tom Thumb. An advertisement dated March 1846 announced that 'the little General's weight is only 15lb, and he is the most enchanting little being living. He has had the distinguished honour of appearing three times before Her Majesty'.[26] Meanwhile, in Baker Street, a shilling was also the price of admittance to an attraction just as popular in the 21st century as in the 19th – Madame Tussaud's waxworks. Set-pieces included Queen Victoria's coronation and a tableau of Victoria and Albert with their children.

Victorian Londoners also loved taking trips on pleasure boats. An excursion to Gravesend in Kent and back left every day in the summer of 1845 from Nicholson's East India and China Wharf, Thames Street.[27] On one of his rare days off, did Clark and his fiancée Elizabeth pay their ninepences, too, and join the crowds of merrymakers on deck? The journey would have taken them downstream past the throng of sailing vessels berthed alongside the busiest docks in the world. At Greenwich the stately buildings of the Royal Observatory and Queen's House appeared, but a little further on there was a tourist attraction of a very different kind. The day-trippers gazed with ghoulish fascination at the prison hulks moored off Woolwich, and craned their necks to catch a glimpse of the convicts being rowed to and from their daily work in the dockyard or the Royal Arsenal.

Back in London, an exhibition at the Cosmorama Rooms, Regent Street, would surely have caught Clark's attention. It featured the work of Eugene-Francois Vidocq, the renowned French investigator. He had been a highwayman and forger before turning informer and eventually becoming the first head of the Brigade de Sureté, the world's first detective force. After his retirement in 1828 the publication of his memoirs caused a sensation. Visitors to the London exhibition shuddered at the array of deadly weapons seized from notorious criminals. A range of disguises worn by Vidocq was also on view, including a priest's robes, peasant's smock and 'every variety of dress worn by the lower orders of Paris'. What was more, the man himself, now over seventy years old, was on hand to answer questions. A newspaper reported that he was 'full of talk of his adventures and curiosities, and altogether, surrounded by so many proofs of his prowess and records of his adventures, he affords a spectacle which when once seen is not easily forgotten'.[28]

As the winter of 1845 approached, the public were eager for news about Sir John Franklin's expedition to the Arctic. This was the latest attempt to discover the fabled North West Passage. Franklin's ships the *Erebus* and

Terror had not been seen since the end of July, when they were sighted in Baffin Bay. Tragically, none of the expedition members were to return alive. On a lighter note, readers were looking forward eagerly to the new Christmas story from the pen of Charles Dickens. This had become a Yuletide tradition, beginning with *A Christmas Carol* in 1843. His offering for 1845 was *Cricket on the Hearth*. As soon as it was published, stage adaptations appeared at the Lyceum and at Covent Garden and also proved tremendously popular.

Five months into 1846, George Clark had been at Arbour Square almost a year. At some point during the week beginning Monday 11th May, he and his fellow constable Isaac Hickton were informed that they were to be transferred to Dagenham, a rural parish on the Essex shore of the Thames about ten miles from Stepney. Hickton also lived at the Arbour Square station. He was 33 years old, unmarried, and had been in the Metropolitan Police since 1842. Like Clark, he was from a far from prosperous background. He had been born in the parish of St Werburgh in Derby. His father Joseph Hickton (sometimes spelt Higton) was a framework knitter or 'stockinger', a notoriously poverty-stricken trade. It was claimed in July 1846 that 'with the exception of the hand-loom weavers of Lancashire, the frame-work knitters of the Midlands are, perhaps, the most desperately depressed body of working men in England'.[29] Whole families toiled together for long hours at home. The father would operate the knitting machine, his wife sewing the seams of the stockings, while the children wound thread onto the bobbins.

Not surprisingly, when Isaac grew up he sought a different career. He was employed for several years at the Derby China Works, then served a five-year apprenticeship to John W. Cock as a currier, a worker who prepares leather so that it is flexible enough for manufacturing purposes. Eventually, though, Isaac too made the decision to join the exodus from the provinces to London and enter the ranks of the New Police.

George Clark carried out his final patrols along the Mile End Road, then on Friday 15th May 1846 he and Hickton said goodbye to their colleagues at Arbour Square before setting off for Dagenham. They probably took the Eastern Counties Railway from Shoreditch to Romford. The opening of this line in 1839 had given passengers an unprecedented glimpse into the poverty of London's East End. From their carriages they could see much detail invisible from the road. A *Weekly Dispatch* journalist noted in September 1846 that when travelling on the Eastern Counties or Blackwall Railway 'what numbers of squalid dwellings meet the view. From the windows of those hovels of the poor, especially in the districts of Whitechapel,

Spitalfields, and Bethnal Green, hang long poles, on which their miserable rags are hung to dry; and beneath the arches of those railways, the pale, emaciated and half-naked children congregate to play'.

Soon, the houses thinned out and were replaced by the wide horizons of the Essex landscape. There was then the shock of the sudden appearance very close to the railway line of Ilford Gaol, a bleak fortress surrounded by a moat. Eventually Hickton and Clark stepped out of the train into the busy market town of Romford, where they were probably met by another officer and taken by horse and cart the final couple of miles towards their new posting in Dagenham. Back at Arbour Square, their old colleagues must have thought the pair extremely lucky to swap the maelstrom of the East End for life in a quiet country village. No one could have suspected what was to follow.

CHAPTER 2

'A sylvan land'

Mention Dagenham today, and two things usually spring to mind. One is the
Ford car factory, which at its height in the 1950s employed more than 50,000
people. The other is the Becontree Estate, Europe's largest public housing
scheme when it was carried out after the First World War. Yet by contrast
here is G.A. Hillyar-Ruell's glowing description of the village in 1912. When
this was written, little would have changed since Clark's arrival in the 1840s:

> Arriving at Dagenham one is in a sylvan[1] land of river, lake,
> coppice, arable and pasture; far, indeed, from the madding
> crowd and the busy mart. Dagenham itself is surrounded by
> cornfields and market gardens. The soil is exceedingly fertile,
> and being flat is easily worked. The village is quaint and old-
> world, many of the houses being boarded, with gable roofs. It
> seems to grow out from a core of quaintly irregular cottages
> clustering around the spire of the church. The more recently
> erected houses – there are but few – are on the outside edges.
> Time alters little of the Dagenham of old![2]

James Thorne's *Handbook to the Environs of London*, published in 1876, was
less enthusiastic. It declared that 'Dagenham is a long straggling village,
chiefly of cottages, some pretty good, some decent, but too many poor, low
and dirty thatched mud huts'.

Dagenham was one of the earliest recorded Saxon settlements in Essex, its
name deriving from the Saxon 'Daeccanham', meaning 'Daecca's home'. In
the 1840s the parish covered 4,550 acres, including about a thousand acres of
Hainault Forest, and the population at the time of the 1841 census was 2,294.
The largest concentration of people was in Dagenham Village, and there were
smaller communities to the north at Beacontree Heath and Chadwell Heath.
James Thorne described Beacontree Heath as 'a collection of mean houses,
with a beer-shop and Wesleyan chapel'. Manor houses and farms were
scattered throughout the rest of the parish. Some agricultural workers still
lived in centuries-old clay cottages, the 'mud huts' referred to by Thorne.
The original builders had used puddled clay as their basic material. To form
the inside walls they plastered over reeds gathered from the river bank.[3]

We have a description of the riverside area from the pen of Katharine Fry,
daughter of the great prison reformer Elizabeth Fry. In the 1820s and 1830s
the Fry family spent their summer holidays at two fishing cottages there.[4]
Katharine remembered that 'It is difficult to convey the sort of enjoyment

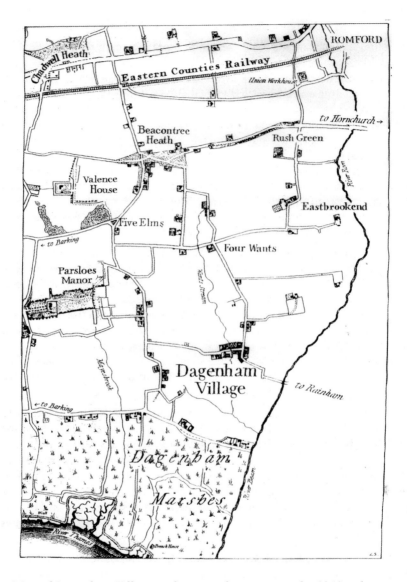

Map of Dagenham Village and surrounding areas in the 1840s, showing places mentioned in this book. It uses elements from Chapman and André's 1777 map of Essex, plus details from early Ordnance Survey maps

Dagenham afforded us...There was fishing, boating, driving and riding inland by day, and when night closed in over the wild marsh scenery the cries of water birds, the rustling of the great beds of reeds, the strange sounds from the shipping on the river, gave the place an indescribable charm'.[5]

Quiet as Dagenham was, it was by no means cut off from the capital city. It was served by a road from London to Tilbury, the Dagenham portion of which had been improved during the Napoleonic Wars. In the 1840s an omnibus from Rainham to London, horse-drawn of course, picked up passengers at 9am each day from the Bull pub in Dagenham Village, returning at 6pm. A carrier's van from Aveley called at the Bull on Thursdays on its way to London, and returned on Saturdays.[6] Travel to London was further improved in 1839 when, as we have seen, the Eastern Counties Railway came to nearby Romford. These good transport links gave Dagenham market gardeners the opportunity to grow vegetables such as peas and beans for the London market.

As he and Hickton walked round the village for the first time, with the station sergeant William Richard Parsons at their side, several buildings would have caught Clark's interest. Foremost of these was the parish church of St Peter and St Paul. This had very nearly become the scene of tragedy back in December 1800, when the tower collapsed, completely demolishing the nave and south aisle. A Sunday morning service ought to have been taking place at the time, but luckily the vicar Edward Chaplin was late in arriving with the key, and the congregation were still waiting in the churchyard. At the reopening of the church four years later, a bellringer was killed in a freak accident when his leg got entangled in the rope and he was tipped onto his head.[7]

Looking round inside the church, Clark would have noted memorials to members of prominent Dagenham families. Most conspicuous were the dazzling life-size marble statues of Sir Richard Alibon, a seventeenth-century judge, and his wife Barbara. There was also a tablet to the memory of William Ford, an eccentric farmer so mean that he used to sit at the rear of the church with his labourers. He knew that the further back you sat, the less you were expected to put into the collection. When Ford died in 1825 he bequeathed £10,000 in trust to establish a free school for 30 Dagenham boys and 20 girls.[8]

In 1846 the vicar of Dagenham was Thomas Lewis Fanshawe. He had by then held the post for thirty years. His ancestors had been prominent in Dagenham affairs since the early seventeenth century. The Reverend Fanshawe lived at the family seat of Parsloes Manor, a mansion about a mile west of the village, and let out the vicarage to tenants.

Watercolour of Dagenham in 1900 by A.B. Bamford, showing the church tower and the back of the Cross Keys Inn

Dagenham Village's two main roads, Crown Street and Bull Street, both took their names from public houses. These were the Rose & Crown, which in 1846 was run by John Key, and the Bull, of which George Kittle was the landlord. The Bull also served as the village post office, Kittle's son James being the letter carrier. Clark's initial tour would have also taken in the third and final alehouse of the village, the half-timbered Cross Keys, facing the church and dating from the 15th century. Landlord of the Cross Keys at the time of Clark's arrival was Yorkshireman Thomas Shutt.

The Wants stream ran across Crown Street. It didn't have a healthy reputation, having been described as 'the ditch called the Common Sewer' in 1564, and was probably also polluted by a tannery a mile upstream. Dagenham Village had no piped water until 1870. The only street lighting would have been one or two oil lamps fixed to walls at intervals along the main thoroughfare.

The western end of Crown Street was called Church Elm Lane, and this was the site of the new school funded by William Ford's very generous legacy. In its early years the school used rented premises, but in 1841 it moved into the purpose-built building designed by John Davis Paine, the architect of London's first Waterloo Station. The boys attending were between 8 and 14 years of age, and the girls from 8 to 12.

No doubt Sergeant Parsons lost no time in introducing the new arrivals to the prominent village tradesmen. These included Benjamin Holgate, a carpenter and undertaker who also served as the parish clerk, blacksmiths William Gann and John Hastin, Thomas Cozens the butcher, William Goddard the baker, and boot and shoe makers Thomas Chase, William Dowsett and James Farrow.[9]

One tradesman who got to know George Clark well was Thomas Smith, a grocer and draper. Earlier that year, in the face of strong opposition from the Reverend Fanshawe, Smith had built a small yellow-brick Wesleyan Methodist chapel, known as the Ebenezer chapel, on the western side of Bull Street. It was part of the Romford section of the Spitalfields Circuit. One of the preachers there in the mid nineteenth century was a man named Chambers, who used to walk from Spitalfields and back. He would leave tracts at the Bull Inn as he passed, and apparently one Sunday evening the drinkers decided to return the favour. They marched unceremoniously down the aisle of the little chapel during Divine service with a full pot of beer, requesting the preacher to refresh himself.[10]

Clark immediately joined the congregation of this chapel. It's not known for certain whether he was a Methodist before coming to Dagenham. His fiancée Elizabeth's grandfather Daniel How is recorded as being an active Methodist, and a chapel was to be built in her home village of Eversholt, Bedfordshire, in the 1850s. This may indicate that a group of Methodists

Looking west along Crown Street, Dagenham, in the early 1900s, with the church spire in the distance

existed in Eversholt in the 1840s and met at that time in private houses. Elizabeth and Clark are likely to have been members of such a group, and may even have first met each other there.

George Clark soon took an active role in the life of the Bull Street chapel, becoming a tract distributor for Dagenham. He was, of course, ideally placed to do this as he journeyed extensively around the area in the course of his duty. Tracts were loaned out on a weekly basis.[11] Each district was served by one or more distributors, who would make sure that every household wanting a tract had one. It was collected the following week, and another left in its place.

Clark could have found himself in deep water had this reached the ears of the Commissioners. It seems that six years earlier a Roman Catholic police officer had been handing out tracts while on patrol in one of London's outer districts. He was possibly one of the many Irishmen who had joined the force. A furious letter-writer wittily made his point in the *Times* on 27th February 1840. 'Sir, I hardly believe it can be by the direction of our present Socialist rulers that the Men in the Metropolitan Police Force in the Suburban Districts add to their other services that of circulating Roman Catholic Tracts as this mode of disorganizing the present institutions of the Country appears to me roundabout and indirect'.

John Wesley, whose work led to the founding of Methodism, had made great use of tracts to back up his preaching. By the 1840s, many hundreds had been published by the Wesleyan Tract Committee. They took the form of pamphlets, of four pages or more, on a wide range of subjects. Some were reprints of Wesley's sermons. Others were biographies of prominent Methodists or anti-Catholic treatises. According to a summary of over 500 tracts in the *Wesleyan-Methodist Magazine* for 1843, 'No. 432 is a good tract on Socialism, and no. 441, on Sunday Newspapers; - nuisances that greatly need to be removed'.

Many tracts warned of the evils of alcoholic drink. This stance led to Methodist street preachers risking life and limb if they set up their stall in certain districts. Heavy drinking was commonplace in all walks of life in early Victorian society, not least because of the impure state of the water supply. It was usual for farm labourers to be given beer in lieu of part of their wages.

At harvest time in particular, farmers supplied their workers with generous amounts of home brew. The *Essex Standard* of 17th July 1846 told its readers that 'we are assured by a highly respectable farmer the other day that he had a labourer who, for a day's work, had cut five acres of oats and drank thirty-two quarts of strong beer, and finished in the evening by betaking himself to the village ale house to enjoy his pint and his pipe'.

The police force attracted many single ex-Army men who were likely to have a more than average fondness for the bottle. Indeed, a large number of early recruits were dismissed for drunkenness. These included the first two men to be enrolled in the Metropolitan Police back in 1829, William Atkinson and William Alcock, who were both sacked after just one day's work.

Policemen were forbidden to drink while on duty, but this regulation was widely flouted and difficult to enforce when keeping a watch on pubs could be one of their chief tasks. On Christmas Eve 1846 Commissioner Mayne warned his officers against entering too much into the festive spirit. 'All must refrain from accepting drink offered to them on duty, and remember that no excuse can be allowed for any man who renders himself unequal to the strictest performance of his duty by drinking; after this caution any man reported for drinking will have no plea against being punished by dismissal'. Would this instruction be heeded? Two days later, alas, came the sequel. 'The Commissioners regret extremely to have had so many constables reported to them this morning for being drunk on duty...The Commissioners have felt it their painful duty to dismiss each man reported for so grave an offence. The Commissioners trust that the examples that have been made will have a due effect...'

Clearly George Clark did not match the stereotype of the hard-drinking policeman. Did his Methodist principles make it difficult for him to fit in, one wonders?

CHAPTER 3

'No Police! No Police!'

Before the Victorian age, the day-to-day system of law enforcement in Dagenham hadn't changed for hundreds of years. An unpaid parish constable, occasionally two, would be elected by the Vestry to hold the office for twelve months. He would normally be one of the local farmers or tradesmen, and would have to carry out the duties in his spare time. Miscreants or drunkards might be placed in the small lockup near the churchyard gate.[1] Beacontree Heath wrongdoers could find themselves in the pair of stocks outside the Three Travellers Inn. These had been presented by the Reverend Fanshawe, in 1819,[2] and he is said to have discussed his plans with Elizabeth Fry one afternoon when she came to tea.

This time-honoured system was clearly not adequate to deal with burgeoning levels of crime and unrest as the nineteenth century wore on. The parish constables of Dagenham and its surrounding areas complained time and time again that they were unable to cope. There was also no method of public prosecution. Individual victims of crime would have to bear the cost of bringing cases to court. Eventually sixty inhabitants of the district, mostly farmers, set up an Association for the Prosecution of Felons in 1835. They paid a subscription, and in return the society bore the expense of prosecuting anyone suspected of stealing from its members, and appointed a secretary to deal with the extensive paperwork involved. The cost of mounting a prosecution was considerable. When Samuel Seabrook of Dagenham brought George Blazeby before the Essex Quarter Sessions in April 1846 accused of theft, his costs for fares for himself and three witnesses, plus police and clerical fees, amounted to £4 11s (£4.55p). Blazeby pleaded guilty and was sentenced to two months' hard labour at Springfield Gaol. Mr Seabrook's expenses were paid to him by the court[4].

The Railway Age began to make its mark on the area in the late 1830s, when the Eastern Counties Railway drove a line through Dagenham towards Romford. It ran just north of Beacontree Heath, and brought with it the Railway Police, described by local historian Cyril Hart as 'Dagenham's first organized law-enforcement agency'. Parliament required each railway company to employ its own constabulary to help quell the fears of people worried by the presence of unruly gangs of railway navvies in the vicinity, especially on pay days when they descended on the beerhouses. As soon as trains began operating on the line in 1839, the Railway Police were also expected to work the points and act as signallers. Cyril Hart tells a dramatic story: 'Once, a constable, running from his post to chase wrongdoers, forgot to put the signals at danger and there was a crash, probably the first one in the Dagenham area'.[5]

An officer of the Bow Street Horse Patrol

Another crime prevention force operating near Dagenham was the Bow Street Horse Patrol. It covered the main highways leading from the capital, such as the London to Colchester road which went through Ilford. These thoroughfares needed to be made safe for travellers, for at this time highwaymen still posed a very real threat.[6] The uniform of the Horse Patrol had a conspicuous red waistcoat which caused the officers to be nicknamed 'Robin Redbreasts'. In the 1830s an officer named George Weston, based at Romford, had the job of patrolling the three miles from Romford to Ilford four times during the night shift.

On 3rd January 1840 Dagenham became part of the Metropolitan Police district. When first founded in 1829 it had covered seven miles from Charing Cross, but its scope was now extended to a fifteen-mile radius from the city centre. Areas now covered for the first time included Barking, Chingford, Chigwell, Dagenham, East Ham, Little Ilford, Loughton, Leyton, Waltham Abbey, West Ham, Walthamstow, Woodford and Wanstead. Together they formed the Great Ilford section of the K Division. The Bow Street Horse Patrol was now discontinued within the enlarged Metropolitan Police area, and many of its officers joined the new force. One of these was Dagenham's first Sergeant, Samuel Tebenham, an ex-butcher from Suffolk. Before taking up his post at Dagenham in January 1840, Tebenham had lived at Great Ilford with his wife Mary Blinco and their children.[7]

When the new detachment of the K Division arrived in Dagenham for the first time it must have been quite an event for the villagers to witness, with popular songs being sung as the men marched in.[8] Sergeant Tebenham was allocated six constables, three for the Dagenham Village area and three for the Beacontree Heath district.[9] His officers did not, however, cover the areas of Chadwell Heath and Marks Gate located in the north of the parish. These were served by a small separate division of the Ilford force.

Local tradition has it that Dagenham's first police station was situated over a greengrocer's shop at the junction of Crown Street and Bull Street.[10] However, when the rate books and the 1844 Tithe records are examined, it becomes clear that the police in fact took up residence elsewhere. They occupied a building on the eastern side of Bull Street. It had formerly been used as a house and shop, and was held on a yearly tenancy from a Dagenham widow named Hannah Wade.[11] As this was not a purpose-built station like Arbour Square, and was relatively small in size, it ought to have been described as a station house rather than a police station, but in practice the terms were interchangeable.

Many people were suspicious of Robert Peel's 'New Police', viewing them as another layer of authority set to keep the poor in their place. Back in 1840, the force[12] had only been in Dagenham a month when an incident occurred which illustrates just how unpopular its arrival was in some quarters. PC Thomas Norton was patrolling Dagenham Village just after midnight when he came across two men, James Harrington and Matthew White, 'in the street causing a great deal of noise and disturbance'. Norton asked them to go home, but they refused, and were soon joined by several others. The gang surrounded the officer and attacked him, chanting 'No Police! No Police!' as they did so.

But I tell you 'tis no use your coming here there is no property left on my land but the old scare Crow - no one will steal him · I should think

EXTENSION of the NEW POLICE

A contemporary cartoon showing the unpopularity of the
New Police in rural areas

Norton later told the Ilford magistrates that he had a loaded pistol in his hand at the time of the incident, and 'he was fearful some serious accident would happen. He told them it was loaded but they still surrounded and assaulted him'.

(According to Douglas G. Browne, pistols were issued to police stations in the early days of the force[12], but there seems to have been no question of George Clark carrying firearms while on patrol five years later.) Luckily for Norton, Sergeant Tebenham was within earshot on horseback, and on hearing cries for help he rode up to give assistance. Eventually he and Norton, who by this time had blood pouring down his face, managed to secure Harrington and White. They were brought before the Ilford Petty Sessions on 15th February 1840. Harrington was fined £5, but being unable to pay he was sentenced to 2 months imprisonment. White was fined £2.[13]

Sometimes the bad feeling was provoked by overbearing behaviour on the part of the police. On 4th March 1840, for example, Charles Rowan gave this instruction: 'It has been stated to the Commissioners that the Police Constables in some of the outer Divisions have stopped and examined the little Bundles of labouring People going to work which bundles generally contain their food and nothing else. The Superintendents will immediately point out to the Constables the absurdity and impropriety of such a practice. It is the business of the Police to know the bad characters in a Rural District and they should not interfere with any others'. The following week he had to remind officers when 'passing people in the streets not to shoulder them off'.

It was not merely the poorer sections of the community who resented the arrival of the Metropolitan Police to this part of Essex in 1840. Many of the leading inhabitants also objected strongly. As ratepayers, they were having to foot the bill for a service that was no longer under local control. The nearby parish of Romford had unsuccessfully applied in September 1839 to be covered by the Metropolitan Police.[14] The Chairman of the Havering Liberty Quarter Sessions declared in January 1840 that he was pleased Romford was not to be included, as 'the rate, in all parishes where the police was established, amounted to 8d in the pound on the rack rent'.[15]

By this time it was accepted that cities needed a professional police force, but many did not want to see it in the countryside. The Rural Police Act came into force in 1840, permitting counties to set up police forces if they so wished. The *Times* of 11th January 1840 contains a glowing review of a pamphlet by a Mr Brereton condemning the decision to adopt the Act in Norfolk. Brereton claimed that the supporters of the new system were 'depriving the people not only of the control of their own expenses, but of the guardians of their own persons and properties...It is the main intention of this change to substitute martial force for civil power. What else can uniform, and arms, and military commanders mean?' Worst of all, according to Brereton, was that it smacked of Frenchness. He made the tongue-in-cheek claim that it wouldn't be long

A group of Romford policemen, 1860s

before the fleur-de-lys appeared on police uniforms. Napoleon had been defeated less than thirty years before, and this argument was guaranteed to inflame opinion among patriotic Englishmen.

The Dagenham police brought its suspected wrongdoers to the Ilford Petty Sessions, held every first and third Saturday of the month at the Angel Inn, and covering the districts of Ilford, Barking, Dagenham and Woodford. A strange case heard there in June 1843 illustrates the lingering animosity felt by some middle-class residents towards the police. Miss Mary Chapman, who lived at the Cross Keys, alleged that PC Timothy Drew of Dagenham had placed a wicket gate in the road, causing her pony and chaise to swerve on to the footpath. It emerged that Drew had been playing a game with the children of his fellow-constable Thomas Kimpton. He would take the gate off its hinges and lay it down, and the children fetched it back. Witnesses Susan Kettle, Thomas Kimpton and Ellen Kimpton all declared that the gate had been placed 'on the footpath as close to the ditch as could be, and not in the centre of the road'. Predictably, the charge was dismissed. According to the Chairman, 'a more paltry case had never come before the bench'.[16]

On the morning of Wednesday 17th September 1845, after almost five years in charge of the Dagenham police, Samuel Tebenham died suddenly aged 47.

A view of the Angel Inn, Ilford, in the 1880s

A newspaper report gave the cause of death as 'a fit of apoplexy', but according to the death certificate he fell victim to a heart attack.[17] Tebenham was buried in the parish churchyard five days later. His 13 year-old daughter Mary Jane, who died of typhus, had been laid to rest there three years before.

The man chosen to replace Tebenham was Constable William Richard Parsons, a farmer's son from Norfolk in his late twenties who had been a miller before joining the police in December 1839.[18] On 29th September 1845 Parsons was promoted to the rank of sergeant and transferred from Barkingside to Dagenham. He had recently married Maria, the daughter of Jonathan Rawlings, landlord of Barkingside's Fairlop Oak pub. On 11th April 1846, seven months after their arrival in Dagenham, Maria gave birth to a daughter, who was to be named after her mother.

Why exactly were George Clark, Isaac Hickton and another officer, Jonas Stevens, transferred to Dagenham in May 1846? A report in the *Times* a few days after Clark's murder gave the official explanation. It told readers that the police had succeeded 'in ridding this portion of the county of some very notorious characters. Some of the police, who had thus rendered themselves obnoxious, were, in consequence of various threats from time to time being held out to them, removed from Dagenham to distant stations, and their places supplied by others, among the latter being the deceased'. However, Dagenham folk who were in the know must have chuckled heartily as they puffed away at their clay tobacco pipes while reading this report. The 'notorious characters' prompting the shake-up were in fact the policemen themselves!

We have noticed the ill-feeling between some Dagenham people and the police. Another example of this occurred in March 1846. PC James Hall, another ex-Horse Patrol officer, spotted a man on the other side of the road carrying a suspicious load over his shoulder. He called over to ask him what it was. The man, John Kemp, told Hall that it was a bullock's head which he had just purchased for two shillings from his employer, Mr Coppen of Beacontree Heath. Kemp then walked on. Hall grew annoyed because Kemp had not stopped. He crossed the road, seized the man by the collar and punched him in the eye. The force of the blow knocked Kemp down. He said later that to save himself from falling into a nearby ditch, he laid hold of the policeman, and the bullock's head went by accident against Hall's uniform. PC Hall then dragged Kemp to the police station. He urged Sergeant Parsons to charge Kemp with assault, but Parsons refused. Instead, it was Hall himself who stood at the bar at the next Ilford Petty Sessions charged with assaulting Kemp. Hall declared he had hit out in self-defence after being struck three times with the bullock's head. When the evidence had been heard, 'the Chairman, to the great surprise of every person in court, said the magistrates were of opinion that no assault had been proved, and they should dismiss the case'. He announced that details would be sent to the Police Commissioners.[19] Hall left Dagenham soon afterwards.

This episode had been unwelcome news for the authorities, but far worse was to come. Two months later, on Saturday 9th May 1846, another three Dagenham constables appeared before the Ilford magistrates, accused of assault and false imprisonment. They were Robert Greaves, Timothy Hayes and James Oliver, and the chief witness against them was Dane Stokely, who worked as an ostler in the stables at the Cross Keys. He told the court that two days before, Greaves, Oliver and Hayes were drinking at the Cross Keys and playing at skittles and quoits. It is likely that this involved some form of gambling. An argument between the officers and Stokely, possibly linked with the policemen having borrowed the landlord's horse and carriage earlier that day, led to a full-scale fight. Greaves struck the ostler on the side of the head, Hayes then knocked him down, and Oliver then jumped with his knees upon him. Hayes was threatening to 'knock his nose off'. The trio were all very drunk.

At this point Constable Thomas Kimpton arrived on the scene. He told his fellow-officers that if they didn't stop the attack immediately he would have them locked up. They reluctantly let go of Stokely, and walked away. Thomas Shutt, landlord of the Cross Keys, asked Kimpton to wait a while to make sure all was quiet. Peace appeared to have been restored, so Kimpton left. He turned the corner only to see Oliver and Hayes coming towards him. They were now wearing their greatcoats and wielding cutlasses, which they had fetched from the police station. They rushed back to the Cross Keys and dragged away Stokely, the terrified ostler, flourishing the cutlasses in the face of anyone who dared oppose them. He was taken the short distance to the lockup at the station house. Greaves, Hayes and Oliver were unable to actually lock the door, as Kimpton had snatched the keys and was determined to hold on to them. Kimpton later told the magistrates that Oliver 'abused him for so doing'. This stand-off lasted for about three quarters of an hour, and was no doubt witnessed by a good many curious and astounded onlookers. Eventually Sergeant Parsons came up and took charge of the situation, and Stokely was then liberated.

When the case was heard, the magistrates returned a guilty verdict, and served constables Greaves, Hayes and Oliver with a fine of 40s (£2) each plus expenses, or a month's imprisonment if they were unable to pay. Greaves handed over the money, but Hayes did not and so had to prepare himself for a few grim weeks within the walls of Ilford Gaol. The third shamed officer,

The only known view of the front of the first Dagenham Police Station (circled). Detail from a photograph taken from the top of the church tower in 1900

James Oliver, did not appear at the trial and a warrant was issued for his arrest.[20] William Richardson, who as Inspector of the Ilford Station held overall responsibility for policing Dagenham, told the court that an account of the incident would be sent to the Police Commissioners. On Monday 11th May the inevitable decision was taken to dismiss the three men.[21]

The whole affair was highly embarrassing to the police authorities, and they sought immediate replacements likely to restore the confidence of the people of Dagenham. George Clark, with his unimpeachable record, was an ideal choice, and four days later he packed his bags and set off for his new post. When Clark arrived at the station house in Bull Street, he would have found it quite a contrast to the modern accommodation back at Arbour Square. An entry in the *Particulars of premises in the occupation of the Metropolitan Police* tells us that the Dagenham building was a 'very old brick wood and lathe and plaster house with stable for one horse and weather board lockup'.[22] The report stresses that its condition left much to be desired. 'Many parts are very dirty...requires cleaning and painting throughout – in cell very bad being built of weather board and decayed...cleaning good as far as the floors are concerned'. The Commissioners were hardly extravagant when it came to cleaning supplies. The Police Orders of 16th March 1840 decreed that each Sergeant's Station was allowed a wool mop and a birch broom every three months, and a new scrubbing brush after six months. Replacement hair brooms and pails were provided once a year. There was also a strictly limited candle allowance for stations without gas lighting: 11 lbs (5 kilos) in January, but only 5lbs during the summer months.

The Dagenham station house had a charge room measuring 168 square feet (just under 16 square metres) plus a scullery and a mess kitchen. It was at that time the custom for police officers to live either at the station itself or as close to their beat as possible. Sergeant Parsons and his family had a set of rooms, and one upper floor room measuring 164 square feet served as accommodation for up to two unmarried constables paying a shilling (5p) per week each in rent. This room was to be Clark's new lodging, which he would share with PC Jonas Stevens. Twenty year-old Stevens was also a newcomer to Dagenham, arriving on Monday 18th May 1846, three days after Clark and Hickton. Clark probably did not intend to live at the station for very long, as he and Elizabeth were shortly going to be married. Isaac Hickton didn't take up residence at the station, but lived in a cottage at Beacontree Heath, a hamlet about two miles (3km) to the north of Dagenham Village.

Many aspects of Clark's work would have changed now that he was in a rural area. Numerous fires were started deliberately in the 1830s and 1840s, as a means of protest against poverty, unemployment and the Poor Law. Arsonists' main targets were hedges, hay-ricks and houses. In the summer of 1849, for example, a large number of fires occurred in Dagenham, including one at a farm run by a Mrs Tuck near the Chequers Inn that engulfed the reed stacks, corn store, stables and other outbuildings.[23] Clark's instruction manual told him to:

> give immediate alarm, by springing his rattle; he should as soon as possible, send information to the Division Station, and, until the arrival of some superior officer from whom he may receive further orders, he will exert himself in any way likely to be most useful, as, in keeping the space near the spot clear, assisting in removing property, sending for a Police force from the nearest Section residences, giving notice to the fire offices, engine keepers, turn-cocks, &c.

Police officers were also expected to round up the numerous homeless people roaming the countryside. The manual quoted extensively from the Vagrancy Act of 1824. Constables had the power to arrest 'every person wandering abroad and lodging in any barn or outhouse, or in any deserted or unoccupied building, or in the open air, or under a tent, or in any cart or waggon, not having any visible means of subsistence, and not giving a good account of himself or herself'. In January 1840 three men who gave their names as James Stebbens, William Newman and Isaac Pepper, were found sleeping in a cow-house in the farmyard of a Mr Collier. They were brought before the Romford Petty Sessions, and 'not being able to give a good account of themselves, were committed as vagrants to the House of Correction at Ilford for one month'.[24]

The authorities also waged a constant battle against poaching and theft of farm animals. The Game Act of 1831, hugely unpopular with country dwellers, imposed heavy fines on people convicted of trespassing in search of game, including rabbits. In June 1847 Charles Wain, a Dagenham farm labourer, was convicted at the Ilford Petty Sessions of 'having set certain snares for the purpose of taking game'. He was fined 40s (£2) plus costs, but could not pay this large sum and so was imprisoned for a month instead.[25] Those caught poaching during the night risked being transported.

Contemporary local newspapers are full of reports of livestock being stolen from farms. In February 1840, for example, we read that three sheep were stolen from Mr John R. Hatch Abdy of Stapleford Abbots. The police were able to follow the footprints of the thieves all the way to a large dung heap at Chadwell Heath. It was being guarded by a growling dog, which had been stolen a few days before from George Edward Pollett, a Dagenham farmer. The policemen now had the unpleasant job of searching the dung heap, and eventually they discovered the carcasses of two of the stolen sheep, tied up in smock frocks. Two men, named Radley and Rudge, described as 'notorious characters residing at Chadwell Heath' were swiftly arrested by 'that indefatigable police officer, Weston', on suspicion of the robbery.[26]

The dog was not the only animal stolen from the unfortunate Mr Pollett. He had a flock of fifty sheep, and on 5th January 1840 one was butchered and its skin, head and entrails left lying in the field. Thomas Pollett, the farmer's son, told the Crown Court that he and PC Cousins, together with another local farmer named Kettle, followed a trail of footprints and blood to the house of John Perkis, a 25 year-old labourer. They went inside, and found a piece of mutton which exactly fitted the carcass. Perkis's shoes also matched the footprints from the field. He was found guilty of the theft, and sentenced to be transported for ten years.[27]

James Parfey Collier of Wheel Farm, Rush Green, was awoken one night towards the end of 1839 by the furious barking of his dog. He looked out of the window to see two men sneaking away. Collier soon realized that the hen-house had been broken into, and that two ducks and a gander were missing. This being just a month before the January 1840 arrival of police forces in Dagenham and Romford, the resourceful farmer immediately mounted his horse and rode off in search of Sergeant George Weston of the Horse Patrol. Weston soon afterwards arrested 28 year-old Dagenham bricklayer James Dowsett, who was found to have a duck and two nets in his possession. We are solemnly told by the *Chelmsford Chronicle* that 'Mrs Collier identified the duck'. Dowsett was tried for theft, found guilty and sentenced to ten years' transportation.

By the time Victoria became queen, the death penalty had been scaled back and was now reserved only for cases of murder or treason. Thieves were now likely to be transported to the Colonies, usually Australia, especially if they had previous convictions. Early in 1840, father and son William and Charles Coe, both described as hay binders, were found guilty of stealing a donkey belonging to John Cole and potatoes from James Grout, both at Hornchurch. The father, despite being 76 years old, was given four months' imprisonment with hard labour, and his son was transported for seven years.[28]   In the summer of 1846, labourer John Poole of Dagenham, aged twenty-three, was sentenced to seven years' transportation for stealing a watch.[29] The shortage of corn has already been mentioned, and anyone convicted of stealing it also faced transportation. This was the fate of 29 year-old William Reed in 1846.

He worked for Messrs Mollett, of Stapleford in Essex. Reed was convicted of stealing two sacks of dressed wheat from them, and was transported for seven years.[30]

Dagenham was, as we have seen, at the outer edge of the Metropolitan Police district from January 1840. This had the immediate effect of causing a crime wave in nearby areas not covered by the new police, particularly the parish of Hornchurch, lying just to the east of Dagenham. Early in January more than a dozen robberies took place in Hornchurch within the space of a single week. Later that month, a brown mare and a set of chaise harness were stolen from Mr Tabrum, of Hornchurch, and nearby on the same night a new light market cart was taken from Mr Newman.[31] Luckily for the owners, the thieves decided to abandon their haul at a public house on the Hackney Road.[32]

Romford, having unsuccessfully applied to be included in the expanded Metropolitan Police area, was instead given a detachment of men from the new Essex Constabulary. There was no shortage of crimes for them to solve. One enterprising Romford farmer, a Mr Stone of Goosehays Farm,[33] whose hen house had been broken into several times, decided to strike back by rigging up his own burglar alarm system. A press report headed 'Spirited capture of a hen-roost robber' described how Mr Stone 'adopted a plan of affixing a bell in his bedroom, with wires leading to the hen house door and a spring attached, so that if any person in the night-time opened the door the bell would give the alarm. 'He was awoken at one o'clock one Saturday morning by the bell. Calling on two of his servants to get up and follow him, he made his way to the hen house. When Mr Stone opened the door, the thief immediately rushed out and gave him a blow in the face, nearly knocking him down. The farmer hung on to his man, though, and 'after a severe struggle he was captured'. Mr Stone then went round the yard and noticed his goose-house had also been broken open. Four live geese and one dead one were found in a bag. Six of his forty hens had also been killed.[34]

Such run-of-the-mill crimes were what George Clark and Isaac Hickton would have expected to find as they settled into their new environment, a world away from the cosmopolitan hustle and bustle of Stepney. Yet it would soon have reached the ears of the new officers that there had been two startling high-profile cases of suspected murder in the Dagenham area within the past few months. In October 1845 Mrs Mary Dunsden, wife of a Chadwell Heath potato salesman, had been found in bed with her throat cut. The scene was dreadful, a witness remembering that 'the wound [was] large enough for a pint bottle to have been put in end ways'. Mrs Dunsden had been sick and bedridden for some time, and the inquest jury returned a verdict of suicide.

Sensationally, two months later her husband Thomas Dunsden was brought before the Ilford magistrates charged with her murder.[35] George Banham, a local linen-draper, and Rachel Summons, a servant in the Dunsden household, both gave evidence against him, but eventually the case was dropped before it could be heard at the Essex Assizes.

Meanwhile, in Dagenham Village, all was not well at the William Ford School in Church Elm Lane, built just a few years before with the eccentric farmer's ten-thousand pound legacy. A bitter feud was raging between Thomas Cutler, who taught the boys, and Ann Bridges, who was in charge of the girl pupils. When 72 year-old Mr Cutler suddenly collapsed and died in December 1845, on returning from a church service with the boys, suspicion immediately fell on Mrs Bridges. Had not the pair had a particularly violent quarrel that very day? Rumours flew about the village that she had poisoned her fellow-teacher. The inquest jury returned a verdict of death by natural causes, but the Trustees of the school asked Mrs Bridges to resign. This she refused to do, and was eventually reinstated.[36]

So all was not sweetness and light in the little village of Dagenham. If gossip was to be believed, a sinister undercurrent lay beneath the quaint rural setting. As Sherlock Holmes was to say to Dr Watson in the short story *The Copper Beeches* as their train sped past picturesque farmsteads and cottages: 'You look at these scattered houses, and you are impressed by their beauty. I look at them, and the only thought which comes to me is a feeling of their isolation, and of the impunity with which crime may be committed there...It is my belief, Watson, founded upon experience, that the lowest and vilest alleys in London do not present a more dreadful record of sin than does the smiling and beautiful countryside'.[37]

Bull Street, c.1910. The Dagenham Police Station where Clark lived is the weatherboarded building on the left, with the two small girls standing outside

CHAPTER 4

'Have you seen my mate?'

Anyone calling at the cottage which served as Dagenham's police station would have heard a variety of English regional accents. The officers came from different parts of the country, and had also followed an assortment of trades during their lives. Their backgrounds were typical of the kind of men joining the Metropolitan Police in its early years.

As we have seen, Clark and Hickton started work at Dagenham 15th May 1846. They were joined three days later by Jonas Stevens. Stevens had just finished his police training and this was his first posting. The remaining three constables had been there since the early days of the Dagenham force some six years before. Unlike the newcomers, they were all married men with families. The oldest and most long-serving was 39 year-old John Burnside Farnes. He was of English and Scottish ancestry and had been born in Southwark, just south of London Bridge. Farnes was a bookbinder by trade. The precise date of his joining the Metropolitan Police isn't clear, but judging by his warrant number it was most likely around the end of 1831 or the beginning of 1832. Farnes had served at Stepney before being posted to Dagenham. He married Anne Isacke in 1830, and in the summer of 1846 they lived in a cottage called Wiseman's in the hamlet of Beacontree Heath with their five children.

Another of Clark's new colleagues was Abia Butfoy. He was 36 years old and from Bethnal Green. The Butfoys were descended from Flemish Huguenot silk weavers who had settled in London's East End at the close of the 17th century. As a young man Abia did try to make a living as a weaver, but these were not prosperous times in that trade, and after a while he opted to take the King's shilling instead. By 1837 he had left the Army and married Elizabeth Burton, also from Bethnal Green. Butfoy was one of many ex-soldiers to join the Metropolitan Police. He and Elizabeth had five children by 1846. They lived in a cottage in Bull Street, just three doors away from Dagenham police station.

As we have seen, there was a rule that candidates for the police force should have no more than three children to support. This was probably a reflection of the low rate of pay. But how could such a rule be enforced? And did men who fathered further children after starting their police career risk dismissal? Probably not, as Farnes, Butfoy and the sixth and final Dagenham constable Thomas Kimpton each had five children by 1846. Indeed, Kimpton seems already to have had one more than the maximum three when he joined the force in January 1840.

Thomas Kimpton was thirty years old and hailed from Hendon in Middlesex. As a young man he followed his father John Kimpton's trade of saddler and

An early 20th century view of the Four Wants junction, showing how isolated and lonely the spot was

harness maker, and was also at some point employed by Hendon surgeon John Wyndham Holgate. At the tender age of 17, Kimpton married Ellen Maria Popham at St Pancras Old Church. He joined the police force in January 1840. By 1846 he and Ellen were living with their family at Rose Cottage, situated on the road which led north from Dagenham Village towards the Four Wants junction. We have already seen how Kimpton stood his ground in a difficult situation during the stand-off with Hayes, Oliver and Greaves the week before Clark's arrival. All sergeants had a nominated deputy, and Kimpton held this post at Dagenham.

Now that his force was back to full strength,[1] Sergeant William Parsons could put the shamed ex-constables firmly out of his mind and hope life at the Bull Street station would be less turbulent in future. One of his first acts was to reshuffle some of the beats. The area known as Eastbrookend,[2] which was some distance to the north-east of Dagenham Village, towards the boundary with the parish of Romford, had previously been patrolled by Abia Butfoy. Parsons now decided to allot Eastbrookend to George Clark.

A circuit of this beat took an hour and a half, making it almost five times as long as Clark's previous patch on the Mile End Road. Such a long beat was quite usual in London's outer districts, however. Clark would patrol it on foot and alone between the hours of nine at night and six in the morning. He would rendezvous with fellow officers at specific times and places during the night to exchange information. At intervals Sergeant Parsons would travel on horseback around each beat, his task according to the *Provisional Instructions* being 'constantly to patrole [sic] his section, and enforce the performance of duty by his Men'.

The constables also acted as a kind of human chain for passing on reports between Dagenham and Ilford, where Parsons' superior officer Inspector William Richardson was based. This was an era long before the invention of the telephone or walkie-talkie. The most up-to-date means of communication in 1846 was the electric telegraph, which was at that time being installed alongside railway lines. It had already proved its usefulness in fighting crime. If a fugitive was known to have caught a particular train, his or her description could be wired to the next station and there was a good chance of an arrest being made.

The starting point for George Clark's Eastbrookend beat was the Four Wants, a crossroads lying a mile (1.5km) north of Dagenham Village. This had been an important junction for many centuries, and roads led from here to Beacontree Heath, Barking and Romford, as well as to Dagenham Village itself. Dagenham was a superstitious community, and Clark would soon have heard that the Four Wants had a sinister reputation. In his *History of Dagenham in the County of Essex,* first published in 1904, J.P. Shawcross tells us that suicides were supposed to have been buried there. 'This tradition', he writes, 'throws light on the belief current among the old inhabitants of the place that ghosts and unnatural spectres have been seen at different times at this spot, and that a coach drawn by four headless horses has been seen there at least twice at midnight, to the great horror of those who witnessed it'.

It's worth noting that there were no public houses at all along the Eastbrookend beat. It's possible that this was one reason why Clark was given this particular route. Being an active Methodist he may well have disapproved of alcoholic drink and preferred to avoid entering pubs wherever possible. The lack of public meeting places such as pubs contributed to a definite air of gloom and isolation about the entire beat. Clark would have been accustomed to gas lamps along the Mile End Road, but there was no street lighting at all at Eastbrookend.

Newspaper reports after Clark's death describe the beat as extending 'a considerable distance along unfrequented roads, having deep ditches on either side, covered with duck-weed, some parts...being extremely lonely'.[3] It was very flat country, like most of this Thames-side parish except the inland area to the north. The roads were not much more than cart tracks. The many ruts would be filled in from time to time with stones collected from the fields for this purpose and piled up by the roadside. This was a job usually done during the winter by farm labourers when other work was scarce.

At the south-west corner of the Four Wants junction was Wants Farm, which belonged to the Gray family. Here every evening Sergeant Parsons would leave Clark to begin his patrol. Wants Farm had been the scene of a burglary five years before. This being the 'Hungry Forties', the thieves had targeted the food supplies, including 'a vast quantity of pickled pork' and 'upwards of 42 store hams'. While there 'they regaled themselves with strong ale and other good things'. The provisions were discovered buried in the gardens of two local men, Joseph Oliver and Abraham Bush. We are told that 'Mrs Gray identified the pork and other things produced as belonging to her husband, and amongst other things was a leg of mutton, which was in the larder, and intended for the next day's dinner'. Whether the meat was still fit to be served up is not recorded.

The descriptions of the beats followed by the Dagenham policemen in 1846 have not survived, but it is possible to reconstruct the overall route that Clark would have taken. Walking as instructed at a steady two and a half miles an hour, and no doubt carrying a ready supply of bread and cheese or pies to sustain him during the long night ahead, Clark would first have struck eastwards along Eastbrookend Road in the direction of Romford. A short distance along, on the left-hand side, was Clark's first port of call, a block of two farm labourers' dwellings known as Four Wants Cottages. The first was occupied by Luke Miller and his family. Living in the next one were three generations of the Page family – a father and son both named William Page, the younger William's wife Mary Ann, and her daughter Mary Ann Brown, by a previous marriage.

On leaving these cottages, the road took Clark through open country, with a wide expanse of cornfields on either side. Local historian J.P. Shawcross wrote that Dagenham produced 'splendid crops of corn'.[4] The next building on the route, on the right-hand side, was one of those thatched clay cottages dismissed by James Thorne in his *Handbook to the Environs of London* as 'mud huts'. It dated back to Tudor times, and its walls were three feet (almost 1 metre) thick. It was occupied by Robert Wright and his family.

Clark passed this clay cottage on his beat. It was hundreds of years old then, and was still habitable when this picture was taken in 1932

As Clark left the cottage, he would have passed a footpath branching off beside it to the right. This provided a short cut to Dagenham Village, avoiding the corner at the Four Wants. If he had been walking without stopping from the Four Wants, Clark would by now have been on the road for about fifteen minutes. He had just left the oldest building in the area, the thatched cottage, and was approaching Eastbrookend Farm, which had been rebuilt just a few years before. It was a smart brick residence, with imposing steps to the front door. It was owned by William Sterry and farmed by widow Rebecca Mihill, who lived there with her son William and daughter Sarah.

Eastbrookend Farm. This was the recently-built home of Rebecca Mihill and her family in 1846. It is now the Farmhouse Tavern

Having shone his lantern at the outbuildings and ensured that the windows and doors were secure, Clark rejoined the road, which now veered northwards to his left. Before heading in that direction, Clark took a track straight ahead called the Chase.[6] It led to Hooks Hall Farm, a timber-framed building dating from at least the 17th century, with a large thatched barn. The farm was run by another widow, Juliana Benton, who lived there with her children.

Another farm on Clark's beat was Hooks Hall, shown here in 1931

Having returned to the main road, Clark soon reached the next area of settlement. Here the road bore sharply to the left, and inside the resulting corner was a cluster of buildings. The first of these, set back from the road, was Eastbrookend Old Hall. Like nearby Hooks Hall it was a 17th-century farmhouse with outbuildings, barn, garden and orchard. It was owned and farmed by Thomas Waters Brittain. Brittain was prominent in Dagenham affairs, being a churchwarden, a member of the Romford Union Board of Guardians, and also holding other public offices such as being one of the Trustees of the William Ford School. He had inherited the Eastbrookend farmhouse and lands through his maternal ancestors the Waters family.

The other substantial house situated inside the bend in the road at this point was Huntings, an old timber-framed building, possibly Tudor, with an 18th-century brick facade. It was owned and occupied by an elderly Bermondsey-born widow named Sarah Stone. She was a niece of William Ford, whose legacy had founded the William Ford School. Opposite Huntings was a large pond where carters paused to allow their horses a well-earned drink. An elderly resident remembers that next to the pond there was 'a sunken barrel of ever-running clean spring water',[7] so perhaps Clark stopped here too, cupping his hands and taking a draught.

Between the prosperous residences of Eastbrookend Old Hall and Huntings, Clark would have passed a small cottage housing Thomas Waters Brittain's horse-keeper, George Blewitt, and his remarkably large family. Blewitt and his wife Alice Brown had seventeen children living in 1846, and another had died in infancy. One can imagine the hustle and bustle of this area during the day, ringing with the sound of children's voices. As Clark passed by on Wednesday 24th June he may have heard even more noise than usual. One of the Blewitt daughters, Rebecca, had married George Cornwall at Dagenham parish church that day, and no doubt the feasting and celebrations continued well into the night.

On rounding the corner to the left and after passing Mrs Stone's barn, Clark would have arrived at Fels Farm, which at that time was uninhabited. This was his last port of call along that particular road. The next buildings, half a mile away, were covered by the Romford contingent of the Essex Constabulary rather than the Metropolitan Police.[8] They were Wheel Farm and Thorntons Farm. We have already met James Parfey Collier and his wife Esther of Wheel Farm. They had been robbed of two ducks and a gander in December 1839. The neighbouring Thorntons Farm was occupied by Southwark-born farmer Ralph Page, his wife Elizabeth and their family. But, as we have seen, Clark's duty did not take him to the Colliers and the Pages. He turned back and retraced his steps towards the Four Wants.

On reaching the Wants junction once again, Clark then followed the next part of his beat, which formed a rectangle. First he turned north along Tanyard Lane, and soon passed a group of farm labourers' cottages on the right hand-side. Living here with their families were William Renn, William Boyton, and Lewis Frost.

Woodlands. Clark would have known this house as Scrimpshires, and it still stands today. Photograph taken in 1931

Clark's next port of call, to the left of the road, was Sparks, an attractive late18th-century house owned and occupied by Joseph Smitherman, a tanner. For hundreds of years a tannery had been situated at this spot next to the Wants Stream. He next passed two cottages on the right, the homes of Edward Clipperton and Sam Boyton.

Another impressive residence then loomed into view. This was Scrimpshires House, a late 18th-century three-storey house named after John Scrimpshire of London.[9] In Clark's day it was home to Samuel Pedley Dodds, a cattle dealer. The policeman then continued north along Tanyard Lane, which curved to the left as it approached a T-junction. Here, straight ahead, was Brown's Farm. In 1846 it was occupied by James Miller and the junction was known locally as Miller's Corner.

It was now less than ten minutes since Clark had left the Four Wants. He turned left at this point and entered Frizlands Lane. He was now walking south. The next building to come into view, on the right-hand side, was Sermons Farm. This was owned and occupied by Samuel Seabrook, a member of a well-established Dagenham family of farmers, landowners and publicans. A few minutes later, Clark could see Frizlands Farm to his right. Its moated site had a long history but the farmhouse itself was modern, having been rebuilt between 1814 and 1828. A sales catalogue of 1841 describes it as 'a superior residence, excellent garden, fish ponds, greenhouse, carriage house, stabling and convenient buildings'.[10]

Another stopping-point on Clark's beat was the smart Frizlands farmhouse, rebuilt between 1814 and 1828

Having passed two farm labourers' cottages on his left, occupied by William White and Charles Mills, Clark headed towards another T-junction where Frizlands Lane met Oxlow Lane. This spot was known as the Three Wants. Straight ahead Clark could now see Hunters Hall Farmhouse, a weatherboarded 18th-century building with four bedrooms and two living rooms. It was owned by the Grays, who also occupied Wants Farm, but currently stood empty. The walk from Miller's Corner to this spot would have taken Clark about ten minutes. He next turned left and five minutes later was back at the Four Wants, the starting point of his whole beat, ninety minutes or so after he had first left it. For the most part during the night Clark was alone, but from time to time would have encountered people such as night watchmen or farm workers preparing for an early departure to market.

Clark's short time in Dagenham had, so far, been uneventful. There are no reports in the local newspapers of his having taken part in any prosecutions. On Tuesday 2nd June 1846 he celebrated his 20th birthday. There was still a year to wait before he reached the age of majority. Clark worked a seven-day week, as we have seen, but he must have had the occasional day off as he is known to have met his cousin William Markham, who lived at Bexley in Kent. To visit William, Clark would have taken the Thames ferry from Coldharbour Point in Rainham over to Erith. No doubt he also met his fiancée Elizabeth How from time to time. There were plenty of decisions to make as the day of their wedding drew closer. He had also made many friends through the chapel, including a young woman his own age named Mary Ann Jones who lived at Folly House in Green Lane, the road between Dagenham and Ilford. At the time of the 1841 census Mary Ann was working as a servant at Valentines Mansion in Ilford.

In June 1846 the talk in England was all of politics. Earlier that year the Conservative Prime Minister, Sir Robert Peel, the driving force behind the creation of the Metropolitan Police back in 1829, had decided to reverse his party's long-standing policy of protection of British agriculture. Peel introduced a bill to repeal the Corn Laws. After fierce debate in Parliament, the bill passed its final reading in the House of Lords on 25th June. Peel was then promptly defeated on an Irish bill, and resigned on 27th June. The change of government saw the premiership pass to the Whig Lord John Russell, who coincidentally had spent part of his childhood at Woburn Abbey, close to George Clark's home village of Battlesden. People debated about what might happen once the Corn Laws were a thing of the past. Some thought it would mean the ruin of British agriculture. Farmers were concerned for their livelihoods. And would bread really become more affordable, or would poor people's hopes be dashed?

Dagenham folk, however, had more than politics to occupy their minds as June 1846 drew to a close. Monday 29th was the feast day of their church's patron saints, Peter and Paul. This event was surrounded by a whole week of merriment and recreation known as the Wakes. In an era when working people didn't enjoy much leisure time, this was a highlight of their year. At the end of the week, just as the festivities in Dagenham were winding down, those with sufficient stamina could have an extra day of enjoyment at the nearby Fairlop Fair, always held on the first Friday in July.

When 20 year-old Julia Parsons, sister of the sergeant, arrived in Dagenham from her home in Whitechapel on Saturday 27th June, she would have entered a village with a distinctly festive atmosphere. In his history of Dagenham, J.P. Shawcross writes that 'The annual "wakes" was a popular institution, with its booths, the fortune-tellers, and the competitions for prizes, such as ploughing for a smock frock, bowling for a tea-kettle, boys racing for a kerchief, or climbing the greasy pole, and girls competing for a scarlet cloak'.[11] That year, the village celebrations enjoyed perfect weather. The hottest June on record was now drawing to a close. There had been sixteen days above 80F (27c) in East London, and temperatures had topped 90 degrees in many places.[12] The extreme weather also brought tragedy in its wake. Around the country labourers were reported to have died in the heat as they toiled in the fields.

The Wakes may also have included less innocent activities such as rabbit coursing, pigeon shooting, dog-fighting and cock-fighting. Men competed in wrestling and single-stick fighting, and drinking contests undoubtedly took place too. In some areas 'great was the renown of the man who could boast the blue ribbon for "tapping the claret"'.[13] Shawcross notes disapprovingly that in Dagenham 'Unfortunately the wakes occasioned much disorder and drunkenness...'[14] The police kept a watchful eye in case the celebrations got out of hand, but some licensed misrule would have been tolerated as being part and parcel of the occasion.

Julia Parsons would be staying at the station house in Bull Street. It's likely that she was there to give some much-needed assistance to the new mother, as Maria had not been well in the two months since the birth. Perhaps Julia had also offered to act as cook to the household. She and the sergeant were half-siblings. William's upbringing had been unconventional. He had been born illegitimate, son of a single mother named Mary Hardingham. His father William Parson[15] married Jemima Whitby soon afterwards, and young William appears to have been brought up by his father and stepmother along with their own brood of children.[16]

Bull Street, Dagenham, in the early 1900s. The Ebenezer Chapel attended by Clark can be seen on the extreme right

Many people, like Julia, made a point of visiting family and friends during Wakes week. It was naturally a popular time for weddings and christenings, and the Parsons family had chosen it for the baptism of baby Maria. On Sunday 28th June, the day following Julia's arrival, the family party walked the short distance to the parish church of St Peter and St Paul where the child was baptised by the Reverend Thomas Lewis Fanshawe. The event was tinged with sadness, however, as one family member was missing. We have already seen that a police constable named Fitz Henry Parsons had lost his life earlier that year after a fall at Woolwich Dockyard. This unfortunate young man had been a brother of William and Julia, and had joined the Metropolitan Police in December 1842. In the early hours of Christmas Day 1845 the 22 year-old constable had been on patrol when dense fog caused him to lose his way and fall ten feet into a dry dock. He was taken to Guy's Hospital but died there on 9th January 1846, fourteen days after the accident. [17]

The actual feast day of St Peter and St Paul was Monday 29th June, the day after the christening of little Maria Parsons. The village would have been alive with music, singing and the excited cries of children enjoying the games. It is doubtful whether George Clark managed to snatch more than a few hours' sleep before his long night duty began. At 8pm he entered the Ebenezer Chapel. It was situated just opposite the police station, and its services drew large congregations. The Ecclesiastical Census of 1851 revealed that 78 people attended the evening service. That summer evening of 29th June 1846, their singing could probably clearly be heard through the open windows of the police station, competing with the tipsy voices and less holy songs wafting out of the Rose and Crown pub just around the corner in Crown Street. Being only a week after the longest day of the year, daylight would have faded slowly. British Summer Time was not then in force, and according to contemporary almanacs the time of sunset at the end of June was just after a quarter past eight. It would, therefore, have been dark when Clark emerged from the chapel.

After the service, Clark collected his truncheon and cutlass, and placed the blue and white striped band on his left arm which indicated he was on duty. He then joined the other officers at about a quarter to nine to line up on parade in the station yard. It was the task of Sergeant Parsons to ensure 'that every man is perfectly sober and correctly dressed'. This inspection was supposed to be repeated when the men went off duty. It was greatly resented by some policemen of the time. For example, PC George Bakewell of the Birmingham force wrote: 'On entering the force I found in the regulations to which I had to conform all the rigour of military discipline, the men being drilled several times every week, without the slightest possible public advantage arising'.[18]

Foxlands Farm. Near here, Clark exchanged pleasantries with Maria and Julia Parsons as he headed towards the start of his beat on the night of his murder

The inspection complete, the sergeant next had to read and explain to the men any orders that had been given out that day by the superintendent of the division or by the Commissioners. Finally, he would march the constables to the starting-point of their beats.

The Dagenham men didn't all begin their shifts at 9pm that night, though. John Farnes had left the station three hours earlier. His beat took him south, along what was known as the Lower Road alongside the Thames-side marshes. Farnes returned to the village from time to time, and ended his shift between two and three o'clock in the morning. He was quite a distance from Clark's beat and would not have been expected to meet him during the night. Isaac Hickton had left the police station at 8pm. This may be because he faced a long walk to the start of his beat at Beacontree (or Bentry) Heath. His beat was adjacent to that of Clark and they would meet at Miller's Corner in Frizlands Lane at allotted times during the night. Hickton could not have found it easy to maintain order in Beacontree Heath. In 1904, J.P. Shawcross noted that 'Until a few years ago, Bentry Heath shared with Chadwell Heath an unenviable reputation by reason of the rough character of those who dwelt in it. The parish constable had anything but a pleasant time of it with these people, if we may judge from his complaints recorded in the annals of the parish'.[19]

Clark's room-mate Jonas Stevens was with him on parade in the station yard that evening. Stevens patrolled the Wood Lane beat to the north-west of the village. On leaving the police station, he walked westwards along Crown Street. This was a different direction to that taken by Clark, and the two would probably not have met up during the night. Thomas Kimpton also set off in another direction to patrol the village. Whether Abia Butfoy was present at all that night is a matter of dispute, as we will discover later. Sergeant Parsons and George Clark were thus quite alone as they left the police station and proceeded northwards along Bull Street towards the Four Wants and the start of Clark's beat.

They were sighted at about a quarter-past nine near Foxlands Farm. This had been the scene of tragedy six years before, in August 1840, when farmer Samuel Thorogood, on his way to one of his harvest fields, received fatal head injuries when his horses bolted and tipped him out of the cart. He left a widow and nine children. A newspaper solemnly noted that 'He quitted his own house in good health and spirits, and in half an hour he was taken home a corpse'.[20]

Foxlands was just over half way between the police station and the Four Wants junction, and the witness was Julia Parsons. She and Maria Parsons, presumably with baby Maria, had been to Romford. Then as now, Romford was a popular shopping centre, and the stores and stalls remained open until

Tanyard Lane in the early years of the 20th century

late in the evening. Walking back to Dagenham with their purchases, the two women had taken a short cut along the footpath which ran from the thatched cottage at Eastbrookend towards Fox Lane and then into Bull Street. As they turned into Bull Street they saw George Clark and Parsons heading towards them. Clark was on foot, with the sergeant beside him on horseback. The four stopped and chatted for a few minutes. Clark, just as the doomed farmer Thorogood had been six years before, was particularly cheerful that evening. Julia Parsons remembered later that he 'appeared to be in very good spirits. My brother's wife expressed that she was very tired and deceased jokingly offered to put her on my brother's horse. She and myself then went home and deceased and my brother went on the contrary way'.[21] After saying their goodbyes, the men continued to the Four Wants, which they would have reached at about 9.20pm. On the way they passed Rose Cottage, where Thomas Kimpton and his family lived.

Just over an hour after parting from Parsons, Clark was seen once more. By this time he had already completed the Eastbrookend circuit of his beat. He was walking north up Tanyard Lane towards Miller's Corner, where he was soon scheduled to meet Isaac Hickton. The man who saw Clark was Luke White, who lived in a cottage in Oxlow Lane. He was apparently in the habit of meeting Clark 'every night and morning'.[22]

White had been working late on 29th June 'in getting the wagon ready for potatoes'. He was heading south along Tanyard Lane towards his own home at 10.30pm when Clark came towards him, singing a hymn to himself. It was 'between Mr Smitherman's gate and the cottage before you come to it... When I met him he was walking towards Beacontree Heath'. The two fell into conversation. 'He asked me how I had toiled the day away, and I said I had had a very long one. He said he had a tract for me, but on feeling his pockets he could not find it'. White then asked Clark to call him in the morning between three and four o'clock, and Clark said he would. 'He had called me several times before'. However, Luke White never saw Clark again after that. He went to bed after 11 o'clock, and later said that he heard 'no noise or hallooing during the night'.

A man named Levy, who lived in a cottage just north of Miller's Corner, towards Beacontree Heath, supported Luke White's statement. He was to tell the coroner that on walking from Dagenham Village to his home 'he passed Clark opposite the Cottages near the Tan-yard on the night of the murder, and that he met Luke White shortly afterwards'.[23] Levy's wife told the police that her husband had mentioned seeing a man wearing a smock frock, a garment worn by agricultural labourers, a short while after he passed Clark.

A few hours later a labourer named Thomas Archer was working in the stables at Wants Farm, beside the Four Wants crossroads. He was busy getting the horses ready to leave for market in London. 'About one o'clock I heard a whistle up the lane, and the trampling of a horse which came Beacontree-Heath way; the whistle was if it was a signal'. Archer told the inquest that about half an hour after this, just before he departed for London, he saw Kimpton 'against our yard gate. He was on horseback. He said "Have you seen my mate this morning?" I told him I had not. He said he could not see him on the beat anywhere, and if I saw him I was to tell him to go to the station house for he wanted him. He then went away and I saw nothing of deceased'.[24] Before Kimpton left, Archer gave him a light for his pipe.

Back at the police station, Julia Parsons woke up at about 6.15am. Her room was next to that of her brother and sister-in-law. She was aware of Parsons telling his wife that Clark was not at home, and that he was going out to look for him.[25] At this point Jonas Stevens returned from his shift, only to hear from Kimpton and Parsons that Clark was missing. Stevens then went to bed at the station to catch a couple of hours' sleep, as later that morning he was due to travel to Ilford to fetch a supply of coal. Kimpton and Parsons left the police station and went around Clark's beat in search of him, taking different directions. Having done this, they met at the Four Wants, but neither of them had found any clue to Clark's whereabouts. Meanwhile, Jonas Stevens was soon out of bed again and on his way to Ilford with a horse and cart for the coal. He stopped at Beacontree Heath before 9am to pick up John Farnes, who was to go with him. Stevens then broke the news to Farnes about Clark's disappearance.

After conferring with Parsons at the Four Wants, Thomas Kimpton returned to the village. He went to Abia Butfoy's house in Bull Street, just three doors away from the police station, and knocked on his door. Butfoy leaned out of the bedroom window. Kimpton called up to him that Clark was missing and that the sergeant wanted him to go round Clark's beat immediately in search of him. It will be remembered that Butfoy had patrolled the Eastbrookend beat before Clark's arrival at Dagenham, and would have known every inch of the area. He did as he was instructed, and whilst engaged in the search he also decided to ask Mrs Elizabeth Page at Thorntons Farm whether she had heard any noise during the night. At lunchtime Butfoy was given a report to be forwarded to Inspector Richardson at Ilford police station informing him that Clark was missing.

There were a good many ponds in the area, and the officers spent the rest of Tuesday 30th June dragging them, probably using long wooden poles with a hook at the end.[26] The deep ditches on both sides of the Eastbrookend main road were also probed. Luke White, the man who apparently had been the last to see Clark alive, first heard he was missing 'as I was returning from my work at Mr Seabrook's, when I saw the constables searching the ponds'. Had Clark perhaps lost his way in the darkness and accidentally plunged into the water?

This was an all-too common occurrence. The Metropolitan Police Book of Remembrance shows that in the previous eight years five officers had drowned while on night duty.[27] Sergeant Parsons must have been forcibly reminded of his brother Fitz Henry's fatal fall into the dry dock at Woolwich a few months before. The *Bedford Mercury* took a less matter-of-fact view. It wrote that the searchers feared Clark to be at risk of suicide. 'As he was of a peculiarly religious turn of mind, it was apprehended that he might have made away with himself in some moment of excitement. All the ponds and canals in the neighbourhood were well dragged; all the copses and wood recesses carefully searched, but to no purpose'.

A letter was sent to George Clark's family in Battlesden, asking whether he had gone home or contacted them at all. As so many people at the time were unable to read, this message was probably delivered by a Bedfordshire police officer, who would have explained the contents and taken note of the reply. Clark's parents, though, had definitely not heard from him. His mother Charlotte, thoroughly alarmed, immediately began making preparations to go to Dagenham herself. There is no record of her husband James Clark making the journey with her. Perhaps he remained behind because of pressure of work, or to look after their daughters, who were aged fourteen and six at the time. Or maybe Charlotte was a forceful woman who would prefer to take action rather than wait passively for news of her missing child. In the event she was not to be left in suspense for very long.

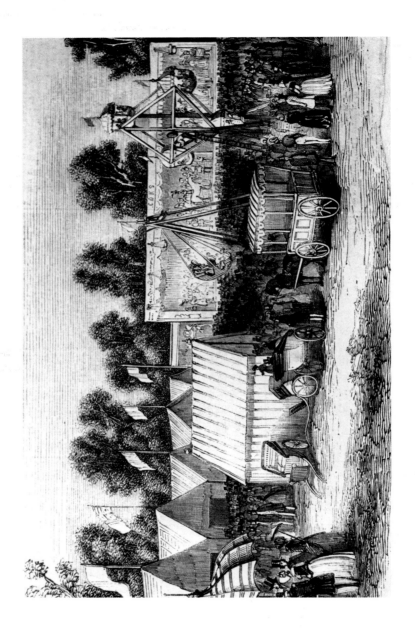

Fairlop Fair in the 1840s

CHAPTER 5

'Horrible and atrocious murder'

It was now 3rd July 1846, Fairlop Fair Day. Together with thousands of others from East London and Essex, Dagenham folk would flock to Hainault Forest, to the north of the parish, for a day of enjoyment. This tradition was begun by Daniel Day in the early eighteenth century. He had a business in Wapping in London's docklands making pumps and blocks for ships, and once a year would treat friends and employees to a feast of bacon and beans under the shade of the mighty Fairlop Oak. Its branches were said to cover an entire acre of ground. The tree itself had been severely damaged by a gale in 1820, but the annual festival continued. There was a procession from Wapping to the forest, with important guests riding in a gaily-decorated boat on wheels. Sometimes things could get out of hand, as Barking-born James Payen recalled in his memoirs. Remembering a visit he made to the fair when a young fishing fleet apprentice, he wrote: 'After this lapse of years, even, my head involuntarily falls with shame as I recall the three days we spent there in the dancing booths and in general rioting. When we reached home on Monday morning, our last farthing had been drained, and morally we were sadly poorer for our "spree"'.[1]

The 1846 event was, unfortunately, dogged by tragedy. It was reported that 'The fair was well laid out. The scenery in the neighbourhood of the forest was most enchanting, and the pleasure-seekers roamed about the woody dells with evident delight. We are sorry to add, that a horse in a gig took fright at the fair, and running over a female caused her death'.[2]

Another fatality occurred several hours later. Constable George Hall, based at Ilford Police Station, had been on duty at the fair and was riding home at 2am on Saturday when he was thrown from his horse. Hall had been working since 11 o'clock Friday morning, and it was thought he had been asleep in the saddle when his horse shied. He was brought to Ilford and attended by 52 year-old local surgeon William Jeremiah Allison, who noted 'a dreadful fracture on the left side of the head under the ear'. Hall died the same afternoon. He was 20 years old, the same age as Clark, and had been married only four months. Three days later, Hall was buried at St Mary's Church in Ilford.

Back in Dagenham, not far from the Fairlop revelry, at around half-past seven on Friday evening, a search party of policemen and some civilian helpers were still looking for George Clark. He had now been missing for four days. The men arrived at Thorntons Farm in Rush Green and asked permission to drag the ponds. Ralph Page, the farmer, is not recorded as being at home at the time. While Parsons, Stevens and Farnes combed a field called the Home

Three Acres, Butfoy and Kimpton dragged the farmyard pond. They found nothing, but the farmer's wife Elizabeth Page told them there was another, smaller pond nearby. Two of her sons would direct them to it.

So twelve year-old William Page, Kimpton, Butfoy, and one of William's brothers, possibly fourteen year-old Ralph, made their way along a track through a potato field called Ten Acres[3]. About seventy yards (65 metres) to their right was a hedge forming a division between their field and the one which their colleagues were searching. At the far end of the potato field, about two hundred yards (185 metres) in front of them, stood a hedge and ditch which formed the boundary of a cornfield known as Barn Field. Like the potato field, this belonged not to the Pages but to James Parfey Collier of nearby Wheel Farm. To get to the pond, the group would have to go through a gap in the hedge, cross over the ditch, turn to the right and then follow the path at the edge of the corn field for about 50 yards (46 metres.) The exceptionally hot and dry summer of 1846 had accelerated the growth of the corn, and newspapers commented that in some parts of Essex it was just a fortnight away from cutting.

On arriving at the cornfield, they were immediately aware of a strong, unpleasant smell. Two people left accounts of what happened next. One was Kimpton in his statement at the inquest into Clark's death. The other witness was young William Page. We have the boy's evidence to the Coroner in 1846, and another account he gave, also on oath, twelve years later. These three versions differ in several respects, and there are even discrepancies between William Page's own two statements. The first account to be given was by Kimpton at the first inquest hearing on 4th July, and made no mention of the boy at all:

> I first saw in a wheat field the staff produced which I knew belonged to him. I then went a little further on and saw the cutlass produced sticking in the hedge about half way up the bank. It was besmeared with blood as it is now. About half a dozen yards from the cutlass I found deceased lying on his back in the wheat about 3 or 4 yards from the ditch.[4]

William Page was called to give evidence at the second hearing, on 14th July. He said:

> Kempton [sic] was walking first up Mr Collier's field and called out 'He is not up here though his staff is here'. Butfoy was close to him and picked the staff up. They turned round then as if to see if they could see him. My brother and myself went on. About 5 yards from where the staff was I found a

cutlas [sic] stuck in the bank. I took this cutlas out of the bank and at the same time I saw deceased lying near where the cutlas was. I then went back to the policemen and told them. Butfoy immediately went right up to him and Kempton to within a few yards. Butfoy called to another policeman in the next field 'Here he lays'. Butfoy then said to Kempton 'You are a pretty sort of a cow hearted policeman'. He made no reply.

Twelve years later Page was quoted in a newspaper as saying:

We (i.e. I and the policemen) smelt a bad smell; and my brother, at the request of the police, went for some tobacco. I kept on, and presently found a staff. I went on about 50 yards further, and saw something shining on the bank. I stepped across the ditch, and found it to be a policeman's sword or cutlass. It was drawn from the scabbard, and I drew it from the bank; and, on turning round, I found Clark lying on his back his hands grasping the corn. I stumbled as it were on his body. I stood still for a few minutes, and on recovering myself I called to the policemen who were coming towards me.[6]

Page's sworn and signed statement from 1858 adds that he 'found the cutlass about 8 or 9 yards from where the body was lying'.[7]

Parsons, Stevens and Farnes immediately made their way to the scene from the adjoining field, as William Page explained at the inquest. 'Then all the policemen came. One of them a little man directly he saw him fell on his back and fainted'.[8] This was Jonas Stevens, Clark's room-mate. In 1858 Page gave extra detail about Stevens's reaction. 'One of them came up, and on seeing the body of the deceased raised his hat and said 'Oh God,' and fainted'.[9]

Although photography had been invented by this time, it was clearly not yet customary to make scene of crime photographs. Kimpton described to the inquest the position of the body. Clark was lying on his back with one leg crossed over the other:

His right hand was clasped hold of a handful of wheat – his left hand close by the side of him…..Just where he lay it appeared as if there had been a skuffle the wheat was quite trodden down 10 or 12 yards round where he lay. There is no foot path in this field and where I found him is a quarter of a mile from the road. Right down the side of the hedge there was a track as if some persons had been walking down – this track extended from where he lay down one side of the field.[10]

The spot where the body was found was in the second field from the road. According to the *Times* reporter George Greene, it must have been chosen by people who knew the area well, being:

> ...admirably calculated for the commission of the crime...the body was found in an extremely large field, and on the western side there is a great bend in the high blackthorn hedge which surrounds it, forming a perfect nook. In this nook the body was found; and, as if it were planned, the spot selected is the farthest point from either of the three farms in the vicinity; and upwards of a quarter of a mile from the main road.[11]

The *Morning Chronicle* asked: 'how is it that he was found in a spot so remote from the beaten track? This can only be accounted for on the supposition that he was first rendered insensible by a heavy blow, inflicted whilst on his beat, and afterwards removed to the spot where the murder was completed – a suspicion which would involve the participation of more than one party'.[12]

It's not surprising that Stevens fainted on seeing Clark's body. The *Times* reports that it was 'in a most dreadful state of decomposition, and so shockingly mutilated and covered with blood that scarcely a single feature was discernible'.[13] According to young William Page, 'the face of the deceased was dreadfully discoloured'.[14] The *Morning Chronicle* told its readers that 'His left eye was forced nearly out of the socket'.[15] The *Times* adds that 'with such violence had the deceased been thrown to the ground, that, notwithstanding its hardness, occasioned by the dryness of the weather, the body had made a complete indentation'. It goes on: 'That there was more than one person engaged in the murder there cannot be the slightest doubt, as the deceased was too powerful a young man for any single individual, armed as he was, to have coped with'.[16]

The policemen's immediate thoughts were that their colleague must have been attacked and robbed. Parsons ordered John Farnes to check Clark's clothes and pockets, telling him 'See if his watch is gone'. Farnes steeled himself to kneel down beside the body and carry out the search. He found Clark's silver pocket watch, and on opening it saw that it had stopped at three o'clock. Clark's clothes did not appear to have been disturbed at all. In one of his pockets they found four half-crowns, four shillings, and a halfpenny.

Clark's rattle was still in his great-coat pocket.[17] Farnes took the rattle out and noticed a small piece of paper wedged inside it. This wouldn't, he judged, have prevented it from making a noise if Clark had tried to use it to raise the alarm. Farnes noticed that 'the scabbard of deceased's cutlass was attached to his belt. The hat was not there. I did not see it at all'.[18]

Back at the farmhouse, Mrs Elizabeth Page heard her boys screaming, amid shouts from the men. She immediately ran to the scene. Thomas Shutt, landlord of the Cross Keys, was also present. A messenger was sent to Romford for a surgeon, and at about half past eight called at the door of Joseph Collin, of North Street.[19] Collin was a bachelor in his early thirties from a well-to-do family of Chickney Hall in Essex. He had served several years of apprenticeship with Mr Gilson of Halstead, followed by formal training at Guy's Hospital in London. When Collin reached the spot and began to examine the body, it was immediately apparent to him that the young man had been the victim of a particularly ferocious attack. It was now getting dark, and a lantern was held up so that the surgeon could carry out his work over the pitiful corpse.

Collin reported to the inquest that there was 'a large opening in the skull six or eight inches in circumference. The scalp was cut off and laying by the side of the head. This wound was likely to have been occasioned by some blunt instrument...this wound of itself would and must have caused death within three or four minutes'.[20]

When the surgeon had made this preliminary examination of the corpse, Mrs Page helped to place it on a door. Her son William was still assisting, in spite of his tender years, and he noted that 'the blood was not seen until the body was moved. When I took the body up there was a pool of blood under the head and neck.[21] John Farnes agreed that there was not a great amount of blood in the area: 'I looked carefully as I went along for marks of blood. I did not find any till we got to the spot where the body was lying. The blood was in one place, just where the head was lying'. He added that the corn was very much trodden down around the body.[22]

Clark's remains were then covered up and lifted on to one of Ralph Page's farm carts. A sad procession then made off. Some people rode in the cart, others walked alongside. Glowing lanterns swung from the vehicle as it was driven along a track eastwards along the side of the cornfield. It then passed through a gate and into a meadow belonging to Thomas Waters Brittain of Eastbrookend Old Hall. From here it went through Mr Brittain's farmyard, then made a right turn into the road and headed towards the Four Wants. Four days previously, Clark had been striding along this road while on his beat.

By now the news had reached Thomas Smith, the Dagenham Village grocer who knew Clark well through the Ebenezer Chapel. Smith made his way to

The path leading out from Eastbrookend Old Hall to the main road. The cart bearing Clark's body came out here and turned right towards the Four Wants. Huntings (now the Bell House) can be seen on the left

Eastbrookend to meet the procession. The eager youngster William Page was still present. At the Rail Pond, not far from the Four Wants, the party halted for a short time, possibly to allow the horse to drink. Here it was joined by James March, a labourer from Dagenham Village. They then went on to Wants Farm. This was the home of the Gray family, who also owned the nearby farmhouse of Hunters Hall, which was at that time unoccupied. Sergeant Parsons was looking for somewhere to leave the body, and was granted permission to use Hunters Hall. The cart took its sad burden the remaining quarter of a mile (400 metres) to the empty farmhouse, situated at the Three Wants. This spot had also of course been on Clark's beat. William Kittle, a Dagenham carpenter, was present at this time, and may have supplied a coffin.

Joseph Collin then carried out a closer examination of the body. This was clearly a case of 'horrible and atrocious murder'.[23] Collin was to tell the inquest that Clark had suffered multiple injuries caused by various different weapons. 'I then discovered at the back part of his neck a wound an inch and a half in depth extending down to the spine. There was also on the top of the head where the scalp had been taken off a deep cut in the bone and extending very nearly through the bone'. The leather stock that Clark wore under the collar of his uniform had not protected him. It had been cut right through, and on removing it, the surgeon noted that 'another deep wound was seen extending down to the vertebrae right through the oesophagus and windpipe then under the right ear there was a wound extending horizontally coming out nearly to the opposite side. This last wound had the appearance of having been occasioned by a double edged knife...the face appeared to have been a good deal bruised, the chest was also bruised and there was a superficial cut over the left shoulder'. He noted that Clark's left forefinger was almost severed. Presumably he had tried to protect his face, perhaps against slashes from his own cutlass.

Collin submitted an expenses claim to the Police Commissioners for his work that night. He wrote that 'In order to furnish a correct account of the wounds inflicted the minutest investigation was necessary and the dreadful state of decomposition in which the body was found rendered the operation one of peculiar hazard to health. My time was occupied the whole of the night in making the examination and in giving directions to the Police in matters connected with the melancholy affair'.[24] Collin requested three guineas for undertaking this task, but was eventually only awarded two. A few years later, Collin abandoned medicine altogether in order to become a clergyman. Perhaps the ghastly experience of carrying out the post-mortem on Clark was the reason behind his change of career. After Collin had eventually departed, the body would not have been left alone. It was the custom to light candles and watch over a corpse in the interval between death and burial.

Between half past eleven and midnight, Kimpton, Stevens and William Kittle the carpenter arrived back at Thorntons Farm to return the borrowed cart. Mrs Page was to tell the inquest that they 'appeared very much exhausted', so she invited them inside and gave them some refreshment. The group sat around the table under the ancient beamed ceiling in the large farmhouse kitchen. Mrs Kittle and Mrs Page's daughter Priscilla were also there, but once again the farmer Ralph Page seems to have been absent. Mrs Page thought Jonas Stevens looked ill and urged Kimpton to take him home. Stevens, it will be remembered, had fainted away on first seeing Clark's body.

Meanwhile, it seems likely that George Clark's mother Charlotte took the train from Leighton Buzzard to London on Friday morning. At that time it would have been frowned upon for a lone woman to stay at a lodging-house, so she may have arranged to stay at Bexley in Kent with her step-sister Elizabeth Markham. This was within easy reach of Dagenham via the Thames ferry from Rainham to Erith. Charlotte arrived in Dagenham on Friday evening and entered the police station in Bull Street. No officers were there to greet her, but she did see Julia Parsons, who was later to tell the inquest that 'I remember the deceased's mother coming to the station on the night he was found. She asked for his things, and they were given to her'.[25] These did not include the box with the broken lock, in which Clark had kept his money. We do not know when the news of George's death was broken to his mother. It is to be hoped that Charlotte's step-sister and nephew were there to support her. The following morning, Saturday, the bereaved mother again visited the station. She begged to be allowed to see her son's body, but was not allowed to do so.

Events now moved swiftly. The Police Commissioners, magistrates and the coroner were alerted. In those days inquest juries had to view the body, so it was necessary to open the proceedings as soon as possible. The Coroner for South and West Essex, which included the heavily-populated area of West Ham, was Charles Carne Lewis, son of a Vicar of Ingatestone. He had been elected to the post of coroner in 1834 at the remarkably young age of 27, and was based in Brentwood. This was the second inquest that Lewis had held that day. In the morning he had dealt with the enquiry into the death of Robert Wilkinson at West Thurrock.[26] At 2 o'clock on the Saturday afternoon, barely eighteen hours after the discovery of his body, the inquest on George Clark opened at Hunters Hall Farmhouse. Press and public were

Hunters Hall Farmhouse.
The first inquest hearing into Clark's death was held here

Hunters Hall cottages.
It is possible that Clark's body was left in one of these for the jurors to view

Wants Farm. This was demolished in the 1940s

out in force. The fourteen-strong jury, all men of course, were local property holders. They included Edward John West, a saddler, who occupied a copyhold cottage and land in Crown Street, and Thomas Waters Brittain of Eastbrookend Old Hall. Once the jurymen had been sworn in, they accompanied the Coroner on the short walk to where Clark's body lay. This was either elsewhere in the farmhouse or inside one of the farm cottages. The *Times* reports, unsurprisingly, that 'the sight was so horrid a one, that the mere cursory glance …was sufficient to render several persons completely heartsick'.

The jury then heard the evidence of the various witnesses summoned to appear that day. Thomas Kimpton was the first to be called. He said he had last seen Clark at 9pm on the 29th, as they were leaving the station to go their separate ways. He explained he 'was in the habit of meeting him at a place called the Four Wants in this parish at one o'clock in the morning and ought to have met him on Tuesday morning last but did not do so'.[27] Kimpton mentioned speaking to Thomas Archer, who had been working in the stables at Wants Farm on the night of the murder. Kimpton said that Archer told him he had seen Clark pass by Wants Farm that night. When the Coroner asked Archer about this, he denied it. He claimed he had not seen Clark at all during the fatal night.

Kimpton described how he gave up waiting at the Four Wants and decided to press on towards Beacontree Heath. There he found Isaac Hickton, gave him the report to pass on, and asked him if he had seen Clark during the night. The answer was a decided 'No'. Hickton was to confirm this. He told the inquest that on handing over the report, Kimpton had asked 'Where's Clark? I can't think where he has got to'.

Next to give evidence was Abia Butfoy, Clark's predecessor on the Eastbrookend beat. As Butfoy's statement unfolded, it must have seemed to his listeners that the murder resulted from a straightforward case of mistaken identity. After all, the attack had taken place at night, and the appearance of a policeman of the time, in the distinctive uniform and top hat, could be almost anyone when seen in silhouette. Certainly the *Essex Herald* reporter thought so. Butfoy gave, he wrote, 'such evidence as will, no doubt, lead to the apprehension of the guilty parties. The name of a person upon whom the strongest suspicion rests was mentioned to the jury'.

This prime suspect was William Walker,[28] a beer-seller and marine stores dealer from Romford. Butfoy explained that four months before, on 4th March 1846, he had stopped Walker on the road leading from Dagenham Village to the Common and questioned him about a bag he was carrying 'upon his shoulders'. According to Butfoy, Walker had said 'it was no business of mine, and he would not show me the contents'. Butfoy then grabbed hold of Walker and tried to drag him to the station. The two men soon came to blows. Eventually, on reaching Workhouse Lane, Walker showed the policeman what was in the bag, and went away saying 'I will be one with you for this'. Butfoy explained that when Clark arrived in Dagenham on 14th May, he took over the Eastbrookend beat and 'continued it from that time until his death'.

Marine store dealers were regarded with great suspicion by the police. Their shabby shops were seen as likely covers for smuggled and stolen goods. The Police Orders of 19th February 1840 declare that new powers have been granted 'especially with regard to searching Carts of Marine store dealers, whom they had reason to suspect'. In *Sketches by Boz* Charles Dickens describes such a store as:

> ...a small dirty shop, exposing for sale the most extraordinary and confused jumble of old, worn-out, wretched articles, that can well be imagined...a board with the squeezed-up inscription 'Dealer in Marine Stores,' in lanky white letters, whose height is strangely out of proportion to their width...Rough blue jackets, with mother-of-pearl buttons, oil-skin hats, coarse checked shirts, and large canvas trousers that look as if they were made for a pair of bodies instead of a pair of legs, are the staple commodities...In the window are a few compasses, a small tray containing silver watches in clumsy thick cases; and tobacco-boxes, the lid of each ornamented with a ship, or an anchor, or some such trophy.[29]

Butfoy having said his piece, Sergeant William Parsons was next to give evidence. He told the jury that after parting with Clark at the start of his beat, 'I saw him again shortly after one on Tuesday morning between the Wants and a cottage standing on the road there close by. That was his time to be there. I proceeded on to his beat and should have met him again at the same spot at three o'clock – he did not come and I went in search of him round his beat but could not find him'. Parsons then gave his account of the discovery of the body, which he said was a quarter of a mile from Clark's beat.

There must have been an appalled silence when the full extent of Clark's injuries was revealed to the gathering. The *Times* reports that at this point the stock that Clark had worn was shown to the jury. 'It was completely saturated with blood. In the centre was a cut five or six inches in length, the leather being cut clean through, whilst above it were several minor cuts, and the holes corresponding with that in the neck of the deceased'.

Parsons said he had returned that morning to the spot where the body was found, and had carried out a painstaking examination of the ground. He told the jury that he 'discovered a great quantity of blood and portions of bone which I know to be skull bones they were laying in the pool of blood where his head lay'. He added the grisly detail that 'some of the pieces of the skull were so firmly embedded in the earth that I was compelled to use a knife to cut them out'.

Joseph Collin then described his examination of the body. He explained that any of the four major injuries would have proved fatal, and could not have been self-inflicted. The neck wound reminded him of the work of a butcher. 'Under the right ear there was another wound, extending horizontally, and coming out on the other side of the neck, just as you would stick a sheep'.[30] Collin stated that he too had re-examined the spot that morning. He thought he could trace marks of scuffling in various parts, but Sergeant Parsons suggested that this might have been caused by the police themselves during the search for Clark.

According to the *Times*, Mrs Elizabeth Page of Thorntons Farm was present at the hearing but wasn't called to give evidence. The *Times* nevertheless revealed a bit of gossip about her to its readers, saying that Mrs Page was rumoured to have been awoken at about 3am on the night of the murder by the violent barking of her dogs in the yard. Apparently she then heard a cry for help, but the noise made by the dogs prevented her from catching anything more distinctly.

No more evidence being given, the Coroner confidently announced that from the clues obtained by the police, there was but little doubt within a few days the parties suspected would be in custody. The inquest was adjourned for a fortnight. The Coroner agreed to the release of the body for burial, and the funeral was fixed for the following day. The *Chelmsford Chronicle* gave the poignant information that 'the unfortunate deceased, it has since been ascertained, was to have been married in a few days to a young woman named Howe, residing near his native place, Woburn'. Weddings at that time were often held on a Sunday, so it's quite possible that the marriage of Clark and Elizabeth had been planned for 5th July. This instead became the date of his burial.

After the inquest proceedings had finished, Charlotte Clark approached the Coroner and begged permission to see George, as he was 'her only son'. Lewis told her he had no power to refuse her request, but strongly advised against it because of the condition of the body. She insisted, and eventually had her way. The *Times* tells what happened next: 'the horrid spectacle, as

A typical country beer house in 1845

was anticipated, having such an effect on her, that she was led away in a state of insensibility'.

The Metropolitan Police Detective Department, which at that time had only been in existence for four years, was already involved in the murder investigation. It was a small unit of two inspectors and six sergeants, and until late 1844 was headed by Superintendent Nicholas Pearce, a Cornishman and ex-Bow Street Runner. Pearce then transferred to the more highly-paid post of Superintendent of the F Division,[31] his replacement being Inspector Joseph Shackell.[32] Pearce continued to involve himself in detective work, though, especially in high-profile cases such as the Clark murder.

Most Victorian newspapers, which incidentally were usually intended for male readers only, devoted large amounts of space to accounts of true crime. *The News of the World* had been founded in 1843 and its output of scandal and crime stories has hardly changed over the years. The detectives were often mentioned by name, and gained celebrity status in the eyes of the avid readers. Two of them, Edward Kendell and Jonathan Whicher, praised by the *Times* as 'two of the most active officers of the detective police force', were sent down to Dagenham for the inquest hearing. Several years later Charles Dickens interviewed seven of the detectives for his magazine *Household Words*. Kendell was given the alias 'Sergeant Fendall' and described as 'a light-haired, well-spoken, polite person, is a prodigious hand at pursuing private enquiries of a delicate nature'. His colleague Whicher (or 'Witchem') was short and thick-set, 'and marked with the small-pox, has something of a reserved and thoughtful air; as if he were engaged in deep arithmetical calculations'.

Having sat through the inquest hearing, no doubt making copious notes as they heard the evidence, Whicher and Kendell then examined the murder scene for themselves. Afterwards they toured the wider area of Dagenham and its surroundings, paying particular attention to the bustling neighbouring town of Romford. As the evening wore on, they visited various pubs and beer houses, accompanied by several local constables in plain clothes. These places, like the marine stores, were frowned on by the authorities. A commentator wrote in 1849 that 'It is in the beer-shops that individuals of notorious character meet, it is here they concoct their plans, and carouse before putting them in execution; the beer retailer is frequently associated with the poachers, and to him they dispose of their plunder in payment for liquor...'[33] Naturally, one of the first places on the detectives' itinerary was prime suspect William Walker's beer shop in London Road, Romford.[34] It was, reported Kendell, 'a place of resort for most of the bad characters in the neighbourhood of Romford'. The drinkers here and elsewhere were no doubt avidly discussing the murder amongst themselves. They were, the *Times* tells us, 'subject to a very scrutinizing inspection, it being believed that in the desperate struggle which had apparently taken place, some of those engaged in it must have been wounded'.

Local tradition has it that coffins were taken to Dagenham Parish Church after dark the night before a funeral. That Saturday evening, therefore, Clark's body would have been removed from Hunters Hall to Dagenham Village and placed inside the church of St Peter and St Paul. The following morning Clark's hat was found by Joseph[35] Palmer, a farm labourer from Beacontree Heath. According to the *Times*, the hat was 'not injured in the slightest degree, and also that when found the deceased's handkerchief was in it'. The hat 'was lying amongst the wheat, about twelve or fourteen yards from the body'.[36] That same morning, Charlotte Clark again appeared at the police station. Either the police officers were not there, or they felt unwilling or unable to speak to Clark's grieving mother. Once more the 20 year-old Julia Parsons appeared. Mrs Clark asked if she could see the box in which George had kept his clothes and valuables, but Julia refused her request.

That day, Sunday 5th July, was one of the warmest days of the long hot summer of 1846. Nearby Hackney recorded a temperature of 94 degrees Fahrenheit (34 degrees Centigrade) at 1pm. We are told by the *Bedford Mercury* that in the afternoon London was 'visited by a thunderstorm, which was most severely felt at the east, and more especially in the neighbourhood of the London docks. Between the hours of two and three, during the time that the storm was at its height, a ball of fire, about the size of a peck[37] measure, fell into the yard of Mr Tugg, a greengrocer'.

It was decided that Clark would be buried at Dagenham, a place he had seen for the first time only six weeks before. Perhaps it was thought best to consign him to the grave quickly rather than transport the coffin back to his home village in Bedfordshire. It's not recorded whether Clark's father, sisters or fiancée were in Dagenham that day. It was not the general custom at the time for women to attend funerals, although this was perhaps a rule adhered to mostly by the middle and upper classes.[38] We cannot be certain whether Charlotte Clark accompanied her son to his final resting place and threw earth upon the coffin. After the dreadful experience of seeing the body the afternoon before, was she strong enough for this next ordeal? William Markham, Clark's cousin from Bexley, was almost certainly present. Clark's grave had been dug at a prominent spot near the path on the south side of the churchyard. The burial service was carried out by Dagenham's vicar, the Rev.

Thomas Lewis Fanshawe, who had recently so vehemently opposed the setting up of the Methodist Chapel attended by Clark. Fanshawe dealt with two interments that day. Both lives had been cut unnaturally short. The other was an eight-month old child, Mary Ann Hawkins, daughter of farm labourer James Hawkins and his wife Elizabeth.

Newspapers across the country devoted many column inches to the murder. They, like the detectives, were convinced that Clark must have been killed in mistake for someone else. The *Sun* described Clark as 'a fine young man'. The *Morning Chronicle* says 'The inhabitants have rendered every assistance to the police for discovery, the deceased being held in much respect'. As we have seen, the Romford beer-shop keeper and marine store dealer William Walker was strongly suspected after his previous run-in with Abia Butfoy. But if people were confidently expecting his quick arrest and charge, they were to be disappointed. The *Times* admitted on 14th July that 'Although he has been under the strictest surveillance of the police since the perpetration of the crime, nothing has been detected in his conduct or transpired otherwise to warrant them in causing his apprehension'.

The day Clark was buried, however, a second mistaken identity theory gained ground. This time, the intended victim was said to be Sergeant Parsons himself. Readers opening the *Morning Chronicle* on Monday 6th July found an account of the inquest hearing, followed by this optimistic paragraph:

> Latest Particulars. – It is expected from the intelligence received in the course of yesterday at Scotland-yard, that by the time your paper is at press the barbarous murderers of poor Clark will have been apprehended…It is a matter of very great doubt whether the deceased was intended as the officer to be murdered, and there is great reason to believe that his identity was mistaken for that of Parsons, his sergeant.

The *Times* explained that Parsons 'has rendered himself obnoxious to some of the notorious characters in the neighbourhood by bringing them up frequently before the Ilford bench of magistrates for drunken and disorderly conduct. A short time since, one of the gang suspected of having been engaged in the murder was brought up to Ilford charged by Parsons with having stolen a quantity of hemlock…'

This refers to a case less than a month before at the Ilford Petty Sessions. On 6th June a Romford man in his mid-twenties named James Young was charged with stealing two pewter pub measures, and other property. Parsons had outlined the case against him. He told the magistrates that at about four

Romford Market

o'clock in the morning of 3rd June, while on duty in Dagenham, he met Young driving a donkey and cart loaded with hemlock and elderberry blossom. The sergeant stopped the cart, and on searching it found rags, bones, brass, and two pewter measures. Believing these to be stolen property, Parsons took Young into custody. One of the measures belonged to a Rainham publican. The owner did not wish to press the case, however, and this resulted in Young being let off lightly. He was found guilty of a misdemeanour rather than a crime, and was fined five shillings plus costs, which he paid at once. James Young had a brother named Thomas who was also known to the police.[39] They both lived in High Street, Romford, and in the 1851 census gave their occupation as 'Herb Collector.'

On Wednesday 8th July George Haslam, confectioner from the Bethnal Green Road, was at Romford Market. Perhaps he had a delicious array of cakes and sweets to sell there. Amongst the noise of the penned animals and buzz of the busy stalls, Haslam overheard the father of the Young brothers saying something which incriminated them. He gave this information to the police, who promptly raided the Youngs' house. They found a weapon which seemed to tally with the 'sharp double-edged instrument' described by the surgeon Joseph Collin as having been used to cut Clark's throat. The *Morning Chronicle* reported that 'among other things they discovered a sword and a stiletto, or Spanish knife, the latter having a sharp double edge, which they took possession of, telling the parties that they should produce them before the coroner'.[40] James and Thomas Young were interrogated by the police, but maintained their innocence. No other evidence had been unearthed against them.

As always happens, when news of the outrage spread, many people wanted to see the scene for themselves. The *Times* reported on 7th July that 'a large number of the inhabitants of Romford, Ilford, Barking, Chigwell, Hornchurch, and the surrounding villages, visited Dagenham for the purpose of viewing the scene of the assassination'. The previous day the appointment was announced of a new Home Secretary, baronet Sir George Grey. The Police Commissioners were answerable to him. He would be kept informed of all developments, and, as we shall see, be expected to make some important decisions about the case.

With their expectations of a swift end to the murder investigation now dwindling, the detectives broadened the range of their enquiries. It was acknowledged that their task was made immeasurably more difficult by the fact that a full four days had elapsed between the crime and the discovery of Clark's body. As the *Times* remarked, the delay 'afforded an opportunity to the murderers to eradicate stains of blood from their clothes and get rid of other evidences of their guilt, thus rendering their detection exceedingly difficult'.

Superintendent Nicholas Pearce urged the Commissioners to publish a newspaper appeal asking medical men to report anyone with suspicious injuries, 'as it is deemed possible the guilty person may have been injured in some way, in conflict with the Deceased'. This was done, but unfortunately the appeal printed in the *Times* wrongly gave 13th June as the date of the murder.[41] Edward Kendell and Jonathan Whicher also did the rounds of local hospitals. Charles Potter, surgeon, of Essex Buildings, came forward to tell them he had treated a man named Henry Clements, who appeared to have received a blow to the neck. This must have seemed a promising lead, as Henry Clements, an auctioneer's porter and hawker, was known to the police, having served several spells inside Ilford Gaol. In June the previous year Clements had appeared in court charged with stealing a saw to the value of six shillings (30p), the property of Romford auctioneer Samuel Henry Leah. This time he was acquitted of the charge.

A popular pub by the name of the Star Tap stood in Romford High Street, near the River Rom. (It was, incidentally, where Edward Ind and the Coope brothers had set up the business that was to develop into the giant Romford Brewery.) Henry Clements must have had a taste for Ind Coope beer, being a regular at the Star Tap. As Clements was enjoying a drink there on Wednesday 8th July he was approached by Thomas Gillman, the landlord, with a message. Apparently the police sergeant from Dagenham wanted to see him nearby about the sale of a Mr Warner's horse. This, however, was a ruse to enable the police to get a closer look at the suspicious wound. Clements later explained that he accordingly left the Star Tap, 'and on walking up the town, a policeman in plain clothes said he wanted to speak to me, and I went with him into the right hand parlour of the Red Lion'.[42] Inspector Richardson of Ilford was there. He asked Clements to confirm his name, then ordered him to show them the wound on his neck. Clements took off his neckerchief, and was found to have an old abcess just under the ear, which had recently been drained. The policemen examined his chest all the way down, then let him go. There were clearly no grounds for linking him to the murder.

It is interesting to note that so far all the men under suspicion lived not in Dagenham itself, but in the nearby town of Romford. The *Times* of Tuesday 14th July, however, pointed the finger closer to home. It stated that it was the general opinion in the Dagenham area that the murderers were connected

The Star Tap Inn

with a 'gang of notorious characters residing in the immediate vicinity of the spot where the murder took place'. The reporter then wrote that local people were saying that if a reward had been offered, one or more of the gang would have informed against their companions before now. Apparently if the government didn't act soon, 'it is understood to be the intention of the jury to send a memorial to Sir George Grey, the new secretary of state for the Home Department, praying that a reward may be offered forthwith'.

Apart from suspecting this 'gang of ruffians infesting the immediate neighbourhood,' local people also told the *Times* reporter that smugglers were likely culprits. 'Some hint very strongly the probability of the real murderers being smugglers infesting Barking and the surrounding villages, Dagenham only lying two miles from the desolate Essex bank of the Thames, and being well adapted for smuggling transactions'. Then as now, tobacco and spirits were heavily taxed and were favoured items for smuggling.

The *Chelmsford Chronicle* of 10th July reported that as a result of Clark's murder, public opinion was in favour of allowing night duty policemen to carry firearms. 'In the present instance, if this had been the case, the report of the pistol must have been heard by some of his brother constables, and if not in time to have succoured him and prevented the murder, certainly in time to have captured some of his assailants'. On the same day, a letter to the *Times* from 'A Friend to the Police' stressed 'the inefficient and unprotected state in which that class of men [i.e. the police] is called upon to perform the most dangerous and desperate services'. The Government announced it was putting up a reward of £100 for information leading to the arrest and conviction of the murderers. Commissioner Mayne suggested that the reward be offered 'with the usual promise of recommendation of Pardon to any Accomplice impeaching the others'. Posters were issued on Saturday 11th July, and were soon 'extensively placarded in and around Dagenham, Romford, Ilford &c &c'.[43]

While Edward Kendell was spending a lot of time in Dagenham itself, 'tracing map of parish and making enquiries' and 'measuring lengths of Beats, distance of places', his detective colleague Frederick Shaw and other officers were despatched to Bedfordshire. Shaw was 38 years old and born at Richmond in Surrey. He was given the alias Straw by Dickens, who described him as 'a little wiry Sergeant of meek demeanour and strong sense, would knock at a door and ask a series of questions in any mild character you choose to prescribe to him, from a charity-boy upwards, and seem as innocent as an infant'. Shaw's aim was to find out more about Clark's private life. His grieving fiancée Elizabeth was interviewed, 'for the purpose of

£100 Reward

WHEREAS on the Night of the 29th JUNE, or the Morning of the 30th,

GEORGE CLARK,

Police Constable of the K Division of Metropolitan Police, was brutally Murdered, when on Duty, by some Person or Persons unknown, in a Field in the Parish of Dagenham, in the County of Essex,

A REWARD

ONE HUNDRED POUNDS

Will be paid by Her Majesty' Government, to any Person who shall give such information as will lead to the Apprehension and Conviction of the Offender or Offenders. And the Right Honourable the Secretary of State for the Home Department will advise the grant of Her Majesty's Pardon to any Accomplice (not being the Person who actually committed the Murder) who will give such information as shall lead to the same result.

Metropolitan Police Office,
4, *Whitehall Place, July* 18, 1846.

This reward poster was displayed widely in the neighbourhood

ascertaining if there was any rival in the love affair, who might, under the feelings of jealousy, have been prompted to commit the deed of violence'.

There was, it seems, no foundation for such a theory. This was confirmed in the *Bedford Mercury* of 18th July, which went on to state that 'the result of their investigation was communicated to town on Saturday, and goes to establish a belief that the track being pursued by Shackell in the neighbourhood of the murder is the right one'. It reported that the mood among the detectives was optimistic. 'It is now confidently hoped that in a very brief space of time the perpetrator of the brutal murder of the policeman George Clark, of the K division, at Dagenham, will be in custody. A chain of circumstantial evidence has come to light which leaves no doubt that the guilty party will shortly be in the hands of justice'.

Then came the bombshell. 'The suspected party is no other than a member of the police!'

CHAPTER 6

'I will swear I did not say it'

On Tuesday 14th July, several days before the appearance of the sensational allegation against a yet-unnamed member of the police, the inquest into Clark's death re-opened. This time the venue was the Cross Keys Inn, opposite Dagenham parish church. Pubs were often chosen for events such as this. Not many public buildings in a country parish could offer rooms large enough for the number of people expected to attend. And a sizeable room was needed here, for people came from far and wide. The *Times* tells us it was 'densely crowded by most respectable inhabitants of Dagenham and the surrounding villages'.[1] Some very un-respectable characters were also to be seen there, which must have lent an extra frisson to the occasion. If the audience were anticipating an afternoon of surprising revelations, they certainly got their money's worth.

The busy coroner, Charles Lewis, came hot-foot from West Ham, where he had been holding an inquest on a man named Michael Hayes, whose death was judged to have been an accident.[2] Lewis made his appearance shortly after two o'clock. He began by announcing that there was a woman in the neighbourhood who hadn't yet been summoned to give evidence, but who might have important information. He and two of the jurors then left the Cross Keys in a chaise to fetch her. No sooner had they returned, than all eyes turned to a man who stood up and insisted on speaking. It was Amos Walker, brother of the prime suspect William. Amos announced that he and others had been 'pointedly alluded to by the public press, and he believed by the jury on the last occasion, as the murderers'. He admitted 'it was quite true that he had been taken up for stealing hemlock, and that his brother had had a quarrel with Butfoy, but they were innocent of the charge'. Walker must have known he was taking a huge gamble by speaking out. Yet he and his brother stood at risk of their lives. The press had more or less taken their guilt for granted, and were probably already drafting vivid reports of a double hanging on the gallows on top of the main entrance block of Springfield Gaol in Chelmsford front of a vengeful crowd.

Once Walker had said his piece, the mystery new witness was called. She turned out to be none other than Elizabeth Page of Thorntons Farm. Mrs Page told of the discovery of Clark's body. She then went on to say that after constables Kimpton and Stevens had brought the borrowed farm cart back later that evening, they stayed a while at the farmhouse. 'I gave them some refreshment as they appeared very much exhausted'.

An early view of the Cross Keys Inn

Nothing she had told the jury so far was at all surprising. However, what Mrs Page said next certainly made everyone sit up and take notice.

Sergeant Parsons had, as we know, told the jury at the previous hearing that on 29th June he had been on duty as usual. He had ridden from beat to beat throughout the night, and had met Clark for the last time shortly after 1am near the Four Wants. Mrs Page, however, was about to undermine this version of events. She said that over supper at the farmhouse Kimpton told her that on the night of the murder Parsons had not been very well, and had asked Kimpton to take the horse and do duty for him. This was, apparently, not the first time it had happened. As we have seen, Kimpton was Parsons' nominated deputy.

Twelve year-old William Page was then called, and described how he had found the body. Jonas Stevens was next to give evidence, and Coroner Lewis asked him about the wooden box in which Clark kept his property. Stevens explained that 'It was a small square box and was always unlocked...He kept all his clothes and other things in his box except his uniform. He used to keep this box very neatly, and doubled up his clothes carefully'. The Coroner was very interested in Clark's financial affairs. How much money had Clark kept in the box? Had he been lending money to many people? The lock of the box was broken – was there a sinister reason behind this?

Stevens replied that 'He kept his money in that box and I kept mine in his box also. He told me he had £1 10s (£1.50) in the box, the day previous to losing his life, I saw him take a sovereign and get change with it. He told me he had lent his cousin money who resided at Bexleyheath. I will swear he did not tell me he had lent anyone else money'.[3] Thomas Kimpton was then called, and stated that Clark had told him he had broken open the lock himself before leaving Arbour Square. 'He did so to shew he had only got his own property – where the key was then I cannot state'. Incidentally, this line of enquiry was followed up by Edward Kendell two days later. His expenses claim reveals that on 16th July he 'went to Bexley in Kent to see Clark's friends, to make enquiries respecting his money'. By 'friends' he means the Markhams, relatives of Clark on his mother's side.

The Coroner then asked Jonas Stevens what he had seen of his fellow-officers during the night of 29th June. Stevens replied that he had not encountered any of the other constables during that time, but that he had seen Sergeant Parsons at about half past 10, and again between twelve and one at Broad Street. On both occasions, he said, the Sergeant was on horseback. He stated that he saw Parsons again at 6am when going off duty.

Was there, the Coroner then wondered, any friction between Clark and the other policemen on account of his active Methodism? Stevens replied that 'Clark was on good terms with the sergeant and all the men as far as I knew. I never heard any of the men quarrel with him about his religion'. Stevens, of course, had been at Mrs Page's when the disputed conversation had taken place, and Coroner Lewis wanted to know whether he had overheard it. The answer was a firm negative. 'I do not remember that Kimpton said anything about doing Parsons's duty on the night of the murder. I don't think such a thing could have been said without my hearing it. I will swear that I did not hear it said'.

Kimpton was then recalled, and asked what he thought about Elizabeth Page's evidence. He denied it all. 'I do not recollect making any statement to Mrs Page that Parsons was ill, and that I did his duty on horseback for him on the night of the murder. I will swear I did not say it'. The feisty Mrs Page took exception to this and was not afraid to say so. She interrupted the proceedings and confronted Kimpton, declaring that what she had stated on oath was true.

Kimpton, however, persisted with his version of events. He stated he had seen Parsons several times on horseback, doing duty himself, throughout the night. 'I saw him last at the station at Dagenham, at a quarter past three o'clock, when I took his horse to the stable. He then said he had not seen Clark during the night, and asked me if I had seen him'.[4] The Coroner and attentive members of the audience must have remembered the evidence of Thomas Archer at the previous hearing. Archer had said Kimpton was on horseback when he stopped at Wants Farm to ask if Archer had seen anything of Clark. Only one horse was kept at the police station, but apparently two officers had been using it at more or less the same time.

Isaac Hickton was then asked to take the oath and give his evidence. He explained he patrolled the Beacontree Heath area, which adjoined Clark's beat. 'I generally was in the habit of meeting deceased during the night at Mr Miller's farm. I went there at about a quarter before 11 o'clock, as there was some singing and a noise, but he did not come.' Hickton said he had met Kimpton at Beacontree Heath about a quarter to one. Kimpton had brought the report to pass on, and had said 'Where's Clark? I can't think where he has got to'.

The Coroner wanted to know whether Hickton had heard anything unusual that night. The constable replied that he had heard 'no report from a gun, or any calls for help or assistance during the night. If there had been a report of fire-arms, I must, I think, have heard it from my beat'. Coroner Lewis had not yet finished with Kimpton. He called him back again, and asked him to elaborate on the subject of the report that Parsons had written to be sent up to his superiors at the Ilford station. Kimpton explained that 'the common way of transferring a report is by passing it to the men on duty from beat to beat'. He said that on the night of the murder he had received the report from Parsons at about 12.15am. 'He told me not to be late with it, but to leave the village a little before one, so as to get at the Wants by one. He had said before if I did not meet Clark to go on to the heath with it'.

Parsons was then recalled, and confirmed that he gave the report to Kimpton at the time stated. The Coroner was also interested in Parsons' statement at the first inquest hearing that his last meeting with Clark took place 'shortly after one on Tuesday morning'.

When asked about this, the Sergeant asserted that 'I saw Clark about 1 o'clock near the Four Wants on the morning of the Tuesday. That was half a mile from the spot where he ought to have met Kimpton at that time'.

The hearing was finally wound up after six o'clock. Lewis announced that 'certain parties' were implicated in the murder, but he was unable to bring the evidence before the jury then and there. An adjournment until 23rd July was necessary to allow time to trace 'some very important witnesses'. One of the Young brothers then asked for the return of the property that had been taken away when the police raided his house the week before. This had, as we know, included a double-edged knife known as a stiletto. His request was turned down. The detectives had an important reason for holding on to the knife. This was soon revealed when the Coroner announced that if one of the Dagenham churchwardens was in the room he wanted to speak to him. Thomas Waters Brittain[5], one of the jurors, came forward. Lewis explained that he thought it would be necessary to exhume the body, and intended to issue warrants to the clergyman and to the churchwardens asking for permission to do so. The *Morning Chronicle* told its readers that this was to enable Joseph Collin to look at Clark's injuries once more, 'and to say whether the weapon in question could have caused such wounds'.[6] Apparently the Coroner made this decision 'after a lengthened interview with Mr Superintendent Pearce'.[7] The results of the second post-mortem would be announced at the next hearing of the inquest.

A week later, on Tuesday 21st July, a band of labourers harvested the wheat in the field where Clark's body had been found. This was done earlier in the season than usual so that the detectives could carry out a fingertip search of the whole area in search of more clues. Edward Kendell and others spent several hours examining the field, but, as the *Morning Chronicle* reported,

An early 20th century photograph of Thorntons Farm. The kitchen where the disputed conversation took place is to the left of the front door

'found nothing tending to show who the perpetrators of the outrage were. Near the spot, however, where the body formerly laid, Kendal [sic] picked up a portion of the deceased's hair and a small piece of his blue coat, which appears to have been cut off with some sharp instrument, and at the same time the wound was inflicted in the throat'.[8]

The following day the same newspaper tried to calm the raging speculation about the involvement of Parsons in the affair. It assured its readers that 'In consequence of the evidence given at the adjourned inquest, tending to throw suspicion on Sergeant Parsons, and also to the effect that he had been guilty of neglecting his duty, a minute investigation was gone into respecting his conduct before Mr Superintendent Pearce, and subsequently before the superintendent of the K Division, Mr Marquard, and the result was, that he had performed his duty properly, and not the slightest suspicion could attach to him'.

At six o'clock on the evening of 23rd July, the inquest opened for the third time. Some days before, there had been a railway disaster not far away at Stratford, and this might have been expected to overtake the Dagenham murder as the current hot news topic. A Mr Hind, a well-known silk fringe manufacturer of Cheapside, had been killed in the accident. The Cross Keys inquest room was as full as ever, though, with an eager public expecting more revelations, fuelled by the rumours of police involvement in the ghastly crime. 'The vast excitement caused by this horrible occurrence has not in the least degree diminished. Before the arrival of the coroner the inquest room was densely crowded by a large number of the magistrates and gentry of the surrounding districts'.[9]

This time three members of the Page family of Thorntons Farm were called for questioning. Priscilla Page, the sixteen year-old daughter of Ralph and Elizabeth, appeared first. She said that she had been at home the evening Clark's body was found but 'I did not see anything of him myself'. Naturally, she was asked about the disputed conversation between her mother and Thomas Kimpton. Priscilla told the jury that she had remained in the room the whole time the men were at supper, and heard everything that passed. She supported her mother's version of events. Apparently, about five minutes before leaving the house 'Mr Kimpton said that on the night of the murder the sergeant came home and asked him to go and do his duty as he was very tired, and that he (Kimpton) did his duty, and that it was not the first time; he said he did the duty on horseback'.

Priscilla was asked about her father Ralph Page's movements on the fatal night. 'I last saw my father at about half past 12 o'clock on the night of the murder in the barn'.[10] She said that due to her father's absence she had slept in her mother's room that night. 'I went to bed between 1 and 2 and my mother with me – we slept in a front room on the first floor'.[11] Priscilla said she was certain she heard no noise of dogs barking, or any disturbance during the night.

Ralph Page himself then came forward for the first time. He told the jury that he had spent the night of the 29th June in his barn guarding his corn as he was afraid of it being stolen. The corn would have been the previous year's harvest, prepared (or 'dressed') and bagged up. Page said he had left the farmhouse between 9 and 10pm, went directly into the barn, and locked himself in. He laid himself on top of some sacks of wheat, and remained there until between five and six the next morning. The only sound he heard during the night was his dog barking between one and two in the morning. 'He made about 4 yelps and then left off'.[12]

Page then spoke about seeing the policemen at various times over the following days as they carried out the search for Clark. He said that on Wednesday 1st July he had met Kimpton 'at the top of the Chase leading to my house'.[13] They had talked about the search, and according to Page, Kimpton told him 'I think it very little use dragging the ponds, for I think he will not be found till harvest time and then I think he will be found in one of the cornfields'. According to Page, in the afternoon of the same day he met three of the other policemen sitting on a gate taking a break from the arduous searching. 'I stated to them what Kimpton had said to me in the morning and I observed that if he is in a corn field he is easy to be traced in the state the corn is now for was a dog to run into standing corn you could track which way he had gone. Parsons then came over to the men and said we have been and look'd round the cornfields and can see no track whatever'. Ralph Page's evidence must have increased the audience's doubts about the behaviour of Parsons and Kimpton.

Mrs Page and Kimpton were then called in, and questioned once again about the disputed conversation. Just as at the previous hearing, there was a confrontation between them. The farmer's wife 'repeated her assertion as to Kimpton doing duty for the sergeant on the night of the murder, and Kimpton as positively denied it'.[14] Mrs Page had so far been on the offensive, not to be shaken from her claim that Kimpton was not telling the truth about what had been said in her farmhouse that night. Yet suddenly the Coroner posed a question that seemed to lay Mrs Page herself open to suspicion. Had she, he asked, told Sarah Scott, the wife of Dagenham farmer William Scott, that she had sat up in her kitchen the whole night of the murder? Indignantly, Mrs Page denied saying any such thing.

Mrs Scott was then called to give her evidence. She at first refused to take the oath. 'She said she was not a Moravian or a Quaker, but would not be sworn'. When the exasperated Coroner threatened to send her to prison she eventually gave way. Mrs Scott told the jury that 'last Sunday week' she went to see the spot where the body was found. She met Mrs Page there, and asked if she had heard any cries for help on the night of the 29th June, her house being so close to the scene. Mrs Page, she claimed, had replied that she hadn't heard anything although she was up in her kitchen all night. According to Mrs Scott, a Mrs Bright and Mr Collier were also present to hear Mrs Page say this. Mrs Jane Bright was then called, but was unwilling or unable to be certain of what exactly had been said. 'I recollect Mrs Page saying that on the night of the 29th she was sitting up in her own room or kitchen – I am not certain which term she made use of'.[15]

The evidence then turned to medical matters. At ten o'clock that morning, Clark's mangled remains had been taken out of his grave. Almost three weeks after the first post-mortem, poor Joseph Collin was obliged to go through the whole grim business once again. This time he was accompanied by fellow Romford surgeon, 57 year-old Charles Cornelius Butler. At the inquest hearing later that day, Collin was called to announce their findings. He said he had been asked to check whether Clark had been shot, but had found no evidence for this. Also, was there a chance he had been killed by his own cutlass? Collin explained that although the cutlass did fit to the depth of an inch and a half into the wound under Clark's right ear, he didn't believe it was sharp enough to have actually been the cause of it. He was also 'satisfied the cutlass could not have cut through the stock and inflicted the wound in front of the neck. That on the back of the neck might have been done by a cutlass. My opinion is the two wounds on the throat – I mean the one through the stock and that under the right ear – were caused after deceased was on the ground and before he was dead'. Charles Butler confirmed his colleague's evidence, and added the gruesome detail that 'that the skull had not a particle of brain left in it'.[16] Nothing at all seems to have been said about the knife belonging to the Young brothers.

The Coroner was determined to get to the bottom of what had been said over supper at Page's farmhouse the night the body was discovered. He summoned the carpenter William Kittle, who had been present at the table that evening. Kittle said he didn't remember hearing Kimpton say he did Parsons' duty on the night of the murder. At this point several members of the jury 'here expressed, very strongly, their opinion that this witness knew a great deal more than he seemed inclined to disclose'. There was then more drama as Mrs Page interrupted to say that the previous Saturday Kittle had admitted that he *did* remember the words being said.

A farm labourer named James March was then called to give evidence. He explained that he had walked with the cart carrying Clark's body from the Rail Pond, and had waited with it at the Four Wants while Parsons sought permission to take the corpse to Hunters Hall. Marsh declared he did not hear Kimpton say he did duty for Parsons on the night of the murder. One of the jury, who we are told was his employer, then challenged this. He 'declared that Marsh had not only declared he heard Kimpton say so once, but many times. The witness here said he did hear Kimpton say he was on the horse that night, but what part of the night he could not say'.

At this point there was uproar as Parsons lost his patience, sprang up and protested that they were 'endeavouring to prove him the murderer'. The coroner tried to calm the sergeant down, but his agitation can only have increased with the evidence of the next witness. This was Thomas Smith, the grocer and promoter of the Ebenezer Chapel which George Clark had so assiduously attended. Smith's statement threw yet more doubt on the policemen's evidence. He stated that he had accompanied the body from Mr Brittain's farm to the Four Wants. Kimpton of course was there too, and had talked about searching for Clark when it was first realized he was missing. 'He said he rode on the horse to see after the deceased on the night he was lost. He said he rode as far as Mrs Myhill's [sic] or Mrs Stone's[17] he there whistled two or three times but heard nothing of him. He said he kept out the horse as long as he dare, and then went home'.[18] When asked whose horse this was, he replied 'I supposed he meant Sergeant Parsons' horse'.

Help was at hand for Parsons, though, in the form of his sister Julia. She gave her address as 49 Oxford Street, Mile End. She began by telling the coroner of her meeting with Parsons and Clark as they strolled towards the Four Wants at about a quarter past nine on the evening of the murder. She said 'Clark appeared very cheerful'. Julia then said that her brother 'came home again to the station about 12 o'clock. He then made the report, and afterwards went out again. That was before 1 o'clock. I did not see him again till about 9 the next morning. I slept in the room adjoining my brother's room'. She said she had heard her brother tell his wife at about 6.15am that Clark had not come home. 'My brother went out, and on coming home, at nine o'clock, had breakfast, and said Clark could not be found'.[19] Julia was asked whether it was possible her brother could come and go from the house during the night without her hearing him, and she admitted that it was.

The Coroner then told Parsons that he would be happy to hear any witnesses he wished to produce. The one person definitely in a position to know whether Parsons had been out at work or home in bed that night would have been his wife, but there seems to have been no question of requiring her to give evidence.[20] The first witness called on behalf of Parsons only spoke of seeing him on duty up to nine o'clock. The second was Thomas Shutt, landlord of the Cross Keys. He told the Coroner he had served Parsons with a pint of porter at midnight when on duty. Finally, a man named James Dale swore that as he passed through Dagenham on his way from Hornchurch to London between three and four o'clock in the morning of 30th June, he had definitely seen Parsons. 'I met him at the corner at the top of the Village. He was on horseback. I did not speak to him but I am sure it was him'.[21]

Coroner Lewis decided to put an end to this knotty subject for the time being. He announced that 'there could be no doubt but Parsons was on duty the whole night'. Several members of the jury also 'expressed themselves fully satisfied that Parsons was performing his duty in a proper manner'.[22] The question at issue was, Lewis declared, whether Kimpton had said those words to Mrs Page. He felt that 'the evidence went to show that Kimpton did make the statement, and why he did make it God only knew'. Kimpton at this point reiterated his claim that he did not say so, but we are told that 'the members of the jury expressed their conviction that he had'.

The coroner then calmed things down by calling another witness, who had written to him offering important new evidence. Her name was Mrs Elizabeth Dodd, and she told a dramatic tale to the jury. She said that on 29th June she had been to Whitechapel for a job interview, and didn't get back to her home in Romford until about 11 o'clock or midnight. She made her way from Rainham across the Dagenham fields, and in 'the second cornfield' she saw a tall man with black whiskers and wearing a fustian[23] coat talking to a policeman. The man asked the officer the time, 'then used an improper expression towards him'. Mrs Dodd recognized the swearer as somebody she had seen several times before, 'in the fields near Mr Lee's, at Romford, eating bread with a very large knife'. She then spotted someone else looking over the hedge, and hurried away. 'As I approached nearer Romford I met two girls, who asked me if I did not hear screams'. Would her story, with its enticing detail of the 'very large knife', provide the much-needed breakthrough? The *Morning Chronicle* reporter thought not. He described Elizabeth Dodd as 'a simple girl' and her statement as 'rambling' and 'vague'.[24]

It was now nearly ten o'clock, and the hearing had been in progress for almost four hours. Inspector William Richardson told the Coroner 'that that was the whole of the evidence he had to offer'. Lewis announced that he had been told that John Anderson, the governor of Ilford Gaol, might have

Woolwich Police Station. This photograph is dated 1908

important information, but was unable to attend that day as he was away in Kent. He went on to say that 'There were also some other matters to be brought before the Jury, which had been found near the spot where the murder was committed. Under these circumstances, he felt it necessary that the enquiry should be adjourned for a month'.[25] If any arrests were made in the meantime, the jury would be called back.

A month had now passed since the discovery of the body. At about eight o'clock in the evening of Saturday 8th August, an Irish boy entered Woolwich police station and insisted on speaking to Inspector Levy. The lad may not have looked very prepossessing, but what he had to say made the officer take him extremely seriously. He said his name was Michael Walsh[26], and he had come to accuse three people of being involved in the murder of George Clark. Apparently two of them, Ellen Rankin and Dennis Flynn, were at that very moment in Denison's lodging-house just a short distance away.

Constables Edwin Horsfall and Edward Palmer were immediately sent out with the boy to the address he had named, reaching there at about half-past eight. Michael Walsh pointed out the suspects. Rankin tried to push past the officers and escape into the street, but she and Flynn were seized and taken away. Dennis Flynn's reaction seemed to point to his guilt. 'On the boy's statement being read over to Flynn, he betrayed very strong emotions, his face became deadly pale, and large drops of perspiration rolled down his face'.[27] He seemed resigned to being arrested. 'On going to the station, Flynn enquired whom he had robbed or injured'. He was overheard to say to Rankin, 'Keep your mouth shut, and they can't hurt us'.[28]

Two days later, on 10th August, the pair were brought before Woolwich Police Court. Flynn was described by a journalist as 'a decent looking Irish labourer', and Rankin as 'a woman who has been cohabiting with him'.[29] It seems she was also known as Ellen Cotter. They were ordered to appear at the Ilford Petty Sessions the following day, and were then removed to Ilford Gaol. The third suspect named by the boy was John Hennessy. It was not long before he too was tracked down and taken into custody at Ilford with the others.

The trio appeared before the magistrates on Tuesday, 11th August at 12 noon, in the justice room at Ilford Gaol.[30] The senior officers involved in the murder investigation were present to listen to the allegations unfold in the courtroom. Could this at last be the breakthrough they were waiting for?

We don't know Michael Walsh's exact age, but his short life had clearly been one of struggle. He had been in England only six months, having arrived on 5th February. It's likely he was one of the many thousands forced to leave their native land during the devastating potato famine. Alone, he had made his way around the country, taking casual jobs such as haymaking. He told the magistrates that a farmer named Giddins of Cudham in Kent had recently employed him to help bring in the corn harvest. His fellow-labourers included Dennis Flynn and Ellen Rankin.

Walsh then reached the crucial point of his story. 'On Tuesday afternoon last I was at work at Hanesty, when the prisoner Dennis Flynn came into the field and got some work also at cutting wheat'. The next day, Walsh claimed, a group of workers were sitting around a fire in the field cooking their lunch. One of these was Ellen Rankin. She was complaining about having to take such a gruelling job. Her companion Flynn had been earning good money in London, she said. Unfortunately, he was being forced to lie low in the country for a while as he had assaulted a policeman. The incident had apparently been sparked off by a fracas in a pub between English and Irish groups. The Irishmen had insisted on singing, and this soon led to a fight. When a police sergeant arrived on horseback to deal with the situation a stone was hurled at him. Michael Walsh then alleged that Rankin had gone on to say that Flynn and Hennessy had later attacked another policeman who was found dead in a field. Hearing this in court, Ellen Rankin 'became greatly agitated'. She asked for a glass of water, and was allowed to sit down.

Michael Walsh then claimed that John Hennessey was also one of the harvesting party. Hennessey immediately protested that he had been at home in Stratford at the time, and had never been to Cudham in his life. A witness was then called who, it seemed, could back up at least part of the boy's story. He was Felix Sweeney, who with his cousin John Sweeney had been amongst the group around the fire. Felix told the magistrates that he remembered Ellen Rankin talking about a policeman being found in a field with his head off. He hadn't really paid much attention to what she said, though. He stated that John Hennessey had definitely not been there. In fact, he had never even seen him before. Dennis Flynn then took the oath. He admitted that he knew Hennessey, but categorically denied the boy's allegations. He screamed 'It is all untruth that he has been stating. I am as innocent of this murder as a man in Smithfield'.

PC Edward Palmer told the court that he had searched Rankin's bag and found 'two odd white gloves, the kind policemen wear'. When the trio were remanded in custody for a week, Hennessey burst into tears. Pointing at Walsh, he cried 'That boy is taking my life away'. Flynn also protested his innocence. He exclaimed 'Your worship, I am a poor hard-working chap, and never hurt the hair of a man's head'. According to the *News of the World* 'the boy Welch was also ordered to be detained, suspicion being entertained that if allowed to go at large he would not be forthcoming'.

At an early hour on Saturday 15th August the three were brought up again before the Ilford magistrates. Dennis Flynn spoke at length about how he had taken Walsh under his wing, sharing his meals with him as they travelled together in search of work. The lad agreed that this had been the case. Flynn explained that it was only when his resources were becoming exhausted, that he told Walsh he couldn't look after him any longer. The boy had then left, muttering that 'he would have a supper of beefsteaks, or rashers, from someone'. Soon afterwards, the two policemen had turned up at Flynn's lodgings in Woolwich and taken him and Rankin away.

Flynn had an ally in Thomas Reed, foreman of the Stratford building firm of Messrs R. & E. Curtis. Reed told the court that from 4th June to 4th July last Flynn had been employed by them as a labourer at Loughton New Church. On 29th and 30th June, far from being absent, Flynn had actually worked overtime. The foreman produced time-books to back up his evidence.[31] In any case, Loughton was the considerable distance of 14 miles (22 km) away from Dagenham. Flynn declared on oath that Ellen Rankin had lodged with him at Loughton on the night of the murder.

John Hennessey's witness was his father-in-law, who swore that Hennessey was at work with him on 29th June at Mortlake, and that he got up at 4.30 the following morning. Ellen Rankin was also able to prove that the suspicious pair of white gloves had in fact been given to her by a woman named Margaret Driscol to prevent her hands being injured by thistles while cutting corn.[32] That energetic detective Edward Kendell told the court that he had travelled to Loughton and Mortlake to enquire into the character of the prisoners and their witnesses, and found them to be 'perfectly correct'. He was convinced, he said, that they were innocent. Kendell explained that Hennessey was indeed on the run from the police, and that Walsh must have known this, but it was for an offence completely unconnected with the murder of Clark. The chairman of the magistrates discharged the trio. Hennessey was then put up again on the charge of assaulting a potboy, to which he pleaded guilty. He was fined 1s with 10s costs, and allowed time to pay. For the detectives, it was back to the drawing board. Another apparently promising lead had come to nothing.

We have seen that after a somewhat shaky start, by the 1840s the press and public saw the Metropolitan Police in a generally favourable light. During the summer of 1846, however, there was a steady stream of incidents bringing nothing but criticism of the force. Commissioners Rowan and Mayne must have been most unhappy to read a lengthy anti-police editorial in the liberal *Morning Chronicle* of Friday 14th August. It contended that 'the humbler and more helpless classes of the community' were sometimes falsely accused. It claimed that to gain a conviction and the reward or promotion that went with it, police officers resorted to perjury (lying when under oath in the courtroom.)

In support of its argument, the *Morning Chronicle* quoted the case of PC Samuel Peyton, of E division. He was accused of assaulting a law-stationer named Samuel Irons, and of using insulting language towards him. It seems that the police had been called to keep order when crowds of sightseers flocked to the scene of a row of houses in Holborn which had suddenly fallen down. Constable Peyton mistook Irons for one of the so-called Swell Mob, well-dressed pickpockets who worked unsuspected in large gatherings. He forcibly dragged Irons out of a confectioner's shop, shouting to the proprietor 'You have a thief in your house!' The policeman had brought forward a Mrs Pounsbury to give evidence in his favour, but the magistrate, Mr Jardine, decided 'she had perjured herself' at his request. Jardine was also convinced that other officers had lied in support of their colleague. Peyton was found guilty of the charge, and sentenced to a month's hard labour in the House of Correction.

The *Morning Chronicle* editorial pulled no punches in its assessment of the situation. It alleged that the magistrates believed 'this practice of perjury was on the increase in the police', but that Mr Jardine's condemnation of Constable Peyton was the first time this had been expressed in public. Not to be outdone, the *Daily News* of the same day thundered that 'The instances of brutality on the part of the police are so common that the force, instead of being regarded as a protection to the public, is to many, and particularly to women having occasion to be out alone in the evening, really an object of terror'. It quoted a case heard the previous day at Clerkenwell Police Court. A Constable Broadridge was charged with 'an assault of a most brutal and wanton character upon Mrs Welch, the wife of a respectable tobacco-manufacturer'. She and a friend, a doctor's wife, were out walking at about 11pm when Broadridge shouted 'Go on, you common women' and shoved the heavily-pregnant Mrs Welch along the street. He and another constable then dragged her to the police station. She caused a sensation in court by showing the injuries they had inflicted on her arms, 'and their appearance shocked the spectators; the upper parts of both arms were quite livid and swollen, not a mere finger mark, but five or six inches in breadth'.

The following Monday the paper returned to the topic, telling its readers that the Commissioners had directed an immediate inquiry into Mrs Welch's case. It urged Rowan and Mayne to dismiss rogue policemen such as Broadridge

The early police uniform, including top hat and truncheon, is shown in this photograph of PC Moses Row of the South Wales Police

rather than just suspending or redeploying them. Apparently 'large numbers of persons, who find themselves obliged to be out at night, consider it very desirable to keep at a civil distance from the policeman whom they pay for protection'. The writer ended by declaring that such evident corruption threw doubts over the future of the Metropolitan Police itself.

Such a press campaign against the force was nothing new. Rowan and Mayne had ridden such storms before from time to time during their seventeen years at the helm. They had, they thought, always acted promptly to weed out the small minority of men revealed to lack the necessary integrity. Yet on Monday 17th August they must have feared a crisis was looming. The allegations in the *Daily News* and *Morning Chronicle* had been bad enough, but the Commissioners had that very weekend been made aware of a devastating new development in the George Clark murder case. They knew that it would soon be exploited to the full in the Press. And they would not in all honesty be able to deny the force of the criticism.

An 1843 cartoon by George Cruickshank demonstrating a widely-held view of the police

*4, Whitehall Place. Butfoy would have walked up the steps on the left for
his fateful interview with the Police Commissioners in August 1846*

CHAPTER 7

"You know you are guilty of it'

Let's now return to the events of Saturday 15th August, two days before the outburst from the *Daily News*. That morning, Dennis Flynn, Ellen Rankin and John Hennessey had been set free by the Ilford magistrates, no evidence having been found to link them to the death of Clark. The murdered man's colleague Abia Butfoy was present at the hearing, no doubt with other Dagenham officers. Butfoy afterwards returned to the Bull Street station house, but when the time came for him to line up with the others in the yard in preparation for going on duty, he was nowhere to be found. The other officers began to panic. Did they now have a second disappearance on their hands?

Butfoy's failure to turn up that evening was indeed cause for alarm, but not in the way his fellow officers first feared. He wasn't lying dead or injured somewhere in a repeat performance of the Clark outrage. Instead, he had travelled to Whitehall Place and insisted upon seeing the Commissioners. What he told them would probably be reported in today's tabloids under the headline 'Butfoy's Bombshell'. He claimed, no less, that the Dagenham police had stood up at the inquest hearings, had solemnly sworn on the Bible that their evidence was nothing but the truth – and then had promptly told a tissue of lies. Perjury, of which the *Morning Chronicle* had said 'there is no crime of more pernicious consequences to the community', had reared its ugly head once more.

One wonders what drove Butfoy to confess all to Rowan and Mayne. Had he been wrestling with a guilty conscience? Or did he perhaps think that the truth was bound to come to light eventually, and that by speaking out voluntarily he might manage to evade punishment? We have seen that as early as the week ending 18th July, the Dagenham police were strongly suspected of involvement in Clark's murder. This was a full four weeks before Butfoy's visit to Scotland Yard. It's quite likely that his revelations, far from being a bombshell, were what the detectives and the Commissioners had been expecting. The only question had been which of the officers would crack first. Whatever Butfoy's motivation, it has to be said that to take such a step certainly required a degree of courage on his part.

Rowan and Mayne immediately informed the Home Secretary, Sir George Grey, of the developments. He agreed that William Parsons and the Dagenham constables be suspended from duty, with pay, from 17th August until the termination of the inquest. The headline of the *Weekly Dispatch* of 23rd August screamed: THE MURDER AT DAGENHAM – APPREHENSION OF FIVE OF THE POLICE.

It reported that Superintendents Marquard and Pearce interrogated Parsons and then ordered him to be taken into custody, along with Hickton, Farnes, Kimpton and Butfoy. Reading this, people must have had a vision of the whole crew being rounded up and carted off to Ilford Gaol. The truth was not quite so dramatic. The men were in fact put under house arrest. Detectives Kendell, Langley and Shaw were instructed not to let Parsons out of their sight, and to make sure he didn't communicate with any of others. Jonas Stevens, who had recently been transferred to D Division, and was now living at a police station at 4, Bryanston Place, Marylebone, was also held. Replacement police officers from the H and K Divisions were drafted to Dagenham.

30 year-old Detective Sergeant Edward Langley was from Stock in Essex. On Tuesday 18th August he took Parsons to the murder scene. As they were leaving, Langley noticed a bloodstained handkerchief in a meadow belonging to Thomas Waters Brittain 'adjoining the field where the murder took place'.[1] He bent down to pick the handkerchief up, and realized it was stuck to the grass, clotted with blood. He described it as 'silk, having a blue ground with a figured orange, yellow and crimson border, very old, and much torn'. The Coroner was told, and ordered the handkerchief to be left at Dagenham station in the hope that it would be identified.

In the meantime, the detectives renewed their enquiries in and around Dagenham itself. In his expenses claim, Frederick Shaw states that he spent the week of 19th-26th August interviewing 'the inhabitants at Wood Lane, Beacontree Heath and Chadwell Heath'. These claims are full of revealing detail.[2] Edward Langley put in for the cost of a 'fly from Romford to Dagenham, 3 and a half miles, there being no other conveyance – 3 shillings'. We learn that on 23rd August and 1st September he travelled from Dagenham to Westminster by omnibus, and paid two shillings and sixpence (12½) for a seat inside. His colleague Shaw claimed one shilling and ninepence for a second-class train ticket from Romford to Shoreditch (the terminus of the Eastern Counties Railway at that time) on 18th August, a distance of 12 miles, followed by an omnibus to Westminster costing sixpence. Henry Smith's expenses bring to mind the fictional journeys of Sherlock Holmes and Dr Watson. He spent eight shillings on one cab journey, firstly from Bow Street to Dean Street Westminster, then to Arbour Square Police Station and finally to Marylebone Police Station. He also paid a sixpenny toll at the Turnpike Gate on the Commercial Road.

On Thursday 20th August, just five days after Butfoy's revelations, the inquest re-opened for the fourth time. It was due to begin at 6 o'clock in the evening, but the Coroner had summoned so many witnesses that he decided to bring the proceedings forward to 2.30pm. We are told that the room was 'crowded to suffocation by magistrates and the resident gentry of the neighbourhood'.[3] By now they had all heard that the Dagenham policemen had been suspended from duty. More than that, the rumour was that they would soon be charged with murder. There must have been gasps when the officers appeared dressed in their own clothes, adding substance to the shocking gossip. As we have seen, police officers were expected to wear the uniform seven days a week, whether they were on duty or not.

Abia Butfoy was the first to give evidence. He began by telling the jury that on the morning of the day of the murder, Monday 29th June, he and Parsons had travelled to Romford in order to attend to some business at the Magistrates' Court. He said they were joined by two constables from Ilford named Belton and Ballard. The court proceedings finished about an hour later, at which point, according to Butfoy, the four policemen embarked on a marathon drinking session. The following memory of the scene at magistrates courts of the 1880s, written by Thomas Holmes, a Police Court Missionary, show that there was nothing unusual about this. He asserts that the police were regularly bribed with free drinks:

> In those days policemen waited for the men and women who had been in their custody, and against whom they had given evidence, and, after their fines were paid, went to the nearest public house and drank at their expense. Hundreds of times I have heard prisoners ask the prosecuting policeman to 'Make it light for me', and many times I have heard the required promise given and an arrangement made. Sometimes I am glad to think that I have heard policemen give the reply: 'I shall speak the truth'; but not often was this straightforward answer given...it is now [1908] a rare occurrence for a policeman to take a drink at his prisoner's expense.[4]

Butfoy doesn't reveal who exactly picked up the drinks bill on this occasion, but it must have been a pretty heavy one. He recounted that the foursome first spent two hours in the Lamb Pub in Romford Market Place. Afterwards they adjourned to the Star Tap in the High Street, where they stayed for about an hour. He explained that they had then taken a horse and cart back to Dagenham, reaching there at about a quarter to one in the afternoon. Butfoy was dropped off near his house in Bull Street, but only stayed there for about five minutes. On re-emerging he made his way to yet another pub, this time the Rose & Crown in Crown Street. The Ilford policemen, Ballard and Belton, were inside and already making short work of more supplies of beer. They asked Butfoy to join them for another drink, but he told the court that this time he refused. The two Ilford constables then finished their beer, took the horse and cart and drove away.

The Rose & Crown ceased to be a pub in the 1880s. By the time this photograph was taken it was the residence of the Bales family

Butfoy staggered out of the Rose and Crown and immediately came up against Sergeant Parsons in the street. It seems that Butfoy was shortly due to go on duty. Parsons could see he was in no fit state to do so, and ordered Butfoy to go straight back home. 'My regular time was to have gone on duty at 3 o'clock, but when we go before the magistrates it is optional with the sergeant what duty we perform; the sergeant gave me leave to go off duty on that day at the Rose & Crown public house; the fact is that I was intoxicated at the time, and he told me to go in, which I did'.[5] Butfoy admitted to the court that 'we were all the worse for the drink but I think I was the most drunk of the party'.[6] He said he returned home at about two o'clock, went to bed around five, and remained there until he was awoken the following morning by Thomas Kimpton with the news that Clark was missing.

Butfoy then went on to give damaging evidence about Sergeant Parsons himself. Apparently Parsons too must have been feeling the worse for wear after that day's tour of Romford pubs. Butfoy announced that 'I have learned from some other constables that Parsons was not on duty after 12 o'clock'. We are told that this created a 'sensation' within the inquest room.[7] It vindicated all that Mrs Page had said.

According to Butfoy, Parsons went into action soon after Clark's disappearance, flatly ordering the constables to say, if asked, that they saw him on duty in the early hours of Tuesday 30th June. 'It has passed between Parsons and me and the other men that "we were all in a mess and must stick to the tale"; that has passed repeatedly'. The Coroner asked Butfoy what exactly was meant by the 'mess' they were in. His reply was 'Why, a mess as to the falsehoods we had told, by saying that we saw him on duty at 12 o'clock and after one, when we did not'. Parsons had also asked Butfoy to pretend that he himself had been on duty as usual that evening, instead of sleeping off the effects of the pub crawl. Butfoy threw even more suspicion on Parsons by commenting that 'It looks strange that the sergeant does not account for his time from half-past 9 o'clock until 11, and that Clark was not seen by a man who was invariably in the habit of seeing him at 11 o'clock at the Four Wants'.

John Farnes then stepped up to give evidence. He backed up what Butfoy had said. He told the Coroner that Parsons didn't ask him personally to vouch for his being on duty the whole of the night, but had relayed the order via Kimpton. 'I met Kimpton between his house and the station. The conversation began about Clark, with one of us saying "This is an unpleasant thing about Clark" and Kimpton said if we did not keep to the statement of what was said with respect to meeting Sergeant Parsons, we should all get into trouble'. A weary Coroner Lewis interrupted Farnes at one point, saying 'We want no more falsehoods, we have had enough already'.

Thomas Kimpton was then called. He began by saying 'I have nothing further to say than to tell the truth'. He stated that at six in the morning of Tuesday 30th June he went into the police station to call the sergeant up. He knocked at the bedroom door, and about five minutes later Parsons appeared. Kimpton told him that Clark was missing. Parsons said 'It is very strange he is not at home; stop a few minutes, and I'll go with you, and we'll look for him'. Kimpton continued, 'We then went round Clark's beat, I one way, and Parsons the other'. He said that when the pair met up again they set off back to the station, calling in at Kimpton's house on the way. It was then that Parsons first broached the subject, saying: 'The man is missing, and I must say I saw him at 1 o'clock, and you must say the same'.

Kimpton and Butfoy disagreed, however, about whether Butfoy had been on duty that night. Kimpton maintained that Butfoy had done his nine-hour shift from 3pm as usual. He told the jury that at midnight he was holding the horse near the door of the police station while Parsons was writing the report. Butfoy then came up, went inside and said to Parsons 'All right, sergeant' to indicate he was now going off duty. Kimpton added 'I was sober at the time'. Butfoy tried to test Kimpton by asking 'Was it a dark or a light night, and can you tell me which way I came?' Kimpton replied that 'It was not very dark, and you came from the direction of your house to the station'. Kimpton went on to deny having called Butfoy up at a quarter to six the following morning to tell him of Clark's disappearance.

Parsons was then called. He too was dressed in plain clothes, and the audience held its breath as it waited to see what he had to say for himself. Parsons kept things short and to the point. He stood by everything he had said at the former hearings. He maintained he was on duty the whole night, up to 6am, and didn't go to bed until after that. Whatever the others had said to the contrary, he claimed, was absolutely untrue. 'Whatever Butfoy states about not being on duty at twelve o'clock is false. He came home at that hour and reported himself to me'. Butfoy retorted 'If I was on duty, what beat was I on?' Parsons' answer is not recorded.

John Farnes then came forward to claim that Parsons had told him to say he had seen him on duty at eleven o'clock, two o'clock and six o'clock. The times had even been written down for him. Coroner Lewis asked 'What do you say to that, Parsons?' The sergeant coolly replied: 'He can say what he likes – I never told him to do it. It is a very hard case for me; I am placed as a sergeant over them, and they state what they like. All they have stated against me is entirely false'. He agreed to sign a declaration to that effect. The Coroner clearly still had his doubts. Farnes had said he had seen Parsons at midnight, so Lewis asked him about the state the horse was in. Farnes replied that 'it did not look unusually hot or warm; when I heard Parsons's horse coming it was at a walking pace'.[8] Jonas Stevens was the next to be called, but was unable to shed any light on the events of the fatal night. He said he and Clark had gone on duty at the same time, but their beats were distant from each other.

Isaac Hickton then came forward. As he was taking the oath, Butfoy claimed that he was only pretending to kiss the Bible. The ritual was then repeated three times. Hickton told the court that he had patrolled the Beacontree Heath beat on the night of the murder. He had left the station at 8pm and returned at about 5am. He said he saw absolutely nothing of Parsons throughout the night. In fact, he did not encounter his sergeant again until past one o'clock on the following afternoon. 'Parsons then came to me in the station yard, and said to me "Say that I saw you during the night" at certain times which he mentioned, they were 3 different times, I think 11 o'clock, between 12 and 1, and 3 o'clock'. Coroner Lewis asked Hickton: 'So you were willing to perjure yourself to screen Parsons?' The constable replied: 'I did so, but with the best intentions'. Hickton said that later that day John Farnes had been ordered by Parsons to write down the times they were to stick to as having seen Parsons on duty. Farnes agreed that this was the case. No copies of this vital piece of paper were produced. Hickton said his copy was lost.

Parsons accounted for this by telling the coroner that 'my superintendent called on me to account for my time, and I put it down on paper for the men, as they contradicted one another'.[9] Then came a moment of pure drama. The Coroner told Parsons 'They all contradict *you*', to which the reply was 'I can't help that'.

Julia Parsons was then called, but loyally admitted to nothing that would compromise her brother. She confirmed her previous statement that she had seen Parsons writing the report at 12 o'clock, when she went to bed, and that she did not see him until after eight the following morning. The next witness was James Dale, the man who had previously sworn positively to seeing Parsons on duty at 3am on horseback in Dagenham Village. He now stated that he certainly saw such a figure, but couldn't be sure that it was definitely Parsons. He was asked whether the rider was wearing a great coat or a cloak. Presumably the sergeant wore a cloak when on horseback. 'Have you been told to say you saw Parsons?' asked the Coroner. Dale denied that this was the case.

If Parsons thought he was in enough trouble, there was even worse to come. The next man to take the stand was Henry Clements, the Romford hawker who shortly after the murder had been decoyed into the Red Lion and questioned about a suspicious wound on his neck. Clements now stated that Parsons himself had been in the pub at the same time. He claimed that Parsons, engrossed in a newspaper, had suddenly said to himself: 'Dear me, poor fellow, I wish I had not done it'. Clements immediately asked him what he meant by that, but there was no answer. Clements said he then went to the Star Tap and told various people there what he had heard, including the landlord Thomas Gillman and the letter carrier William Spencer. The story soon got round, for according to Clements, he was confronted by Parsons and Kimpton in the Star Tap some weeks later. They had just brought two young men over to the Romford magistrates on a charge of housebreaking. Clements alleged that Kimpton said to him: 'I understand you've got something to say against Parsons. What do you want to interfere with it for, what is that to do with you? If any one asks anything of you, say you don't know nothing about it'.

The coroner asked Clements why he hadn't come forward with this information before. Clements replied that he had come to the previous hearing but Inspector Richardson had refused to let him in. Richardson then told the court that yes, this was true, but he had had no idea Clements wanted to make a statement. At this point Clements offered to answer any questions which might be put to him by Parsons, but the sergeant said he had none to put, and knew nothing at all about it. He denied having made the comment at all. William Spencer, a Romford letter-carrier, confirmed that he heard Clements state publicly in the Star Tap that Parsons had said while reading the paper 'Poor fellow, I wish I hadn't done it now'. It was past 7 o'clock when the hearing was eventually brought to a close, after 4½ hours of pure drama. Lewis announced he was adjourning the inquest for another three weeks.

Newspapers fell over each other to blacken the names of Parsons and the Dagenham constables. The *Weekly Dispatch* claimed that after Clements' evidence 'Another witness deposed to having heard Parsons make a similar exclamation in the parlour of the Red Lion'. It also hinted that Clark's rattle had been sabotaged: 'Policeman Farnes said that when the body of Clark was found the rattle was in his pocket, but that a piece of paper was wedged in that part of it where the tongue of the rattle was fixed, and thereby preventing it making a noise'.[10] Another newspaper alleged that Clark was killed for the 'quantity of sovereigns' that he was known to keep in his box. Apparently, 'the failure to obtain the key by some of his comrades induced the murder'. The *Times* remained level-headed, reminding its rivals that there was nothing

The Red Lion (now the Golden Lion), Romford, where Sergeant Parsons allegedly said 'Dear me, poor fellow, I wish I had not done it'.

sinister about the broken lock since Clark himself had lost the key, and 'being unable to find it when he left Arbour-square, he himself burst it open to show his comrades that he was taking nothing away but his own'.[11] *Douglas Jerrold's Weekly Newspaper* contented itself by saying: 'There are many rumours concerning this mysterious affair which we do not think it right to give. A strict enquiry is going on, and the scene of the murder has been more particularly examined'.[12]

Home Secretary Sir George Grey ordered details of the events to be sent to the Attorney General and Solicitor General, John Jervis and David Dundas. On 26th August they gave their opinion that Parsons 'has been guilty of subornation[13] of perjury and that he probably would be convicted of that offence...we likewise think that Parsons has been guilty of perjury but doubt whether there is sufficient evidence against him to warrant a conviction'.[14] They considered that Parsons, Hickton, Butfoy, Kimpton and Farnes would probably be convicted of conspiracy, and that the four constables 'may' be found guilty of perjury. It seemed that no criminal proceedings could be taken against them before the winding-up of the inquest.

There now followed a renewed anti-police press campaign. On Thursday 27th August the *Daily News* quoted John Rawlinson, a Marylebone magistrate, as saying that 'the police had lately got into the way of being exceedingly violent'. Other magistrates, according to the paper, take the opposite tack and 'bolster up the police in the exercise of their authority'. It goes on to suggest that the working-class background of the typical police recruit was a significant factor. 'The feeling that he wields the baton of the law, is in itself a strong temptation to an uneducated man to use it rather freely...let any of our readers take a tour of police observation in the low neighbourhoods of London...he will find the bluecoated functionary exercising a very terrible despotism over basket women and little boys...In this sort of empire he acquires a sense of his own importance, which breaks out against less submissive objects'. It was summed up as 'ignorant, low-bred, often brutal, tyranny'.

The article then discussed the culture of perjury: 'He acquires also an esprit de corps, which aggravates the tendencies of his position. He feels it his duty to stick to his brethren through thick and thin; and to swear to the truth of a policeman's statement, though a hundred unofficial voices contradict it'. Perhaps worried that he had gone too far, the writer added this disclaimer: 'Of course, the exceptions to this charge are numerous. Indeed the habits we are describing may be rather called the exception; civility, self-restraint and sobriety, the rule. We do not believe so good a municipal force exists anywhere as the New Police. But they have besetting sins...'

Richard Mayne responded on 2nd September by urging police officers to show 'forbearance and good temper' even under extreme provocation, and when giving evidence 'not to overstate or shew desire to obtain a conviction'. He acknowledged that 'late newspaper paragraphs and articles shew that there is a feeling in some of the public to impute blame to the Police in those heads, which however undeserved should make all the police especially cautious'.

Ten days later, however, there was more embarrassment for K Division. Police Constable John Francis of Loughton had been having an affair with a married woman named Elizabeth Serjeant. Her husband William found out what was going on, and warned Francis 'not to encourage his wife'. On the evening of Monday 7th September, Serjeant was sitting outside the King's Head in Loughton when he saw his wife and Francis strolling along together. He went up to them and tried to pull his wife away. A fight then broke out between the two men. Francis gained the upper hand, and, according to a witness, Mrs Serjeant urged him to give her husband a good beating: 'Well, come Jack, knock him down again!' With his rival sprawled on the ground, Constable Francis whisked Mrs Serjeant back to his own house. Her husband dusted himself down and promptly marched off to find Sergeant Edwards. The policeman must have been taken aback to hear the story, as he had marched Francis off on duty three hours before with instructions to go to Buckhurst Hill, then return into Loughton and continue his patrol until 5am. The men then went to Francis's house. The love-struck constable refused their pleas to make Mrs Serjeant leave, declaring he 'would lose his life first'. He said he was resigning from the police force there and then, and would do no more duty. Francis then hurled his uniform out of the window at the sergeant.

Eventually the situation was brought under control. Constable Francis did not die in defence of his lady love, as he had threatened, but allowed himself to be hauled before the Ilford magistrates on 12th September. Like the Dagenham constables, he had clearly been suspended from the force, as he appeared in court in plain clothes. He faced two charges, one of assault and the other of neglect of duty. We are told that the abandoned husband's 'left eye and cheek bore marks of severe punishment'. Francis was found guilty on both counts. For the assault on William Serjeant he was fined £3 plus expenses, or two months' imprisonment if he could not pay. His punishment for the second charge demonstrates that in the wake of the Dagenham case there was a determined crackdown on shirkers in the police. According to the *Globe*: 'with respect to the neglect of duty, and in order to act as an example to others, the magistrates were unanimous not to inflict any fine, but to commit him to the House of Correction for one month with hard labour'.[15]

There was even more drama to come, this time from the two wives. Elizabeth Serjeant, described as 'most showily dressed,' was accused of assaulting Elizabeth Francis on the same night. It seems that Mrs Francis had also confronted the couple in the street, and Mrs Serjeant had then 'seized her by the throat and knocked her down'. To add insult to injury, she was forced to spend the night in the kitchen while her husband entertained his lover elsewhere in the house. Mrs Francis alleged in court that Mrs Serjeant 'had seduced all the men in the neighbourhood'. Mrs Serjeant denied the assault but the magistrates found her guilty. She was fined £1 plus expenses, and was also ordered to find bail to keep the peace for 12 months. The forbearing William Serjeant was willing to give his errant wife another chance. We are told that he paid the fine, and also entered into security for his wife's good behaviour.[16]

Two days later, on Monday 14th September, the Clark inquest opened for the fifth time. The room at the Cross Keys was again 'much crowded by the gentry and inhabitants of the district anxious to hear the proceedings'. They were to be disappointed this time, however. A Mr Samuels,[17] one of the 14 jurors, did not appear due to illness. Coroner Lewis told the audience that 'it was true that there was still sufficient to form a competent jury, but having begun with 14 jurymen, he considered he would not be doing his duty to proceed with a smaller number'.[18] He announced an adjournment of a week.

Sergeant Parsons now had a legal representative, Benjamin Rawlings, a Romford solicitor.[19] Rawlings sprang into action on his client's behalf, urging the Coroner not to postpone the hearing. Parsons, he said, had now been under 'strict surveillance' at the police station without charge for over a month. This 'had tended to increase a strong prejudice in the public mind against him. His being continued still under surveillance of the police would only tend to increase that prejudice'. The *Bedford Mercury* told its readers that 'Sergeant Parsons was not in attendance: he is so closely watched that he is not allowed to go to sleep but in company of one of the police'.[20] Coroner Lewis was not to be swayed. He declared that Parsons had only himself to blame, and no right to complain. He added that 'Supposing him to be innocent of any participation in the murder, there was another charge which he would be called upon to answer'.

Parsons must also have been worried about the effect his situation was having on the health of his wife Maria. According to the *Bedford Mercury*, 'It appears that when Parsons could not move without a constable being in attendance on him, it began to make such a visible effect on his wife, that it was thought advisable to move her to her father's house at Barking Side'.

This was the Fairlop Oak pub, of which Jonathan Rawlings was landlord. The newspaper also stated that 'in addition to the bloodstained handkerchief found in the field adjoining that where the murder was perpetrated, other articles have been discovered likely to throw a light on this cruel and mysterious murder'. It did not reveal what these articles were.

In the meantime, the team of detectives were still busy dashing from place to place following up leads. Edward Kendell wrote that his duty was to investigate 'every report that I heard in any way relating to the Murder'. He alleged that 'in many instances after walking a great many miles' he found 'that they emanated only from idle taproom talk'. He had been ordered by Superintendent Pearce to take the Dagenham constables around with him while he made his enquiries. Their company was not always welcome. In submitting his claim for expenses, Kendell complained that 'the false statements of the Constables occasioned me a deal of trouble, and expense, and whenever they accompanied me in any of my enquiries, I was obliged to pay their expenses as well as my own, most of them having large families and consequently no money to spend'.

Kendell was asked particularly to investigate a woman named Susan Perry. She had met Clark at Arbour Square Police Station, where she was one of the domestic staff. Apparently she had been to Dagenham while Clark was there and had been seen in company with him. Susan had been separated from her husband James Perry for about two years. What was more, it was reported that James and three other men had been seen leaving a Beacontree Heath public house on the night of Clark's murder. On 22nd August Kendell fetched Susan Perry from Arbour Square to be questioned by Pearce. Her husband had left the district, and the detectives were told to lose no time in tracking him down. Some years before, the couple had lived at Corbets Tey,[21] just outside Upminster in Essex. Sergeant Henry Smith, described by Dickens in *Household Words* as 'a smooth-faced man with a fresh bright complexion, and a strange air of simplicity', stayed at the George Inn at Corbets Tey for four nights during the hunt for Perry. Thirty-four year old Smith must have known the area, as he had been born in nearby Purfleet. He is said to have been a butcher before joining the police force.

In the meantime his colleague Frederick Shaw was also on the case, making enquiries at Hornchurch, Upminster and West Thurrock. At last, 'after considerable trouble', he succeeded in tracing James Perry. The man was just across the Thames in Greenhithe, Kent, working for cement manufacturers White & Sons. Shaw spent the week of 13th-18th September in Greenhithe. He reported that he interviewed Perry several times but 'could not obtain any

The George Inn, Corbets Tey, where Sergeant Henry Smith stayed while searching for the murder suspect James Perry

Information to justify his Apprehension'. It seemed that a man named James Everett, not George Clark, was the cause of the Perrys' separation. Sergeant Kendell followed up James and his brothers Jeremiah and Oswald, all said to be friends of Susan Perry, but to no avail. Yet again a seemingly promising line of enquiry had resulted in a dead end.

A few days after the abortive fifth hearing, Coroner Lewis was called back to Dagenham to hold another inquest. The dead man, moreover, was linked to the George Clark case. He was Joseph Palmer, the farm labourer who had found Clark's hat in the cornfield on 5th July. Palmer was 36 years old and lived at Beacontree Heath. His wife had discovered his body on 18th September hanging from a rafter in the privy. The inquest jury was told that Palmer 'had been rather low-spirited since the Monday, in hot weather his head was bad, and about 2 or 3 months since he stated to his wife the devil told him to kill himself'.[22] Is it a coincidence that Palmer's suicidal feelings began at about the time of Clark's murder? Mrs Palmer told the inquest that her husband was also unhappy in his job. Other witnesses spoke of his 'low and unsettled state'. The jury returned a verdict of 'temporary insanity', and Palmer was laid to rest in Dagenham Parish Churchyard on Tuesday 22nd September.

The date of Palmer's burial also saw the sixth and final inquest hearing into George Clark's death. It began at the earlier time of 10am. The general public had not started to lose their fascination with the case. Far from it. The *Essex Standard* reported that 'Long before that time not only was this inquest room, but every avenue leading thereto, densely crowded...the interest felt in the proceedings seems to have increased with each adjournment of the inquest, more particularly among the resident gentry and more respectable classes resident in Dagenham and the surrounding villages...'[23] The massed ranks inside the Cross Keys must have gasped in horror when Detective Sergeant Langley showed the jurors the bloodied handkerchief he had found on 18th August in the meadow next to the cornfield where Clark's body had lain.[24]

A new witness now appeared and took the oath. This was Constable George Dunning, who had joined the force on 6th July that year, only to be posted to Dagenham shortly afterwards. Dunning told the jury he had been there for just over nine weeks. They then heard yet another sensational allegation against Parsons. Dunning said that on Thursday 27th August Maria Parsons was with her parents at Barkingside, but the sergeant's sister Julia Parsons was staying at the police station. On entering the station just after 11pm, Dunning was aware of a heated argument between Parsons and Julia in an upstairs room. He heard Parsons scream that he would throw Julia down the stairs if she didn't hold her tongue. About a quarter of an hour later Dunning was in a downstairs back room and could still hear their raised voices. The acting Sergeant at that time was 28 year-old George Corbin.[25] Dunning and Corbin stood on the stairs inside the police station listening to the quarrel raging between brother and sister.

But what precisely had they heard? Corbin told the jury that he himself couldn't distinctly make out what was being said. He could only relate what Dunning had told him. This was that Julia had said: 'You know you are guilty of it.' Parsons answered: 'Do you mean this affair?' to which she replied: 'Yes, and other things too'. Parsons, it seemed, had then called her 'a bloody bitch' and burst into tears. The Coroner called Dunning back, but instead of confirming the damning phrase 'You know you are guilty of it', the constable denied hearing the words at all, or telling Corbin that he had. Corbin maintained his account was correct, and the Coroner and Sergeant Thomas Pearson both added that Dunning had told them the same. Coroner Lewis grew annoyed. Here was yet another unreliable witness in this case. He said Dunning 'must recollect one thing or another…and if you do not you are a most unfit person to give evidence either before this or any other jury'. When Dunning was eventually allowed to step down, he decided to submit his resignation almost immediately – a wise course of action in the light of the existing perjury allegations. He was allowed to leave the force four days later.

Julia was then called, and admitted that she and Parsons had argued for about half an hour, but she firmly maintained that the quarrel was nothing to do with the death of Clark. The truth was, she said, that since Parsons had been 'under arrest' his brothers had not been in touch, and this had upset him. 'He called me some names I cannot mention, and at the end of the quarrel he cried; all I accused him of was concerning our family'.[26] Julia said she had been 'in a great passion at the time, and may not recollect all that was said between us'. She was certain, though, that she had never uttered the words 'You know you are guilty of it'.

The question of whether the Romford hawker Henry Clements had heard Parsons say 'I wish I had not done it' in the Red Lion was again raised. Benjamin Rawlings, the Romford solicitor appearing for Parsons, declared he could prove that his client was never left in the room alone with Clements. Sergeant Thomas Pearson backed him up, telling the jury that he went out of the room for about half a minute, during which time Inspector Richardson was at the door, grasping the handle. Neither Richardson nor Pearson heard Parsons utter anything, though they did recall him being immersed in the newspaper.

Kimpton, Farnes, Hickton and Butfoy weren't present whilst the evidence was being given. The coroner then ordered them to be brought the short distance from the police station. He then asked if they had anything more to add. They all said they had not, and repeated that their last evidence was the truth.

Coroner Lewis then summed up the case. Addressing the jury 'at some length', he gave his opinion that if Clark were killed during an ordinary quarrel, or in the course of his police duty, then the attacker would have given one blow or cut, and then made his escape. However, the murderer or murderers had not been satisfied with killing their victim, but had mangled and mutilated him in such a way that suggested they were motivated by some personal animosity. In short, it was a revenge attack.

The Coroner then considered the movements of Clark's colleagues on the fatal night, concentrating particularly on Parsons and Butfoy. 'It appeared clear that during portions of the night of the murder Sergeant Parsons was not on duty. What became of Parsons between half past 10 and 12 on that night, and between 1 and 6 the next morning did not appear; nor did Parsons exhibit any disposition to inform the jury. Again, the constable Butfoy endeavoured to make it appear that he was not on duty the night of the murder, having, as he said, got drunk at Romford...now this was positively contradicted by Kimpton and by Parsons himself, who said Butfoy came to the station at 12 and said "All right, Sergeant.".[27] In short, if Butfoy could not prove he was in bed at the time, perhaps he as well as Parsons should be under suspicion.

The inquest room was cleared so that the jury could deliberate. The crowd of press, public and police waited anxiously outside the Cross Keys for the verdict. We do not know whether any members of Clark's family were present. That it would be ruled a case of murder was a foregone conclusion, but would the jury feel they could put a name to the killer or killers? After an interval of more than an hour, the court re-opened. Coroner Lewis then announced that the jury had come to a verdict of 'wilful murder against some person or persons unknown'. Parsons and Butfoy must of course have breathed a sigh of relief, but not for long. The coroner immediately announced that Parsons and the constables 'would be indicted forthwith for perjury'.

On the morning of that final hearing, the *Times* reporter George Greene had been speaking to John Lewis, the Vicar of Ingatestone in Essex and brother of the Coroner. The Reverend Lewis had let Greene know he had a number of accusations against the police. He alleged that the bloodstained handkerchief found in a meadow near the site of the murder had been deliberately put there by the police 'to mislead'. Lewis also claimed that Superintendent Pearce had visited his brother, the Coroner, at Brentwood to tell him that there was not going to be any charge against the police whilst knowing full well that there was. Apparently the vicar was so incensed that he intended to make a formal complaint, bringing Pearce's conduct 'before the public'.

Soon after the inquest jury had returned their verdict, Greene went up to Superintendent Pearce, told him about the allegations and said Lewis had given him permission to publicize them. A worried Pearce immediately reported the conversation to the Commissioners. He wrote that the Coroner's brother alleged 'that I was as bad as any of the rest, and the Police were all alike from the highest to the lowest...That I had been called before Colonel Rowan to answer for my conduct'. Richard Mayne felt that leaping to the defence of the beleaguered Superintendent might inflame public opinion even more. He added a note in the margin of Pearce's report, explaining that 'taking into consideration the bad conduct of several of the Police at Dagenham, which give some apparent grounds for unfavourable opinions of the Police with reference to this case, I thought it not advisable to take any step upon this'. He added he had assured Pearce 'that of course it is not necessary for him to clear himself to the Com[missioner]s of such an accusation'.

This was not the only time Superintendent Pearce came in for harsh criticism that day. Benjamin Rawlings, the Romford solicitor appearing for Sergeant Parsons, announced at the inquest that the health of Mrs Maria Parsons had declined, and she was now 'in an exceedingly dangerous state'. Rawlings blamed this on the 'harsh treatment' ordered by Pearce. The Coroner sprang to Pearce's defence. He declared that 'from what he had seen of Mr Pearce, he felt satisfied that he was incapable of acting in a harsh manner towards any female, especially to Mrs Parsons, who was placed in her present situation by the misconduct of her husband'. Pearce defended himself by stressing that he was sympathetic to the plight of Mrs Parsons, and 'had treated her with the greatest kindness, consistent with the duty he had to perform, which was one of great importance and responsibility'.

Maria's father Jonathan Rawlings was having none of this. He declared that Pearce had ordered the police to keep his daughter under constant watch. This, added to a slow recovery from childbirth, had triggered her illness. Rawlings said he had medical opinion on his side, and threatened that 'if anything serious happened to her, he should insist on having a coroner's inquest on her'. Pearce retorted that he had never ordered a watch to be kept on Maria, but admitted that a policeman had been under orders to report 'any communication that might pass between her and her husband'. This, he said, was 'no more than his duty'.

Two days later, on 24th September, Maria died at the age of only 24. This latest twist to the story was enthusiastically reported in the *Bedford Mercury* in language worthy of the most melodramatic Victorian novel. 'The fright and grief at her husband's situation had, however, taken so deep an effect upon her system, that despite the active attendance of a medical gentleman, death terminated her mental and bodily sufferings late on Thursday night'. The *Illustrated London News* went one better with an unspoken suggestion of suicide. It stated that she died 'under melancholy circumstances...she had recently been confined, and it is supposed that the particulars connected with the melancholy event had such an effect upon her feelings as to accelerate her death'.[28]

Maria's father Jonathan was present when she died, and he registered the death six days later. His call for an inquest on his daughter was not successful. According to the death certificate, there were no suspicious circumstances. The cause was given as 'remittent fever, typhus, one month, certified'. On Thursday 1st October Maria's coffin was taken from the Fairlop Oak to Barkingside Church. The burial service was taken by Perpetual Curate John Budgen, who had officiated at her marriage to Parsons at that very church just fifteen months before. Maria's bereaved husband Parsons was probably still surrounded by a phalanx of watchful officers. We have no record of Parsons' reaction to Maria's death, but the quarrel with his sister reveals something of his fragile state of mind during the previous weeks. The sad news had been announced at the Ilford Petty Sessions on Saturday 26th September. The court was crowded that morning, due to a rumour, which turned out to be untrue, that Sergeant Parsons and the Dagenham constables would be brought before the magistrates and charged with murder.[29]

The killing continued to fascinate armchair detectives among the public. The Commissioners received an anonymous letter dated 25th September, allegedly written from Russell Square. It expressed the opinion that Clark was murdered by smugglers, who carried on their trade 'with the connivance of the Police'. The writer claimed that Clark had refused to co-operate with this, and 'it was considered by all parties the best plan to put him out of the way'. The smugglers carried out the killing, but 'the Police were well privy'. A note written by Richard Mayne attached to the letter dismisses the theory. 'The enquiry as to smugglers was carefully made in the first occurrence of suspicion immediately after the murder, but no grounds whatever could be obtained to support such'.

In the aftermath of the inquest, Rowan and Mayne met several Divisional Superintendents to discuss the progress of the murder enquiry. So far, the

Holy Trinity Church, Barkingside, where Maria Parsons was buried 1st October 1846

£100 reward for information had not produced the desired results. The outcome of the meeting was a proposal to raise it to £400, by asking for voluntary subscriptions from the police themselves. In a letter to the Home Secretary asking permission for this scheme, the Commissioners remarked that 'a certain odium has been cast upon the force generally by the non-discovery of the murder....the misconduct of some individuals of the Police at Dagenham reflects badly on the whole force. The proposed reward will show that the Police desire that the guilty should be discovered'.[30]

Police officers gave generously to the collection. The donations from each Division ranged between £20 and £70. These contributions meant that very soon the total reward had shot up to £675.[31] The Home Secretary, however, demanded that the idea be dropped. Richard Mayne wrote on 8th October that: 'the Commissioners having laid before the Secretary of State the proposal...Sir George Grey directs in reply, that while he fully appreciates the motives which have led to this proposal, he thinks it is one of a novel character, and open to some objections, which would not justify him in sanctioning it'.[32]

The critics continued their attacks on the police. Towards the end of September, Rowan and Mayne were faced with accusations that prostitutes were 'oppressively dealt with by the police, or unduly favoured if they pay the constable'. The *News of the World* weighed in on 27th September with a front-page article headlined 'Ferocity of the Police'. The Commissioners must have drawn some comfort from the fact that this particular incident took place not in London but in the country town of Northleach in Gloucestershire. A disturbance broke out in a pub after a drinker broke a glass and refused to pay for the damage. The police were called, and a Constable James Probert was seen to push an old man, who fell to the floor. When onlookers protested, Probert 'drew out his truncheon, and struck out right and left'. A man named Reuben Busby, who was said to be sitting quietly at a table, died of head injuries. The coroner's jury returned a verdict of manslaughter against Probert.

Even the *Times*, not normally known as a critic of the Establishment, was stirred to anger by this case. It compared Probert's overreaction in the Northleach pub with the suspiciously easy escape from custody of three well-known members of the swell-mob as they were being taken in handcuffs from Hammersmith Police Court to Newgate Prison. The language used in the *Times* on this occasion echoed that of the left-wing *Daily News* and *Morning Chronicle*: 'We see in one instance imbecility sufficient to raise a suspicion of collusion, and on the other rigour carried to a degree which renders those the terror of society who should be confidently looked upon as its safeguards…'[33]

Three days later, the *Times* leader-writer returned to the subject with refuelled indignation. 'Such an atrocity as that perpetrated at Dagenham it has not been our duty to chronicle for many years, if all the circumstances attending to it be but duly considered'. The inquest revelations tended 'to shake our confidence in that system on which we now entirely rely for the security of life and property'. After recounting once more the lies told by the Dagenham officers, it looked back at the state of affairs that had existed before Peel's New Police were introduced. It described the previous system as 'frightfully vicious' and full of corrupt thief-takers such as the notorious Jonathan Wild,[34] then went on:

> It was confidently presumed that with the establishment of our present corps we had stifled for ever those nefarious practises under which crime was carefully bred at the expense of society for the profit of its paid protectors. But what shall we say now? Are we better off…when we are encompassed by a body to whom an oath in a case of murder is a thing of no moment at all?[35]

The previous day, the *Morning Chronicle* had argued for a public enquiry into police corruption: 'the public interest imperatively requires an investigation of a more free, searching and extensive character than can possibly be had upon the trial of such an indictment [of perjury]'.[36]

Meanwhile, the detective Edward Kendell was hard at work following up the evidence given by Elizabeth Dodd at the third inquest hearing on 23rd July. Mrs Dodd, it will be remembered, had recounted how she was walking home to Romford from Whitechapel across some fields on the night of the murder when she saw a tall man in a fustian coat swear at a policeman. She had seen the same man several times in the fields, eating bread with a very large knife.

Alas, Kendell was to discover that Elizabeth Dodd's story was, to say the least, far-fetched. He found that her interview at Whitechapel had in fact taken place on 13th July, two weeks after the murder. It was for the post of a servant in the household of a Mrs Elton, at 122 High Street. Mrs Dodd started the job on the afternoon of 16th July and had left, or was perhaps dismissed, the following day. Kendell reported wearily to the Commissioners on 9th October 1846 that the whole thing had been a wild goose chase. Elizabeth Dodd, he wrote, was 'a person of bad character, and is considered by many in Romford, to be of unsound mind'. She had had at least one spell in Ilford Gaol, 17th to 23rd October 1845.[37] She had admitted to Kendell that she was living at the Canteen at Warley Barracks at the time of the murder, and her story was 'all imagination'.[38]

The following day, Saturday 10th October, an extraordinary incident occurred which led to yet more criticism of the Metropolitan Police, and especially of K Division. An officer on horseback was said to have ridden at full gallop down White Street in Bethnal Green, causing terrified pedestrians to scatter in all directions. People came out to see what was the matter, and 'the adjoining shopkeepers ran out and advised him to dismount from his horse, as he was manifestly so much intoxicated that he could scarcely retain his seat'. The policeman then apparently spurred his horse directly at a group of people talking together 'rode in amongst them like a madman, driving them from one side of the street to the other, and loudly exclaimed "Back, all of you, or I'll run over you"…a scene of indescribable tumult and indignation ensued'.

To everyone's astonishment, the miscreant was a high-ranking officer. He was Inspector John Julian, a man with a 15-year career in the force behind him. Julian's version of events, given to Worship Street Police Court magistrate Robert Edward Broughton, was very different. He said he had come upon a man struggling violently with a constable, egged on by a threatening crowd. The rabble had hissed and hooted the inspector, threatening to drag him off his horse. Julian and the constable took a man named William Scott into custody as the alleged ringleader. Three sergeants and three constables backed up the Inspector's story. Ranged against them were a number of witnesses. The *Daily News* left readers in no doubt which version it believed:

> Here is manifest perjury either on the part of the Bethnal Green shopkeepers or the police….The reputation of the K division is at stake….the witnesses for Julian are all of a trade, and a trade proved to be not very scrupulous in the matter of perjury…On the other hand we have, among the householders, an undertaker and a surgeon (who, though they may be popularly considered members of two branches of one profession, are of two trades by the Directory), and a watchmaker; men of probable substance, intelligence, and respectability; strangers to the prisoner; who testify in the teeth of the police statement...the account they give is consistent with itself, and probable.

The magistrate found Scott guilty and fined him five shillings. The allegations against Inspector Julian were ignored. 'His verdict is sheer nonsense' thundered the *Daily News*. A few days later, another hearing arose from the same incident. A watchmaker named Thomas Blake accused Inspector Julian of rearing the horse at him and chasing him along the road, almost trampling him in the process. Julian in his defence said the horse was unmanageable. Once more several witnesses backed up the accusation, and this time Mr Broughton found Julian guilty. Delivering judgement, 'he was bound to say that he firmly believed every word that had been stated by the witnesses' and called it 'most extraordinary and unwarrantable behaviour' and fined him £5 plus costs. The inspector was immediately suspended from duty.

According to the *Morning Chronicle* the very existence of the Metropolitan Police was now under threat. It wrote ominously on 27th October that perjury in the police, 'if not effectually repressed will very soon compel the public to demand the dissolution of a force which, according to its present constitution and conduct, exposes the community to greater evils than those which it professes to prevent'.

In the meantime, the police authorities wondered whether Sergeant Parsons was alone in failing to supervise his night duty men. They ordered spot checks on other K Division sergeants. The results were disappointing, as can be seen in the Police Orders files. On 16th October 1846 Sergeant James Mann was reduced to the rank of Constable 2nd Class 'for being found in the Station at Barking at 5 minutes before 6am yesterday when on out-door duty, and not visiting any of the men of his section after 2am'. Three days later, Sergeant Robert Backhouse of Chadwell Heath was demoted to the rank of Constable 'for being absent from the appointed meeting place at 12.30 am'. It perhaps comes as no surprise to learn that Inspector William Richardson, who as head of the Ilford station had overall responsibility for policing in these places as well as Dagenham, was allowed to retire on 26th October on health grounds, being 'worn out'.[39] Whether he was in fact eased out we do not know. Richardson was 55 years old, and had begun his police service in the Horse Patrol twenty years before. He was awarded a pension of £64 per annum. His successor was Henry Procter, a 30 year-old R Division Sergeant born in Boston, Lincolnshire, and now awarded promotion to Inspector after only six years in the force.

Meanwhile, the public urged the authorities to hurry up and deal with the disgraced Dagenham officers. On 21st October the *Times* reported that 'Nothing can exceed the displeasure of the inhabitants of Dagenham, Romford, Ilford and the surrounding villages, at the tardiness shown by the Government in taking proceedings against Sgt Parsons and constables...The men are still at Dagenham, under strict surveillance, doing nothing but receive their pay, or a greater portion of it, and, to use the remark of a gentleman living in the neighbourhood, "getting fat upon idleness"'.

In fact the case had not been forgotten but was being slowly chewed over by the Attorney-General and the Solicitor-General. At last, 'after mature deliberation', they gave their opinion.

This was that only three out of the six Dagenham officers were to be prosecuted. These were Parsons, Kimpton and Hickton. Incredibly, it seemed that the remaining three, Butfoy, Farnes and Stevens, had not been properly sworn at the first inquest hearing. Although they had admitted giving untrue statements, apparently 'the charge of perjury could not be sustained'.[40] Butfoy, Farnes and Stevens were dismissed with effect from 8th November 1846, and were now free to go.

Their colleagues remained suspended from duty and under house arrest while legal proceedings were prepared against them. Their pay was now stopped. As the alleged offences had taken place in Essex, outside the jurisdiction of the Central Criminal Court, they faced a long wait before the cases came to trial. It was first thought that they could be heard at the next Essex Quarter Sessions, in early January 1847. The Home Secretary, Sir George Grey, seems to have been the first to realize that the Court of Quarter sessions was not actually allowed to try perjury cases. The delay would therefore be even longer, until the Essex Lent Assizes, in March 1847. That was a full six months in the future. The Commissioners fretted, urging the Solicitor of the Treasury 'as to the importance on several accounts of the legal proceedings being carried on with the least possible delay…'[41]

Meanwhile, the ever-energetic Edward Kendell had journeyed to the West Country in pursuit of yet another promising lead. A man named Richard Bragg was a clerk for the foremost Victorian engineer Isambard Kingdom Brunel, and lodged with 'a female named Williams' at 5 Old Park Hill, Bristol. On 10th November, Mr Bragg must have been astonished to find the detective on his doorstep requesting an interview. He would have been taken aback even more when Kendell produced a letter supposedly written by himself, offering 'some reliable information' about the Clark murder. Mr Bragg wrote indignantly to the Commissioners that 'the letter purporting to be written by me and offering to give certain information respecting the late murder at Dagenham, is not in my handwriting, nor am I at all able to recognise whose it is'.[42] He went on to say that beyond having read of the case in the newspapers, he knew nothing whatever of the murder, 'and would cheerfully lend every assistance in my power to punish the party who has

A group of early policemen, two of whom are wearing the summer uniform of white trousers

been guilty of bringing my name before you in reference to it'. Kendell tracked down three other people in Bristol by the name of Bragg – one an accountant, one a shoemaker and the other an ironmonger - but none could help in any way. The culprit behind the hoax was never discovered.

The following week Kendell followed up a statement made by a Bethnal Green cabman who had heard another Cabman 'say that about the time of the murder he brought two gents from near the East India Dock Wall to the West End of Town. They were very tipsy and covered with blood'. The men told the startled cab-driver that they had been fighting. Unsurprisingly, the pair were never traced.

On 18th November Inspector John Julian, who as we have seen was convicted the previous month of deliberately charging his horse at the citizens of Bethnal Green, was reinstated. He was to be transferred to Clerkenwell, in G Division. Five days later the disgusted *Morning Chronicle* told its readers that 'Inspector Julian is once more to have the opportunity of enjoying, should he be in the mind, those exciting nocturnal recreations which are now doubly recommended to his taste by the charms of cheapness and safety…We trust that Sir George Grey will find some early opportunity of acquainting the public with the grounds on which he deems himself justified in re-instating this man…'[43]

Five days later, the same newspaper returned to the attack. 'It was hardly in the nature of things, that the public should remain for any considerable time without hearing something to the disadvantage of K division…Some surplusage of licence, in the use of both truncheon and tongue, might be naturally counted on, as a distinctive characteristic of the moral being and doing of division K…Division K is again in court, already, in the person of No. 210, testing the value of its lately-renewed license of outrage and perjury'. It quoted a case in which a Constable Montford was allegedly seen to be engaged in 'improper conduct with a woman' down a dark alley. A Mr and Mrs Blundell passed by, and when Mrs Blundell commented about what was going on, the policeman swore at her. The couple announced they would report him for this insolence, at which he is said to have rushed at them, hit out with his truncheon and knocked down a woman and a baby.

As the year of 1846 drew to a close, the *Times* gave its readers an update on the situation at Dagenham. It reported that the constables faced problems making ends meet now that they were no longer being paid. Apparently Kimpton and Farnes, with eleven children between them, had 'been compelled to apply to the board of guardians to the Romford Union for relief…altogether, the men and their families are described as being in the most destitute state. One of the men states that, but for this unfortunate occurrence, he would have been entitled to a retiring pension of £28 per annum for length of service'. This was presumably John Farnes, who had been a policeman for fifteen years.

For his colleagues Thomas Kimpton and Isaac Hickton, the loss of a pension would soon be the least of their worries.

CHAPTER 8

'Told a falsehood, not knowing the consequences'

The rather beleaguered Superintendent of K Division was 42 year-old Cort Henry Marquard, an East Londoner who had joined the Metropolitan Police as a constable in 1830 and worked his way up the ranks. On 2nd February 1847 Marquard steeled himself to write to the Commissioners with yet more humiliating news. The disgraced officers Parsons, Kimpton and Hickton had managed to slip away from Dagenham after being held under house arrest for the past four months. Julia Parsons was immediately pulled in and questioned about her brother. She told them that as far as she knew he was making his way to Liverpool. This was a major port, and so perhaps Parsons was intending to leave the country. Marquard reported that Julia 'does not know his address, expecting a letter in a few days'.

Marquard also forwarded a letter of resignation from Hickton. It read 'Isaac Hickton late PC 85 K Division but at present suspended from duty begs leave to give the required notice to resign (that is) one month commencing on Monday the 1st Feb 1847'.[1] The address on the letter was a coffee house at 8 Fairfield Terrace, Stepney. This was run by a Mr Sadler, who was quick to defend himself against any suspicion of involvement. Hickton, he said, had not actually been staying at the coffee house but had sent the note to him through the post to be forwarded to the police authorities.

Preparations for the prosecution of the trio at the approaching Essex Lent Assizes continued unabated, and eventually on 9th March[2] the Grand Jury of prominent county landowners considered the indictments against the three men in their absence. This was a preliminary to the actual trial. If the Grand Jury thought the evidence on each count was sufficient to warrant a trial, it would announce that a True Bill had been found. The *Times* reported the same day that Sergeant Edward Kendell and others had been busy gathering evidence during the past week, and that various witnesses had been subpoenaed to appear. Seven duly did so – Charles Carne Lewis, John Farnes, Jonas Stevens, Abia Butfoy, Elizabeth Page, Priscilla Page and Thomas Archer. Their evidence was not given in open court. Instead, they entered the jury room individually and alone, unaccompanied by lawyers.

After listening to their evidence, the Grand Jury gave its decision. Parsons, Kimpton and Hickton were to be prosecuted for conspiracy ('conspiring together for the purpose of committing wilful and corrupt perjury'). Kimpton and Hickton were also to be tried for perjury itself. This offence apparently could not be maintained against Parsons, 'who did not commit perjury, he having "stuck to his tale" from first to last, declaring most

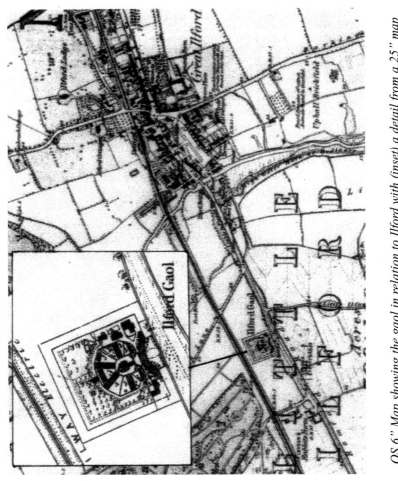

OS 6" Map showing the gaol in relation to Ilford with (inset) a detail from a 25" map of the same period showing the gaol itself

vehemently that he had spoken the truth'.[3] The two indictments against Parsons for subornation of perjury were also ignored. The trials were appointed to take place at the Summer Assizes four months later. According to the *Times*, 'In the neighbourhood of Dagenham the determination of the Government to prosecute in this case has given great satisfaction'.[4]

Marquard wrote to the Commissioners on 11th March to bring them up to date with the search for the fugitives. He wrote that 'PC Kimpton was two or three days past living in the parish of Bethnal Green'. The whereabouts of Parsons were unknown, but 'his sister has stated he has written to his brother, who is Coach Man to Sir George Grey'.[5]

On the final day of the Assizes, the three accused men were called. The only one to appear was Thomas Kimpton, who had given himself up. Kimpton was offered bail for £400, but not surprisingly was unable to afford this sum. He was ordered to be remanded in custody at Ilford Gaol. Kimpton was probably then handcuffed to a police officer and despatched to Ilford on the Eastern Counties Railway. As they travelled the short distance from Ilford Station to the gaol, Kimpton must have grown more and more nervous at the prospect awaiting him there. For the past few years he had regularly hauled suspected criminals to that very place. In July 1845, for example, Kimpton took James Boyce and George Revell to the gaol charged with stealing potatoes, and was given a receipt for travelling expenses of 5s 10d.[6] Now the boot was on the other foot. Everyone at the prison, both staff and inmates, must have been well aware of the twists and turns of the Clark murder investigation. Kimpton's name was now notorious, and life was not likely to be very pleasant for him behind those walls.

Barking local historian William Holmes Frogley, writing in the early 20th century, described Ilford Gaol as 'surrounded by a strong stone wall and moat over which was a drawbridge...There are today (1908) a few large stones having the broad arrow on them still laying carelessly near the path in the Romford Road. They were a part of the Gaol...'[7] At the time of Kimpton's arrival, Ilford Gaol had stood for around seventeen years. In 1851 it was reported that the average number of prisoners was 46.[8] Being only on remand, Kimpton was able to wear his own clothes, mingle with unconvicted prisoners and enjoy food brought in from outside. He was not given work to do. Elsewhere in the building there were many prisoners doing time with hard labour. Some spent endless hours on the treadmill, at a regular 48 steps per minute. Others, condemned to labour in solitary confinement, turned the crank of a 'punishing machine'.[9] The place was not popular. 'Much better known than liked' was the verdict in 1880 as it was being demolished.[10]

An amusing contemporary ballad gave an inmate's view:

'Such a rattling of clogs, clinking of keys, quaking of bellies, and shaking of knees,

And cussing of beds as hard as a nail oh! 'twould kill the devil in Ilford Gaol'.

And to round it off:

'Jonah lived inside a whale, he was better off there than in Ilford Gaol'.[11]

Meanwhile, the investigation into George Clark's murder had taken on a new impetus. At the end of December 1846, Charles and Mary Ann Pollett of 23 Oxford Street, New Road, Whitechapel, let out their front parlour to a recently-married couple named Vincent for five shillings and sixpence per week. A few weeks after their arrival, Mrs Pollett was standing by the fire in her lodgers' room when she noticed a penknife with a white handle on the mantelpiece. She picked up the object, and George Vincent, a tall, well-dressed man of about 35, told her it had belonged to George Clark. He declared: 'I took it out of his pocket myself. Me and someone else whose name I now forget found the body'.[12] Vincent added some gruesome details. 'They had to cut his boots to get them off, and the earthworms was coming out of his mouth and nose'. The landlady could only reply 'Indeed, I should think he must have been a shocking sight'. Her lodger told her it was so dreadful that he was ill for a week afterwards. He then stated that the people taken up on suspicion of the murder so far were all innocent, and hinted that he knew the identities of the killers.

About a month after this, in late February 1847, Vincent vanished from the lodgings owing a fortnight's rent, and leaving behind his sick and destitute wife Hannah. The abandoned woman was fetched away by her mother ten days later. The Polletts alerted the police about their strange guest and his sinister story. Soon the indefatigable Edward Kendell was on the trail, and uncovered a tale of almost Dickensian weirdness. The missing man, it turned out, also went by the names of George Allison and George Allison Overton. He was an ex-policeman,[13] and had even spent some time serving at Buckingham Palace. Kendell was told to look out for a man with 'his little fingers turned inwards, one eyebrow higher than the other, a scar at the back of his neck'.

The fugitive had been on the run for two months when Kendell finally caught up with him at a dockside as he was about to take ship for Quebec. A warrant was out for his arrest, not for involvement in the murder of Clark, but for bigamy! Apparently when he wed Hannah he was already married to a

Harriett Ives who was also his step-sister. He and Harriet had wed in July 1839 at St John's Church in Bethnal Green. Four years later, following a violent marital quarrel in the street, Allison had abruptly put his possessions in a handcart and left. In the summer of 1845 he began courting Hannah Louisa Foster, a customer at the draper's shop where he worked, and they married at Whitechapel Church a year later. Hannah told the Thames Police court that 'On or about Christmas he told her that he was married to another woman, and that he did not like to mention it before as he feared the news would distress her. She continued to live with him until the 23rd of February last, when they had a few words, and, after kissing her, he said she would never see him again, and left home'. Poor Hannah, who had suffered a mental breakdown since her abandonment, fainted away after giving evidence and had to be carried out of court.[14]

The magistrate sent Allison alias Vincent alias Overton to Newgate Gaol to await trial for bigamy. When asked by Kendell about his conversation with Mrs Pollett, the prisoner said he couldn't remember anything about it. He believed that if he really had said such things then he must have been drunk at the time. Allison maintained he was living at Poplar when the murder took place, had never been to Dagenham in his life and had not even met George Clark. 'All he knew about Clark's death was from the newspapers and conversation with the K Division constables'. It seems very likely that he did get information from people close to the investigation, judging by the details he gave about the decomposed state of the corpse. It may also be significant that his lodgings in Oxford Street, Whitechapel were not far from the home of Sergeant Parsons' stepmother Jemima and her younger children. These included Julia Parsons, who had, as we know, been living at the Dagenham station at the time of the murder. The white-handled knife in question was found on Allison when he was arrested. Kendell showed it to Jonas Stevens, Clark's room-mate at Dagenham. Stevens was adamant that he had never seen Clark with such a knife, and Kendell then abandoned this whole line of enquiry.

Back at Scotland Yard, Rowan and Mayne decided to step up the hunt for Parsons and Hickton. With the Essex Summer Assizes at Chelmsford fast approaching, finding them now became a matter of urgency. On 18th June 1847 the Home Secretary authorized a reward of fifty pounds for their recapture. Superintendent Marquard, probably still smarting from the humiliation of their escape from custody, personally gave five pounds towards this sum. On Tuesday 22nd June large placards were circulated to all London police stations and towns around the country. They gave details of the reward and descriptions of the fugitives. Photographs or identikit

£50 Reward.

WHEREAS

William Parsons,

a Police Serjeant, and

Isaac Hickton,

a Police Constable,

lately in the *K Division* of the Metropolitan Police, stand charged with Conspiracy and Perjury at the Inquest held at Dagenham, in the County of Essex, upon the body of GEORGE CLARK, a Police Constable, who was Murdered on the 29th June, 1846.

Her Majesty's Government

will give the above REWARD, to any Person who shall give such Information as will lead to the Apprehension of these Men, or a proportion of it for the Apprehension of either of them.

Description of Parsons,

Aged 30 Years, Height 5 feet 7½ Inches, Fresh Complexion, small Grey Eyes, Sandy Hair and Whiskers, much freckled, walks upright, and is well proportioned, by Trade a Miller, Born in Saint Peter's, Norwich.

Description of Hickton,

Aged 33 Years, Height 5 feet 9½ Inches, Fair Complexion, Grey Eyes, light Brown Hair, small Sandy Whiskers, round Shouldered, draws his Mouth on one side when talking, especially when excited, by Trade a Currier, and was employed at a Tanner's at Hales Owen, near Birmingham, about 3 Months since, Born in Saint Warbut, Derby.

Information to be given at the Police Office, Great Scotland Yard, to the Police Station, K Division, Arbour-square, Stepney, or any of the Police Stations.

Metropolitan Police Office,
4, Whitehall Place.

The wanted poster for Hickton and Parsons

pictures were not used on wanted posters at that time. Hickton was described as '5 feet 9 and a quarter inches, fair complexion, grey eyes, light brown hair, small shady whiskers, round shouldered, draws his mouth on one side while talking, especially when excited…' The last sighting of him had apparently been in his native Midlands. According to the poster, he was 'employed at a Tanner's at Hales Owen, near Birmingham, about 3 months since'. National newspapers and the daily *Police Gazette* also carried the descriptions.

Hickton had in fact moved to North Wales, where he found work at his trade of a currier. In March 1847 he heard about the True Bill being found against him for perjury. He grew worried because he had become known to the Welsh police, so rather than wait for the inevitable knock on the door he left and made his way to the densely-populated city of Liverpool. For three months all went well for Hickton there. He obtained work, and his true identity was not suspected. When the posters appeared, however, Hickton guessed the game would soon be up. Perhaps drawing his mouth to one side while talking was something no amount of disguise could prevent. On 29th June the fugitive sat down to write to his father Joseph, who lived at Derby. Was it a coincidence that this was a year to the day since George Clark's murder? Hickton explained that he was ready to give himself up, but mindful of the reward offered he wanted to be arrested by an old school friend, Sergeant George Hardy of the Derby Police. Joseph Hickton followed his instructions, and the following day Sergeant Hardy travelled to Liverpool, met Hickton and immediately took him by train to London. That same evening, Wednesday 30th June, there must have been a great commotion at Arbour Square police station, when Hardy entered with the wanted man.

Having spent a night in the cells at the very place where he had himself been happily working not so long before, Hickton was taken up the following day before Mr Justice Erle, at the Judges' Chambers. It was ordered that Hickton should be sent to Ilford Gaol to join Thomas Kimpton pending their appearance at the forthcoming Assizes. The *Times* reported of Hickton that 'He is stated, by those whose duty it is to attend on him, to be in a most depressed state of mind'.[15]

Sergeant Hardy had apparently promised to divide the reward with Hickton's father, 'a very poor man'. Hickton senior – who was, as we have seen, a badly-paid framework knitter – wasted no time in attempting to claim the reward money. He wrote to Marquard: 'Sir, I take the liberty of writing to you respecting the reward which I am entitled to for the Caption[sic] of my son Isaac Higton[sic] and will thank you to drop me a line to say whether I shall have to come to Chelmsford to receive the reward or whether it will be paid to me through a Banker in Derby and whether there are any necessary forms to be attended to respecting the receiving of the reward. Signed Joseph Higton'. The letter was passed to Richard Mayne, who dismissed it with a cursory note. 'It appears to me he is not entitled to the reward'. The following month, Hardy was awarded the entire £25. We do not know whether he carried out his promise to share it with Hickton's father.

Back at Dagenham, the first anniversary of the murder was marked by the unveiling of a permanent memorial in the shape of an obelisk over Clark's grave. It was described by the *Times* as 'A very handsome monument, surmounted by an urn'.[16] John Peter Shawcross, author of an early 20th-century history of Dagenham (he was also, incidentally, Vicar of Chadwell Heath), did not share the enthusiasm for this type of memorial. He wrote that:

> The churchyard contains a large number of tombstones. The majority of these are plain marble crosses, which speak of Christian hope; others are simple upright stones; and others again, not many, are merely pedestals supporting urns, suggestive of pagan despair.[17]

The inscription left no room for doubt about how Clark met his death, stating that he 'was inhumanly and barbarously murdered in a field at Eastbrook End'. His character was summed up in glowing terms. 'His uniform good conduct gained him the respect of all who knew him and his melancholy end was universally deplored'. On the other side of the memorial are the words: 'This tribute of respect was erected by the inhabitants of this parish and his brother officers of the K Division of the Metropolitan Police'. It has been stated that the memorial cost the massive sum of £450,[18] but no information survives about its design and installation. It's possible that it was partly paid for out of the reward money that had been raised by the police themselves. As we have seen, the Home Secretary had vetoed adding this sum to the official reward of £100.

Reading the inscription, one is struck by the lack of Christian sentiment and its failure to mention Clark's family. Where is the usual personal information such as 'Beloved son of James and Charlotte Clark' or 'Of Battlesden in the county of Bedfordshire?' Perhaps the Clarks erected a stone to his memory themselves in his home village, but if they did it has now disappeared.[19] In fact, the family seem to have been sidelined altogether in the aftermath of the murder. We have seen that Clark's mother called at Dagenham police station on three separate occasions before his funeral, but no officer had the courtesy even to speak to her. There is also no surviving record of any compensation being awarded to the Clarks.

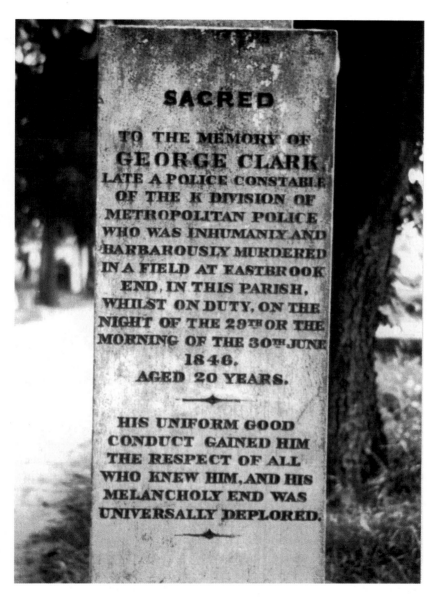

The obelisk over Clark's grave

Later that month, the Essex Summer Assizes began at last. The great and the good of Chelmsford were at the railway station on Monday 12th July to meet the two judges, Mr Baron Parke and Mr Justice Coltman, when they arrived at ten minutes past midday. They were greeted by the High Sheriff and Under-Sheriff, and their ceremonial carriage was escorted to the Shire Hall by the traditional phalanx of 'Javelin-Men', an echo of the bodyguard which once accompanied and protected the representatives of the sovereign through the country. Hickton and Kimpton had by now been transferred to Chelmsford's Springfield Gaol, and on Wednesday 14th July they were brought from there to the Shire Hall and put on trial for 'wilful and corrupt perjury'. The judge was James Parke, who had since 1834 sat as Baron Parke in the Court of Exchequer.

Kimpton's case was the first to be heard. He had a defence counsel, Mr Hawkins, whose fee was probably paid by Kimpton's family in Hendon. The prosecution lawyers were Mr Clarkson, Mr Bodkin and Mr Clark. This echo of the name of the murdered man must surely not have gone unnoticed. The first witness to be called was Charles C. Lewis, the coroner at the Clark inquest. He produced the sworn statements that Kimpton had made at the time, in which he had denied doing Parsons' duty on the night of the murder or telling Mrs Page of Thorntons Farm that he had. Lewis' time was clearly precious, as his expenses for attending the trial amounted to the huge sum of £21 9s 6d.[20]

Mrs Elizabeth Page then described yet again the conversation in the farmhouse after Stevens and Kimpton returned the cart that had been used to carry Clark's body away. 'Whilst they were eating, I asked prisoner where his sergeant saw the deceased last, and he answered – "To tell you the truth, Mrs Page, he did not see Clark that night after he went on duty; my sergeant was very poorly, and asked me to do his duty, and I took his horse and did his duty for him"'. The other witnesses were Priscilla Page, Thomas Archer, Jonas Stevens, John Farnes and Abia Butfoy. They were well paid for their trouble. Farnes was given expenses of £3 10s, Butfoy £2 16s, and the Pages and Thomas Archer were awarded £2 6s each. Stevens, Farnes and Butfoy must have felt the awkwardness of their position. It was only by sheer luck that they were not standing trial themselves. As we have seen, they had escaped on a technicality. Having been subpoenaed to give evidence against their colleagues, they were forced to comply on pain of being thrown into prison themselves for contempt of court.

Jonas Stevens stated that he had heard nothing of the disputed conversation at Thorntons Farm. He said he saw Parsons on horseback at about half-past ten on the night on the murder, but did not see Kimpton at all. It will be remembered that Stevens had fainted at the sight of Clark's body, and that Mrs Page had urged Kimpton to take the young man home as he was obviously not at all well. It's possible that Stevens had been in such a state at the time that he wasn't aware of what was being said.

When the prosecution had finished their case, Mr Hawkins 'addressed the jury at considerable length for the prisoner'. He could not call Kimpton to give evidence in his own defence. This was not allowed for another half-century, until the Criminal Evidence Act of 1898. The lengthy speech did not impress the jury, who returned a guilty verdict. Mr Hawkins then tried to get his client off on a technicality by arguing that the indictment did not contain the essential words 'in the year of our Lord' when giving the date of the offence.

Isaac Hickton was then brought into the dock. A no doubt unwilling Butfoy was forced to admit to the court that Hickton told him he had lied to the inquest about having seen Parsons between one and two o'clock on the night of the murder. Hickton had no lawyer to represent him. He carried out his own defence, and it was reported that he did so with 'great vehemence'. He said, 'My Lord, we screened the sergeant in his neglect of duty, and told a falsehood, not knowing the consequences; the sergeants make a report and have us turned out of our situations if we do not say what they please to order'. He called on Abia Butfoy to back him up. Butfoy confirmed that 'there was great strictness in the metropolitan police', and asserted that 'Parsons neglecting his duty was the cause of all their trouble'.

Hickton then called two character witnesses on his behalf. One was John Willsher, a Romford policeman, and the other was Mrs Elizabeth Page herself, who had apparently known Hickton for two years. He rounded off his defence by 'complaining bitterly' and protesting that 'what he had done was through fear of losing his situation, and to screen Parsons'. The jury bore this in mind when considering their verdict. They announced that they had found Hickton guilty as charged, but recommended him to mercy. Mr Baron Parke, the judge, said he would sentence Kimpton and Hickton after their trial on the second count, that of conspiracy, which would be heard the following day. Would he heed the jury's opinion?

After doubtless spending a sleepless night in their cells at Springfield, the pair were brought back into court the next morning. The judge dashed the hopes of Kimpton and his lawyer by announcing that he would reject the claim that the wording of the indictment was invalid. He said if the prisoners wished to take it further it was up to them to issue a writ of error.

CHELMSFORD, SHIRE HALL.

E.T.W.

The Shire Hall, Chelmsford

154

Mr Clarkson was about to launch the prosecution's case in the second trial, when he was interrupted by the judge. Mr Baron Parke said he saw no point in carrying on with the proceedings. He explained that the sentence he was going to pass on Kimpton and Hickton for perjury would be the same whether or not they were also convicted of conspiracy. The prosecuting lawyer agreed not to proceed any further provided the conviction for perjury was not disputed. This was settled, and the jury were discharged.

Later that day the prisoners were brought up for sentence. The judge was then 65 years old, but was not to retire for another eight years, after which as Lord Wensleydale he made history by being the first commoner since Medieval times to be elevated to the peerage. Judge Parke had a reputation for doing things by the book. His obituary in the *Times* over twenty years later, in 1868, pulled no punches. It said he 'retained to the very last that partiality for precedent and form to which the interests of justice were too often sacrificed' and was 'always on the side of adherence to the letter, even when it conflicted with the spirit, of the law'.[21]

The letter of the law was very much in Mr Baron Parke's mind as Kimpton and Hickton stood before him that day. He told them that perjury was a 'very grave offence….a most serious breach of the laws of both God and Man – because upon the truth all our rights as men rely'. He made it clear he had no intention of following the jury's recommendation of mercy to Hickton. The two men's hearts must have sunk when they heard the judge say that 'In all cases of this kind I have felt it my duty to inflict the extreme punishment of the law, and I see no reason why I should make an exception in this case'. He told Hickton he believed his version of events, 'but before the Coroner you had no reason to suppose that Parsons was guilty of this murder, and you persisted in what you had previously stated, instead of speaking the truth and exposing your superior officer, and the consequence was that great difficulty was thrown in the way of the enquiry, and probably the ends of justice were defeated'. So to add to Hickton's troubles, he was now held partly to blame for the failure of the investigation into the murder of the man he had worked with for a year at Stepney.

The judge then told the pair that 'Had you not been filling a public office, I should not have passed so severe a sentence, but the object is to deter others from a similar offence, for if we cannot have truth from police officers what guarantee have we for the security of either our persons or our property? Under these circumstances, I feel that I should not be doing my duty unless I inflicted upon you the heaviest punishment for this offence'.[22] They were to be fined one shilling, [5p], given a week's imprisonment, then 'to be transported beyond the seas for a term of seven years'. They could not appeal against the sentence, as this was not allowed until the Court of Criminal Appeal was set up in 1907.

There is no doubting that Kimpton and Hickton were guilty of perjury as charged. They had, by their own admission, lied when under oath at the inquest. Kimpton was seen as Parsons' sidekick, and had incriminated himself time and time again. We can probably rely on Henry Clements when he recounted at the fourth inquest hearing that Kimpton said to him: 'I understand you've got something to say against Parsons. What do you want to interfere with it for, what is that to do with you? If any one asks anything of you, say you don't know nothing about it'. There was also no avoiding the fact that he had repeatedly and publicly denied telling Elizabeth Page about Parsons not being on duty after midnight on the fatal night.

Isaac Hickton's involvement, on the other hand, was surely on a different scale. The judge and jury accepted his claim that he was afraid of losing his job if he didn't go along with what Parsons wanted him to say, and there can be no doubting the truth of this. We have seen that the police force was run along military lines, and the ethos of the army seems to be that orders are obeyed without question. Hickton was used to doing whatever his superior officer, the sergeant, told him to do. He had, as we have seen, been brought up in desperate poverty. His wages as a police constable, though not large, did offer the kind of steady and reliable income his father had never enjoyed, and he would have been loath to lose it. Also, it is worth remembering that Hickton and Clark had both been selected to work at Dagenham because of their unimpeachable records.

Kimpton and Hickton, still reeling from the impact of hearing the sentence, were taken back to Springfield, and through the arched, heavily studded entrance door with the words 'Convict Gaol' above it. They were now indeed convicts, with all that the word entailed. They faced a very different regime from the one they had become used to while on remand. Their hair was cut very short. At a time when men wore their hair almost shoulder length, such a style marked out convicts from the rest of the population even without the prison uniform. Along with their hair, they also lost their names. From now on, Kimpton and Hickton would be known only by number.

They would not be transported immediately, if at all. By the late 1840s it was usual for convicts to pass a considerable part of their sentence in England. They were compelled to spend the first portion of it in solitude under the so-called 'separate system'. This had been made legal in 1839 with the aim of preventing prisoners from communicating or even recognizing one another. They were only allowed to see and speak to prison staff. The advocates of this system, which was pioneered at Pentonville Gaol, claimed that when a prisoner was taken out of criminal society and left alone to reflect on his behaviour, 'it is almost universally found that such self-communion is the precursor of moral amendment'.[23] The anonymous author of *Five years' penal servitude, by one who has endured it*, published in the 1870s, agreed:

> A man's whole life passes like a panorama before him. This mistake and that failure – the error of judgement in this case and miscalculation in that – all come up and are plainly seen now it is too late. Lost or misapplied opportunities rise in judgement against the man as he sits in his horrid convict dress over his solitary work in prison.[24]

However, many commentators pointed to an increased rate of mental illness among such prisoners, and by the late 1840s there was much debate in the *Times* and elsewhere about the alleged inhumanity of the regime.

Springfield was originally built in the 1820s, but had recently been remodelled to adapt it to the separate system. Every cell now served as both bedroom and workshop. The rooms were 13 feet long, 7 feet wide and 9 feet high.[25] They contained a table, stool, shelves, WC and washbasin. There was a flap in the door for delivering meals and work materials. Prisoners slept in a hammock which was folded up during the day. The cells were fitted with one gaslight, so that work such as shoemaking, bookbinding and tailoring could be carried on into the evening. If an inmate wanted to call an officer, he pressed a button which triggered a signal outside the door. When taking their morning and afternoon exercise in the yard, the convicts were made to wear special caps which pulled down over their faces, and had to keep a fixed distance apart from each other.

This was also done when they walked to chapel every morning. Once inside the chapel, they were still unable to see each other's faces as they were within individual partitions. The chapel had been revamped in 1845 to house 400 prisoners at a time, arranged on eleven tiers.[26] No doubt the convicts sometimes managed to speak to each other here under the pretence of loud and enthusiastic hymn singing.

Hickton and Kimpton knew that their stay in Springfield would be temporary. They probably received similar advice to that given by the prison chaplain to the author of *Five years' penal servitude:*

> 'You must,' said he, 'just consider yourself a slave till your time is out. Every action of your life will have to be just what your taskmasters may command you to do. Try to bear up meekly and submissively. Avoid giving offence to any of the officials…'[27]

While Kimpton and Hickton were coming to terms with their new way of life, the spotlight turned again to the search for the final fugitive, William Parsons. Parsons himself was described on the wanted posters as being '5 feet 7 and a half inches, fresh complexion, small grey eyes, sandy hair and whiskers, much freckled'. In the town of Windsor, in Berkshire, PC William Cooper had obviously memorized this description. As he paced his beat, on Thursday 15th July, he noticed a man acting suspiciously who seemed to bear a strong resemblance to Parsons. He had 'small grey eyes, sandy hair and whiskers, [and was] freckled'. Perhaps the errant sergeant was intending to approach Windsor Castle and appeal to the Queen herself? The man's appearance was bizarre, to say the least. He had no shoes or stockings, and wore a wig on his recently shaved head. PC Cooper didn't hesitate, and arrested the fellow immediately. When challenged with being Parsons 'he hesitated and was very much confused'. He gave his name as John Luff Churchill, and his age as 24, but appeared older than this.

The next day, 16th July, a letter was written to Scotland Yard on behalf of the governor of Windsor Gaol, William Simms, informing the Commissioners of the arrest. Sergeant Jonathan Whicher was quickly sent to Windsor to view the prisoner, but he reported back to Inspector Haynes that the man was not Parsons. The prisoner had the letter D tattooed under his left armpit, and was taken before the magistrates on suspicion of having deserted from the army.

William Parsons' freedom was in fact coming to an end. He had moved from place to place since slipping away from Dagenham, taking advantage of the plentiful casual work available in railway building. Britain's rail network was booming in the 1840s, and it was estimated in 1846 that the industry employed 200,000 labourers.[28] Parsons had some narrow escapes during that time. The most dramatic incident was when he was arrested by a policeman in the streets of Chester. Luckily for Parsons, a quick-thinking companion threw some snuff into the officer's eyes, enabling the fugitive to get away.

Parsons eventually made his way to Lincoln. News of his whereabouts reached the ears of William Goodrich, a baker of Jubilee Street in Stepney, who passed the information on to the police. Superintendent Marquard promptly despatched 33 year-old Sergeant Thomas Forck up to Lincoln, accompanied by Constable Henry Barnes. These two 'intelligent officers', in the words of the *Essex Herald*, went undercover disguised as labourers. Forck and Barnes called at many places where casual workers were likely to be taken on, including the engineering and iron founding business of Clayton & Shuttleworth. They spoke to the factory time-keeper, James Grantham, who told them a man answering Parsons' description had been working there for about three months. They then arranged to come back early the following morning, Monday 26th July, when Grantham would point out the man to them.

In the meantime Forck and Barnes followed up another lead. A person matching the description of Parsons had apparently been working for the past three weeks or so on the Lincoln to Grimsby railway, then under construction about six miles outside the city. This man, they were told, was staying at a beer house called the Steam Packet, near the canal. On the Sunday evening the two resourceful officers, in their labourers' clothes, 'dropped in as if by accident' at the pub. They sipped drink after drink, keeping an eye on the comings and goings, but there was no sign of anyone resembling Parsons. Their spirits fell. Perhaps it had been yet another false trail.

It was nearly ten o'clock when they suddenly heard the landlady comment that her new lodger hadn't returned home. Another boarder asked whom she meant, and she replied 'The one with the red whiskers'. This was music to the ears of Forck and Barnes. Just a few minutes later, the latecomer entered, and they immediately recognized him as Parsons. The shocked landlady then watched as the men pounced on her lodger and handcuffed him in a trice before he had time to recover from the surprise. Forck and Barnes dragged Parsons out of the Steam Packet and took him to a new, less congenial billet at the Lincoln station house. Even in this awkward situation, Parsons had not lost his characteristic self-assurance. According to the *Essex Herald*, 'Before he was locked up he boasted that he would not have permitted any two men in England to have arrested him, except two of the division to which he formerly belonged'.[29]

The following morning, Monday 26th July, Parsons was brought before magistrate John Snow at the Lincoln Police Office.[30] He was despatched to Lincoln Gaol for a few hours to await police reinforcements who were making their way up from London to remove him. That same evening Forck and Barnes arrived in triumph with their prisoner at the K Division headquarters at Arbour Square, causing 'considerable excitement' in the neighbourhood of Stepney. The following afternoon Parsons was taken before Mr Justice Erle, who told him that unless he could come up with sureties amounting to £200 he would be committed to Ilford Gaol until his trial. Unsurprisingly, Parsons could not comply, and his captors were soon escorting him across the moat and through the entrance gates of Ilford Gaol, out of which Kimpton and Hickton had been taken just a fortnight before. It was going to be a long wait, almost eight months, until his trial. The Essex Summer Assizes having now finished, the next opportunity for his case to be heard was not until the Lent session in the following March.

Two Essex officers on plain-clothes duty, c.1880s. Forck and Barnes adopted similar disguise as they prepared to apprehend Parsons

On the way down to London, Parsons spoke about the 'great hardship' he had endured in the six months he had been on the run. It was noted that 'he appeared much depressed'. Even if Parsons had not already seen the fate of Kimpton and Hickton in the newspapers, he would have been brought up to date by Forck and Barnes, and must have brooded on his own future prospects. The *Essex Herald* told its readers that 'He continues to deny all knowledge of the brutal murder of Clark, and repeatedly declared that he had no suspicion of any one'.

At Scotland Yard, the Commissioners now faced a stream of letters from James Grantham, of Clayton & Shuttleworth, who claimed the reward on the grounds that he had tipped off the police about the whereabouts of Parsons.[31] Thomas Forck wrote in a report dated 7th August that Mr Grantham 'gave me no information whatever'. Rowan wrote to Grantham two days later saying his claim would be passed on to the Home Secretary, but that the Commissioners saw no grounds for endorsing it. Not to be daunted, Grantham protested that 'I caused him to be taken'. He insisted that the police were about to give up the search and leave the next morning, and that he could produce 'respectable testimony' to back up his story. Rowan (surely not at all pleased to see that the letter was addressed to C. Rowan Esquire instead of Sir Charles) then forwarded the whole of the correspondence to Sir George Grey. Following advice from Mr Maule, Solicitor to the Treasury, on 23rd August the announcement was made that the reward of £25 for the recapture of Parsons was to be divided three ways. William Goodridge, the informant, would get £20. The enterprising Sergeant Forck was awarded £3, and Constable Henry Barnes was given £2, amounting to just under a fortnight's wages. As a result of their efforts, the notorious sergeant was now under lock and key at last.

High Street, Romford, with the White Hart Inn on the extreme right

CHAPTER 9

'Under great suspicion of death by laudanum'

Britain was at this time gearing up for its first general election in six years.[1] Dagenham fell into the constituency of South Essex, where two seats were being fought over by three candidates. On Wednesday 4th August 1847, the campaign trail reached Romford. An animated crowd, only some of whom of course actually had the vote at that time, gathered in front of the White Hart Inn in the High Street to await the contenders. The only Parliamentary hopeful to turn up was the Liberal candidate Sir Edward Buxton, whose arrival at 2pm was heralded by a marching band and a long procession of carriages. Romford was known to favour the Liberal cause, and doubtless its orange flags were waving throughout the town. After Sir Edward and his father-in-law, the financier and philanthropist Samuel Gurney, had spoken to the cheering crowds from their carriage, a Captain Cox stood up on behalf of the Tories but could scarcely make himself heard. He was followed by Romford chemist James Macarthy, who jumped up on a wagon to make 'a humorous speech' in support of the Liberal candidate.[2]

Polling took place on the Friday and Saturday. There was no secret ballot in those days. The parties quite openly plied the voters with drinks, and it was quite common for the atmosphere to turn ugly. On the second day of polling, the Saturday, there was a brawl in which Ralph Page of Thorntons Farm cracked a rib. The voting figures show that Page was a supporter of the Liberal candidate, as was his neighbour Thomas Waters Brittain.[3]

Three days later, on Tuesday 10th August, Page and his wife Elizabeth watched proudly from the front pew of St Mark's Church in Clerkenwell as their eldest daughter Elizabeth Bennett Page exchanged her wedding vows with coal dealer William Frost. The ceremony was followed by a reception back at Thorntons Farm. At 2am, while the party was still going strong, Ralph Page went to bed. Not long afterwards he was dead. He was 49 years old. An inquest was of course necessary. Charles Carne Lewis, who had chaired the inquiry into Clark's death, was now to do the same for the man whose twelve year-old son had discovered Clark's body. The hearing was briefly opened at Thornton's Farm, and then adjourned for a week to allow time for a post-mortem.

Rumours flew around the district that Page had committed suicide by taking an overdose of laudanum. The *Chelmsford Chronicle* wrote that he 'had expressed a determination to commit self-destruction', and its description of his final hours brings to mind the scene in Macbeth when the king sees the ghost of the murdered Banquo. 'Suddenly in the midst of the merriment of the party Mr Page left the festive scene and went home. Soon after he was found suffering from a strong narcotic. Mr Butler, surgeon, of Romford, was called in, and applied the stomach pump, but without effect'. This was Charles Butler, who had helped Joseph Collin conduct the second post-mortem on George Clark.

When the inquest resumed, this time at the Cross Keys, the police were interested enough in the circumstances of the death for Superintendent Marquard to attend in person. It will be remembered that Ralph Page had stated that he spent the night of Clark's murder not asleep in his own bed, but in his barn guarding the valuable corn. Was he now suspected of involvement in the crime? Butler explained that an examination of the contents of Page's stomach showed that he had indeed taken laudanum. Butler stated that he didn't believe, however, that the death had been caused by either the drug or the fractured rib. Butler reported that Page had complained of chest pains, and was 'doubtless excited by his daughter's marriage'. Page's medical history included two attacks of apoplexy, and Butler's opinion was that he 'had died from a similar attack'.

The inquest jury were nonplussed, and returned a verdict of 'not sufficient evidence to satisfy the Jury as to the cause'. According to Page's death certificate, the cause of death 'could not be ascertained'. Marquard wrote a report on the inquest to the Police Commissioners, and rounded it off with the comment that 'from the evidence given the deceased had made no allusion to the murder of PC Clark'. Perhaps he had been hoping to hear of a deathbed confession. Ralph Page left no will, but was clearly not a poor man. His goods were valued at up to £600, and letters of administration were granted to his widow Elizabeth.

The dead man may not have admitted being involved in the killing of Clark, but an article in the *Chelmsford Chronicle* on 3rd September, syndicated from a London paper, stoked up the rumours:

> During the last few days the interest connected with the murder at Dagenham has been revived, in consequence of the suicide of one of the principal witnesses in that case. In the opinion of many, the sergeant, who still remains in Ilford Gaol, unable to procure bail, has been relieved of much of the suspicion against him...Since the death rumours have been propagated of the most extraordinary character, and many remarks have been made in reference to the circumstance that Mr Page should have happened to have been in his barn on the night of the murder for the purpose of there looking after his crops.

Page, however, had his defenders. James Macarthy, whom we have already met giving an election speech in Romford on behalf of the Liberal candidate, sent a letter of protest which was published in the *Chronicle* the following week. He wrote that Page had a 'harmless and kindly disposition' and explained that he could not have committed the murder because 'he was physically incapable of doing a deed of such atrocity and requiring much bodily strength'. Apparently two or three years before Page had severely injured his spine in a fall and had been left permanently disabled. He was subject to fits, and 'in the paroxysms of his agony he had frequently taken, by medical advice, tincture of opium'. Macarthy was probably the chemist who dispensed the drug to Page. Page's poor health is, incidentally, confirmed by an entry in the minute book of the trustees of Dagenham's William Ford School on 17th June 1847, almost two months before his death. It reads 'The Master reports the general attendance and conduct of the Boys to be good with the exception of Samuel and William Page their Father being sick and required their attendance'.[4]

Macarthy then described the dead man's widow as 'a most respectable and industrious woman, with a family well brought up; revenge, no doubt, with a desire to divert public attention from Parsons, prompted the paragraph'. He reminded readers that it was Mrs Page who 'was mainly instrumental in bringing the perjured policemen to justice', and wrote that her 'mental sufferings have been much increased' by the article in the *Chronicle*. In rounding off his letter, however, Macarthy made the false assertion that the inquest jury returned a verdict that Page's death was due to apoplexy.

The next issue of the newspaper brought another protest in defence of Page, this time by his Eastbrookend neighbour Thomas Waters Brittain and dated 15th September. Brittain revealed he had been the jury foreman at the inquest on Page. He stated that the medical evidence 'left no doubt whatever upon our minds that the quantity [of laudanum] was insufficient to cause death'. Brittain also denied that there was anything odd about Page being in his barn guarding his crops on the night of Clark's murder, explaining that 'it was his usual custom when he threshed corn in his barn to sleep there to protect it from depredation, and he was doing so on this occasion'. He described the rumour linking Page with the killing as 'one of the most unfounded libels ever issued' and wrote that this was also 'the opinion of our worthy vicar, and the whole body of parishioners'. Page had been 'a respectable farmer and neighbour'. No more correspondence was printed on the subject.

While this was going on, the investigation into Clark's murder was revived in another direction. This had begun the previous winter. One day towards the end of 1846, two labourers named William Roots and John Fuller had been mending a road at Eastbrookend. While they toiled away filling in the worst ruts using the piles of stones left by the roadside, they naturally began to talk. Conversation turned to the George Clark murder, and William Roots told a dramatic story. He began by assuring Fuller that 'if he'd been called he could say more than Archer could, or several others of the witnesses...'

Romford had its own detachment of police, part of the Essex Constabulary. By August 1847 the story had reached their ears, and they seem to have mentioned it to Hornchurch squire and magistrate John Bearblock. Obviously thinking that the Romford officers weren't acting quickly enough, Bearblock decided to take matters into his own hands. Having tracked down Fuller he questioned him about his story. Bearblock then penned an urgent note from his home, Hornchurch Hall, to Nicholas Pearce, 'to be instantly placed in his hands'. He wrote: 'I have this day seen an old harvest man who positively asserts that working in company with a Dagenham man some months since he was told by that person that a smock frock jacket and trousers were by him picked up or found hid about 100 yards from Dagenham village a few days after the murder they were very bloody and offensive he washed them a good deal but could not clean them...' Bearblock rounded off the letter by telling Pearce that 'Ralph Page died on Wednesday last under great suspicion of death by laudanum'.

Edward Kendell was sent to Romford on an early train the following morning and began following up the story. First of all he tracked down and questioned William Roots. The elderly farm labourer explained that one morning, shortly after the murder of Clark, he was walking from his home in Dagenham Village to work at James Miller's gravel pits close to the Four Wants. Roots was with his son and two men named William Edwards and William Jealous. When nearly opposite the cottage where Thomas Kimpton used to live, he saw 'part of an old corduroy trowsers, and parts of an old shirt laying by the side of the road, having been thrown over the hedge from a heap of manure which had been brought from London by Mrs Grays carts at different times, and was Night Soil and other kinds of manure mixed together'. In this statement to Kendell, he does not mention that the items were covered in blood.

Roots picked the clothes up with a pitchfork. William Jealous asked him 'what he was going to do with those beastly things and he said he should try to clean them and get some pieces out to mend his old clothes'. This is striking evidence of the poverty of the times. Once more we are reminded of scenes of wretchedness in Dickens. When they got to the gravel pit, the manure-caked clothes smelt so bad that Jealous persuaded Roots to throw them in.

Edward Kendell could not interview the younger Roots or William Edwards as they were 'away in the country at harvesting'. Kendell enquired about Roots's reputation, and reported that the man 'bears an indifferent character, and much confidence would not be placed in any statement made by him by parties who know him'.

Ilford's Inspector Henry Procter was then sent to ask William Roots if there was any possibility of extricating the clothes from the gravel pit. The prospects of this were not good. 'He says the place where they were buried was very wet and being more than a year ago must be entirely rotten to pieces. He further states that he laid them about seven feet from the surface of the ground and he could not tell the exact spot within two or three rods'.[5] So once more the detectives faced a dead end with their enquiries.

Back at Springfield Gaol, the routine of the imprisoned men Kimpton and Hickton was abruptly broken off. On 29th September 1847, ten weeks after their conviction, they were taken out of their cells and lined up with a large number of fellow inmates. As the men were being handcuffed together, the question 'Where are we going?' must have gone up and down the line. The consignment of shaven-headed convicts was escorted to Chelmsford railway station and then put on a train to London. Not having spoken to anyone but prison staff for months, the men must have been eager to chat to each other, and it was impossible for the warders to enforce silence on the train. They would also have gazed out at the early autumn landscape sweeping by, a welcome change of view from the stone walls of their Springfield cells. Familiar country greeted Hickton and Kimpton as the train stopped at Romford and then sped through part of the parish of Dagenham, not far from Hickton's old home at Beacontree Heath.

It soon entered London's East End, and as it passed Bethnal Green, Kimpton must have longed to be able to jump out and return to his wife and children living nearby. All too soon, the train pulled in at the Shoreditch terminus and the men were transferred to a horse-drawn prison van or 'Her Majesty's Carriage', later known by the American nickname of the Black Maria.[6] Their destination was Millbank, the largest prison in the country. An ex-prisoner describes the journey:

> By standing up I could, through the top ventilating grating, just catch a glimpse of the streets we passed through – over Blackfriars Bridge, along Stamford Street, York Road, over Westminster Bridge, past the Abbey and Parliament Houses, down the Horseferry Road, and in due time we drove within the portals of the Millbank Penitentiary. [7]

View of Millbank Prison from the river

*Plate 1: Exterior of Battlesden Church. Watercolour
by George Shepherd*

*Plate 2: Watercolour of Thorntons Farm by Thomas Dibdin, 1864
(entitled 'A farmhouse near Dagenham')*

Plate 3: Sir Charles Rowan

Plate 4: Richard Mayne

Plate 5: The Reverend Thomas Lewis Fanshawe, Vicar of Dagenham from 1816 to 1857

Plate 6: Sampler in tribute to George Clark, worked by his friend Mary Ann Jones

Completed in 1816, Millbank assumed the role of a 'convict assembly depot'[8] in 1843. As the contemporary writer Hepworth Dixon colourfully put it: 'To Millbank prison, the very lowest, the most reckless, most hardened criminals are sent from all parts of the country: the men who are sentenced to forced expatriation – cast out by the land which gave them birth'.[9]

This huge starfish-shaped fortress of yellow-brown brickwork, with its three miles of corridors, was situated where the Tate Britain art gallery is now. The site was viewed as a very unhealthy one. Dixon wrote that 'Not many years ago, the whole neighbourhood was one extended swamp...the rate of mortality is commonly very high in Millbank prison. If an epidemic visit London, Millbank prison is one of the first places in which its presence is detected'.

The management of the prison had also recently come under fire in a critical report published by the prison commissioners early in 1847.[10] Altogether its reputation was poor. A month previous to Kimpton and Hickton's arrival, the Reverend Whitworth Russell committed suicide by firing a pistol into his mouth, whilst visiting the prison, of which he was an Inspector.[11] The troop of new convicts from Springfield cannot have been looking forward to their arrival. They were given a bath and then, naked, were examined by the prison surgeon before being handed a uniform of grey jacket, brown trousers with a thin red stripe, blue cravats and grey Scotch caps.[12] No personal possessions of any kind were allowed. The writer of *Five years penal servitude* begged to keep his toothbrush, only to be told by the chief warder: 'If you are particular about your teeth, my man, use a corner of your towel'.[13]

Brief details of each new arrival were put into the admissions register.[14] Kimpton was prisoner number 12731 and placed in cell 2 A 11. It was noted that he had seven children and could read and write imperfectly. Hickton's number was 12732. He was given cell 4 B 20 and was also described as having imperfect reading and writing skills. Their physical descriptions were not given.

Each cell had an iron gate opening outwards into the corridor, and then a wooden door opening inwards. The stone-flagged rooms were slightly smaller than at Springfield, but were otherwise very similar. A high window looked towards the central inner tower. The routine for the inmates followed the same pattern as at Springfield. They worked in their cells for twelve hours every day except Sundays, Christmas Day, Good Friday and public holidays. Most were 'employed in making soldiers' clothing, biscuit-bags, hammocks, and miscellaneous articles for the army and navy, and other prisons, as well as the shirts, handkerchiefs, cloth coats and trousers worn by the prisoners themselves'.[15] Weaving and mat-making were also carried out, and there were carpenters' and blacksmiths' workshops on site. A number of trusted inmates helped with the cleaning or worked in the kitchens. Convicts whose literacy was poor were given a reading and writing lesson of an hour once a week.

To modern eyes there seems to have been an alarming lack of attention to personal hygiene. We read that 'Once every week during the exercise hour the men go to the bath – once a fortnight for a wash all over, and the alternate week feet washing only'.[16] They were given a change of clothes every Saturday, and their hair was cropped every ten days or so.

Kimpton and Hickton would have been allowed to write one letter home during the first two weeks after their arrival. Correspondence was vetted by the governor or chaplain, who made sure that 'All letters of an improper or idle tendency, either to or from convicts, or containing slang or other objectionable expressions, will be suppressed'.[17]

Friends and relatives writing in were 'not to say anything about the general news of the day. Anything of this sort would be struck out or the letter returned to sender.....Nothing was allowed to be sent to any prisoner, not even the photograph of a wife or child'.[18] Occasional visits were allowed. The convict and his or her friends were kept apart by a grated compartment in which sat a warder listening to the conversation. The warders were all armed in some way. When on duty inside the prison, they carried truncheons, and when supervising the convicts outside in the exercise yard they held a rifle and bayonet. The inmates had to address the prison officers as 'Sir'.[19]

Tobacco was banned inside Millbank, a move which caused wide discontent. Some inmates had contacts outside who bribed the warders to smuggle it in to them. The 'baccy' was then surreptitiously chewed rather than smoked. Another example of how conditions may not have been as bad as first meets the eye is that the cells were not soundproof and prisoners could communicate merely by tapping on the walls.[20]

When Henry Mayhew and John Binny were gathering material for their monumental 1862 work *The Criminal Prisons of London*, they interviewed the Millbank governor. He explained that 'We pursue the separate system for the first six months, unless the medical officer certifies that the prisoner cannot bear it, in which case we move him immediately into association'.[21] We have already noted that some commentators rejected the separate system as inhumane. Mayhew and Binny themselves concluded that they could not 'see one Christian reason to justify the discipline.' Hepworth Dixon claimed that some inmates put their lives on the line in a desperate attempt to escape their isolation:

> Suicides and attempted suicides are among the ordinary events of this great prison; and they are accounted for by the strong desire of the prisoners to be taken out of solitude and placed in human society....The plan adopted is generally this: the convict listens at the door of his cell for the footsteps of the warder heard coming along the gallery; when he believes him just at the distance which he will traverse in his round before anything fatal can occur, he swings himself up. The warder arrives at his cell – finds him hanging – gives an alarm – assistance is procured – he is cut down, and carried to the hospital, where, if he be lucky, he recovers in a week or ten days, and is then placed in a workroom with a number of his fellows. Sometimes the poor wretch makes a mistake; the warder does not come up in time...'[22]

On Friday 15th October 1847, only two weeks after arriving at Millbank, Isaac Hickton was moved from his solitary cell to the General Ward. This was made up of four cells knocked into one, where a group of prisoners lived and worked together. This transfer would have been authorized by the Medical Officer. Whether Hickton had attempted suicide we do not know. It will be remembered that back in July, after giving himself up, Hickton had been reported in the *Times* as being in 'a most depressed state of mind', so it is very possible.

Elsewhere in London during that same month, the detectives still investigating Clark's murder received some exciting news. A letter arrived from Colonel James Simpson, Commander of the Chatham Garrison. It enclosed a statement beginning: 'I solemnly declare that I was accessory to the murder of Police Constable George Clark'. This was signed by 24 year-old Private Robert Carter, alias George Harrod, of the 1st Battalion Rifle Brigade. Carter had recently been brought to Chatham from Bristol in order to be court-martialled for alleged desertion.

Nicholas Pearce and Edward Kendell quickly made their way to Chatham. Carter told them that back in June 1846 he had been lodging at the Bull Inn in Barking, where he fell into company with three men named John May, William Edwards and William Thomson. The four went on a night-time poaching expedition in Dagenham, and caught 'several pheasants and hares'. They were, he said, on the road back to Barking between two and three o'clock in the morning when they were stopped by Clark. He saw they were carrying game and tried to arrest them. Carter's statement, as reported by Nicholas Pearce, describes what happened next:

> William Edwards who carried a Gun struck the Policeman
> Clark with the Butt of the Gun which knocked him down, and
> William Thomson drew the Policeman's sword from the
> scabbard and struck him several blows about the Head and
> Neck, May assisting. Himself he states attempted to make his
> escape but Edwards presented the Gun at him and told him if
> he did not assist he should Shoot him as they all should be
> alike...after leaving him Dead, they sold their Game and spent
> the Money on Drink together.[23]

The detectives had their doubts about this 'confession' from the outset.
There were some glaring inconsistencies between Carter's story and the
actual circumstances of the murder, and someone has noted these in the
margin. For example, game is not in season in June. Nicholas Pearce was
dismissive. 'He does not appear to know anything of Dagenham or its
neighbourhood, and that he has trumped up this tale to screen himself from
the punishment likely to be awarded him by the General Court Martial, this
being his 5th time of desertion'.

Edward Kendell investigated Carter's background. He travelled to Grays in
Essex, where Carter had worked with his father for a firm of maltsters named
Gosling & Downs. Carter had left his post at the end of February 1841, and
was not known to have been in the neighbourhood since then. His fellow
workmen did not consider him to be 'of sound intellect'.

Kendell then made enquiries at Barking. What he found out there lent even
less credence to Carter's story. He found out that 'he never lodged at the Bull
Public House there, nor is there such persons there as he states he was
employed by (Viz) Hunt, a Shipwright, and Anderson a Block and Pump
maker'. As for the alleged accomplices, 'the only man named John May
known there, is master of the smack Antelope, there is no such person as
William Thompson, there was a young man named William Edwards,
residing there about that time, but no harm was known of him'.[24]

Kendell also made himself known to Carter's brother and mother. They
agreed that Carter was not of 'sound intellect' due to 'small pox in his youth'.
He had apparently drifted from job to job, and had not been seen by any of
his family since February.

They had no idea he had even joined the Army until getting a letter from him
the month before, informing them he had deserted from his regiment and had
been caught at Cardiff. They had since heard that he had been sentenced to
be transported for 14 years. Probably he was at that time imprisoned
alongside Kimpton and Hickton at Millbank. The pitiable young man's story

now fades from view. Whether his life eventually took a turn for the better is not recorded.

Towards the end of the year, Thomas Kimpton was about to leave his solitary cell after three months. Unlike Hickton, he had not been selected to work elsewhere in the prison. Instead, he was about to leave Millbank altogether. On Christmas Eve 1847 Kimpton and a batch of other convicts were ordered to assemble in the prison foyer. Handcuffed, they were taken to the riverside steps where a chartered vessel was waiting. On shore, the brightly-lit shops and bustling market stalls were thronging with excited Christmas shoppers and families making their way to pantomimes. How the boatload of convicts must have yearned for just a few moments with their own families at this festive season, especially in the knowledge that they were being taken to a place with a far worse reputation than even Millbank could boast.

When Thomas Kimpton woke up Christmas Day, he was in a very different environment from the one he had just left. Rather than being alone, he was in a hammock surrounded by dozens of others slung close together. He was now on board the *Justitia,* a convict hulk moored opposite the Woolwich Arsenal. This vessel was the third *Justitia* since the disused ships had first been used to house convicts as a temporary measure a full seventy years before. These floating dungeons had been described in the House of Commons by the MP for Finsbury Thomas Duncombe just a few months previously, in July 1847, as 'disgraceful to a civilized community, and were the more incredible from…being within a few miles from London Bridge'.[25] Hundreds of men were crowded together in squalid conditions. They were sent ashore each day and put to heavy manual work. In 1829 the regime was described by John Wade:

> On their arrival at the hulks, from the different Gaols, they are immediately stripped and washed, clothed in coarse grey jackets and breeches, and two irons placed on one of the legs, to which degradation every one must submit, let his previous rank have been what it may. They are then sent out in gangs of a certain number to work on shore, guarded by soldiers.[26]

In *Great Expectations*, set in the 1830s, Dickens describes a hulk through the eyes of the boy Pip:

> By the light of the torches, we saw the black hulk lying a little way from the mud of the shore, like a wicked Noah's Ark. Cribbed and barred and moored by massive rusty chains, the prison-ship seemed in my young eyes to be ironed like the prisoners…

On first arriving, a convict was given a berth on the lower deck. If he behaved well he would be gradually promoted to the middle and then the upper deck, which was more airy and less crowded. The guards wore a uniform of a frock coat and dark trousers, which according to the *Times* made them resemble Chelsea Pensioners.[27]

Isaac Hickton was not sent to join his comrade in the hulks. The Medical Officer had to pass men as fit to withstand the hard manual labour, and it seems that Hickton was not judged to be physically strong enough. Instead, it was decided that he should continue his imprisonment at Northampton Gaol. This was one of six prisons (the others being Wakefield, Leicester, Reading, Leeds and Bath[28]) with cells used to accommodate the overflow of inmates from Millbank. On Monday 17th January 1848 Hickton, like Kimpton three weeks before, joined a group of fellow inmates in the entrance lobby. They were handcuffed and taken away in a prison van through Central London towards Euston station and the London to Birmingham Railway. As they waited on the platform, the convict band must have been the objects of much pointing and staring, like animals in a zoo. At this spot George Clark had taken the steam train back to Leighton Buzzard after his successful interview at Scotland Yard two and a half years before. When Hickton arrived at Northampton Gaol later that day he must have been devastated to find himself locked in a separate cell once more. The admissions register shows he kept his Millbank prison number of 12732.[29]

So Kimpton and Hickton had to steel themselves to endure their long punishment. The only consolation was surely that it would only be a matter of time before William Parsons joined them.

CHAPTER 10

'Loaded with dirt and infested with vermin'

The wheels of justice were turning very slowly for William Parsons. It was now the spring of 1848, and he had been behind bars since his recapture at Lincoln the previous July. At last, on 7th March, the day of his trial at Chelmsford dawned.[1] As we have seen, the Grand Jury had rejected the charge of subornation (that is, inducement) of perjury. The one remaining indictment was, as given on the Gaol Calendar, for 'conspiracy to impede and prevent the due course of law and justice, by giving and causing to be given, false and perjured evidence before the Coroner, upon a certain inquest upon the body of a dead person, at Dagenham'.[2] It was noted that Parsons, unlike the other defendants, could read and write well. Oddly enough a George Clark also appears on the list. He was accused of stealing a bag, bread and cheese and a smock frock at Cold Norton.

The prosecutor was Mr Clarkson, who had also conducted the case against Kimpton and Hickton the year before. He began by stressing that Parsons and his fellow police officers were not suspected of carrying out the murder. He said that 'there did not appear reason to suppose, although there might have been rumours, that the police of Dagenham were in any degree participating by knowledge, act, or deed, with the fate of the unfortunate man...'[3] Their behaviour may, however, have thwarted the murder investigation. 'The effect of these false statements might have been to prevent the discovery of some or any of the persons concerned...' As for the reason for Parsons going off duty early in the first place, the prosecutor chose not to mention the heavy drinking that Parsons had indulged in throughout the day. He merely said that the sergeant had been 'fatigued by his day's labour'.

The first witness was Charles C. Lewis, the coroner. He read out the statements Parsons had made at the inquest about meeting George Clark and the other constables at various times during the night of the murder. John Farnes was then called. He said he had served in the force for nearly fifteen years before being dismissed, and was at present working as a labourer, 'getting my living now by honest employment'. Farnes told the court that the day after Clark's disappearance he, Hickton and Stevens were called into the charge room at the police station. Sergeant Parsons gave Farnes a piece of paper with a list of beats and times written on it, and said 'You will say that you saw me at such and such times'. Farnes's beat was number 3. Parsons then told Hickton what times he wanted him to say. Hickton was worried he would forget them, so Farnes wrote the times down for him at the dictation of Parsons. Kimpton and Hickton were not summoned to give evidence, although the prosecutor did mention their convictions for perjury.

Abia Butfoy also confirmed having been shown the list by Parsons. He went on to declare that Parsons had admitted to him several times that he went off duty after writing the report at midnight. He added that 'during the adjournment of the inquest, I heard it said that we must be very careful in giving evidence, and keep it from the young hands who had recently joined the force'. Detective Sergeant Edward Kendell was also called. He told the court that he had hunted high and low for the list but without success. He said he had served Parsons with a formal notice to hand it over, to which Parsons had merely replied 'You know I can't produce the paper'.

The evidence for the prosecution having finished, the lawyer for Parsons was about start the defence case when the presiding judge unexpectedly intervened. This was Thomas Denman, the Lord Chief Justice, who was then seventy years old. Lord Denman had been prominent in the campaign against slavery, and was not at all a stickler for rule and procedure like Mr Baron Parke who had overseen the trial of Kimpton and Hickton eight months before. When he finally retired in March 1850, the *Times* paid tribute. 'If Lord Denman has no pre-eminent claim to be reckoned among the subtlest lawyers who have adorned the bench, at least his robust good

Lord Denman. Engraving by Thomas Hodgetts of a
painting by Thomas Barber

sense and sound constitutional views have rendered him a far fitter person to preside in chief over the Court of Queen's Bench than any mere lawyer could have been'.[4] And when he died on 22nd September 1854, the *Times* remarked in its obituary that 'To the cause of toleration and freedom within the boundaries of the law he at all times gave his hearty support'.

Lord Denman announced that he was stopping the trial. This was not because he believed Parsons to be entirely innocent. It was, he said, 'extremely painful to see a case of this kind in a court of justice, where one man had induced others to give falsehoods; and the more so that it was a policeman'. He was calling a halt to the proceedings because he felt the evidence he had just heard did not support the charge of conspiracy. The constables had lied in order 'to screen their officer and themselves, and not to obstruct the course of justice, or throw any obstacle in the way of discovering the perpetrator of this dreadful deed'. He ordered that a verdict of Not Guilty must be recorded. A relieved and delighted William Parsons was then able to walk from the Shire Hall a free man. Four months before, the Grand Jury had listened to substantially the same evidence and had rejected the charge of subornation of perjury. Yet it is hard to think how Parsons could have mounted a defence if this accusation had after all been brought.

Although the prison rules forbade Kimpton and Hickton from hearing about events happening in the outside world, their jailers would surely have told them the outcome of the case against Parsons. It was widely reported in the national newspapers, which had followed every twist and turn of this extraordinary murder case.

The shock waves from this turn of events reached Thomas Kimpton's parents in Hendon. Their son was going through hell on the hulks, and expecting to be shipped off to Australia at any time. It must have seemed beyond belief that the prime mover in the whole disastrous course of events had been set free. Parsons hadn't been charged with perjury for the simple reason that he had never actually admitted lying, whereas their son had been punished for agreeing to tell the truth. After their initial anger at the unfairness of it all had died down, the Kimpton family then considered how the acquittal of Parsons could be turned to their advantage.

As we have seen, no appeal was allowed at that time against a conviction or length of sentence. However, one hope remained. This was to draw up a petition for mercy and get it signed by as many prominent people as possible. David T. Hawkings notes that 'there are tens of thousands of these petitions in the Public Record Office; there is little evidence to show that many of these petitions were effective. Most appear to have been filed away without further action…'[5]

However small the chances of success, anything was worth trying. The family were well known in Hendon, where John Kimpton had been a saddler for many years. He approached the town's Member of Parliament, Charles Gore, who agreed to lend his support by presenting the petition to the Home Secretary. Help was also provided by Hendon's maverick vicar Dr Theodore Williams, who worked as a prison visitor and had even served time himself in debtors' gaols.[6] John Kimpton campaigned for his son's release in the spring of 1848 against a backdrop of a society in ferment. On 10th April 1848 there was a huge rally at Kennington Common in support of the Chartists, who were demanding a range of reforms which at the time caused horror among the governing classes. These aims included every man being given the vote, secret ballots, and salaries for MPs. To the government's relief the demonstration passed off peacefully, aided by a heavy police presence and wet weather.

On 1st May the petition was sent to the Home Secretary, Sir George Grey.[7] John Kimpton had drummed up an impressive 28 signatures. In his covering letter, the Hendon MP noted that they included 'all the respectable people of the parish'. The vicars of Hendon, Edgware, Stanmore and Kensal Green lent their support, as did the surgeon John Wyndham Holgate, who added that he was Kimpton's 'former master who recommended for the police'. Another name on the list was that of George Tanqueray, who was now living in Hendon but had previously rented Dagenham Vicarage.

John Kimpton kept the petition brief and to the point. He put the blame firmly on the shoulders of Parsons, and then pointed out that 'at the Lent Assizes 1848 the Sergeant, who was the Real and Only Cause of your petitioner's son so offending, has been tried and acquitted'. He declared that Thomas and his family 'have lived in credit and respectability up to this unfortunate transaction'.

The Home Secretary duly transmitted the petition to the Commissioners for their comments. Richard Mayne asked his Chief Clerk Charles Yardley to draw up a list of facts relating to the case, making sure to include 'period of service in the Police and good conduct'. Yardley did so, adding that 'Kimpton after confessed to Superintendent Pearce that it was untrue, and that he had been induced to tell the falsehood by Sergeant Parsons to screen him from neglect of duty; that he began with this lie which led to others, until he did not know when to stop, and that he was truly sorry for it, and was ready as far as lay in his power to tell all he knew'.

On 10th May 1848 Richard Mayne sent his views on the case to Sir George Grey. He agreed that Parsons had induced the constables to lie at the inquest. He also noted that Kimpton had served in the police from 6th January 1840 with only one report of neglect of duty. So far, so good. After these positive comments, though, Mayne added:

> The Commissioners feel it their duty however to observe that besides the infamy of the offence of these individuals and the scandal that it cast upon the police force, the false statement misled the officers engaged at first in making enquiry and prevented them taking such steps as they otherwise would have done in endeavouring to detect the murderers who have not yet been discovered.

The Home Secretary took the hint and promptly rejected the petition. Kimpton, no doubt devastated, was forced to grit his teeth and make the best of it on board the *Justitia*. His mood may have been lightened for a while, though, by an episode of high drama on the hulk later that same month. A man named Richard Loder, whose previous jobs had included being governor of Horsham Gaol and a sergeant in the A division of the Metropolitan Police, was overseer of the *Justitia*. His duties included handling the payment of tradesmen's bills and staff wages. Loder was paid £200 per annum. In May 1848 he collected £735 in gold plus £15 in Bank of England notes to be used for settling the previous month's accounts. The atmosphere of criminality on board the floating dungeon proved to be contagious, for the apparently ultra-respectable overseer suddenly vanished along with the money. He also had the effrontery to steal a watch and chain belonging to a convict, which had been placed with him for safekeeping.

Several months later, in spite of the failure of Kimpton's petition, Isaac Hickton's parents Joseph and Elizabeth decided to take the same course on behalf of their son. They sought and gained the help of South Derbyshire MP Charles Robert Colvile, who presented the petition to the Home Secretary on 19th October. Signatories included clergymen from several Derby parishes and three of Hickton's previous employers.

The petition acknowledged that the murder investigation had been hampered by the lies told at the inquest. It then stressed that Hickton had been afraid of losing his job if he did not follow orders from Parsons:

> That the said Isaac Hickton in a letter to his Father states 'that he was not aware of the danger he was running himself into by saying what he did and he was quite ignorant of what he was doing, he did as his superior officer ordered him which he was compelled to do as it was in his power to get him dismissed from the force'.

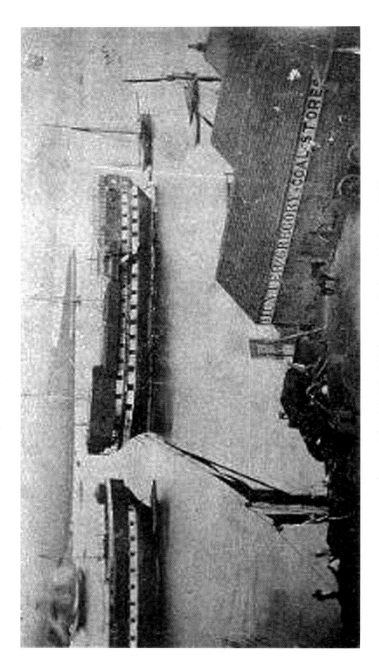

A photograph of the Woolwich convict hulks taken in the 1850s

It was pointed out that the trial judge, Mr Baron Parke, had believed Hickton's version of events. Finally, the petition reminded the Home Secretary that the jury had recommended Hickton to mercy.

We have already seen that Hickton had been 'in a most depressed state of mind' after giving himself up in June 1847, and that he had lasted only two weeks in a solitary cell before being moved to shared accommodation. Unsurprisingly, the petition emphasised the effect that imprisonment was having on Hickton's health. He was now at Northampton Gaol, and it seems that another crisis had occurred, leading to him being transferred to the kitchens where he could work alongside other inmates. A poignant note from Charles Dodd, the medical officer, is attached to the petition. He writes:

> The convict Hickton's mind appears more at rest since he has been fulfilling his new occupation of cook to our gaol. But I do not consider his health at all improved, he is extremely nervous and also very weak. His nervousness is so great that if you speak…quick to him he does not appear to know what he is doing. I have ordered him a pint of beer daily which I trust may accelerate his recovery.

However, once again the Home Secretary did not feel there were grounds for reducing the sentence.

Hickton's disappointment must have been overwhelming, but at least he did not face the danger that Kimpton was now in. The hulks had always had the reputation of being unhealthy, but in October 1848 there was an outbreak of cholera. This dreaded disease could kill in a few hours. We now know that cholera is caused by bacteria ingested in food or more frequently drinking water, but this had not yet been realised in the 1840s.

On 9th October 1848 there were three fatal cases on the *Justitia*. One man was taken ill while at work in the Royal Arsenal. He returned to the ship, and two hours later was dead. He would have been laid to rest at the convict burial ground on Plumstead Marshes, a place described by Mayhew as 'one of the dreariest spots we had ever seen'.[8] It held no memorials, not even simple wooden crosses or numbered signs. The bleakness was only enlivened by a little pale-blue flower, known locally as the convict's flower because it was thought to grow nowhere else but on the graves. The lack of ceremony also extended to the burial service. During a previous outbreak of cholera in 1832, the clergyman did not go to the graveside but read the burial service from the deck of the hulk a distance away, dropping his handkerchief as a signal for the body to be lowered into the grave.[9]

The dead man's fellow convicts were kept in quarantine on board the vessel. As well as being spared their back-breaking labour onshore at the 'public works', the men were allowed other perks at this time. Tobacco had been banned on the hulks in 1832, and this was so resented that it had caused a riot on the *Warrior* on Christmas Eve 1846. Believing that some kind of 'miasma' in the atmosphere was to blame for the cholera, the authorities hoped that smoking might help cleanse the air and repel the contagion. The convicts were also allowed tea or cocoa in place of their usual gruel. The *Times* noted on 11th October that 'The indulgence of being able to smoke has had a wonderful effect, and the men seem to enjoy themselves very much'. One wonders whether the writer of this would have found much enjoyment in being trapped on a filthy ship amidst raging cholera.

The *Times* followed the progress of the outbreak, and by the end of the month was able to claim that the worst was over. On 29th October it reported that the 'total number of cases is 44 attacked, 14 deaths, 14 recoveries, 10 convalescent, all convicts'. At some point during the emergency, the *Justitia* was temporarily abandoned and Kimpton and his fellow prisoners were moved to two smaller deactivated navy ships called the *Hebe* and the *Sulphur*. In January 1849 a violent incident took place on the aptly-named *Sulphur*, when some convicts with a grudge against a quartermaster named Webb attacked their guards. A detachment of Royal Marines had to be brought on board to restore order. The ringleaders were then each given 50 lashes.[10] The *Sulphur* later became the laundry ship for the Woolwich hulks. At the end of every quarter the behaviour of each convict was assessed. In December 1848 Kimpton's conduct, usually good, was judged to be 'indifferent', but we are not given further details. The stress caused by the cholera outbreak no doubt took its toll on many on board the hulk at that time.

As Wednesday 7th February 1849 dawned, Isaac Hickton lay asleep in his cell. Perhaps he was dreaming of his relatively carefree days at Arbour Square alongside George Clark before their ill-fated move to Dagenham. He was abruptly awoken at 6am by the loud prison bell. Hickton quickly washed, then cleaned the floor of his cell with the same water. Chapel followed at 7am, after which Hickton made his way to the kitchen and set to work helping to prepare dinner for the other inmates. This was served at midday. If meat was on the menu, the prisoners were given tin knives to cut it with. They often took the opportunity of scratching graffiti on the knives such as names, grievances and even 'expletives and anathemas against the prison authorities, that they did not dare speak'.[11]

Meanwhile, the normal routine had been resumed on board the *Justitia*. Thomas Kimpton slept in a hammock which had his prison number stitched on it along with the name of the hulk. At 5.30 the ringing of a bell announced that it was time to get up. After a quick wash, Kimpton pulled on the uniform of rusty brown with red stripes.[12] On his left arm was a leather badge with a sequence of letters and numbers on it and on the right was a number of rings. These indicated the length of his sentence, the number of months he had been on the hulk, and his good conduct marks.

Rowan and Mayne, recognising the importance of a smart and professional appearance, had stressed that police officers should be clean and presentable at all times. Now, after a year and two months on the hulks, Kimpton would have been covered with grime despite his best efforts. In 1847 the Williams report had revealed a shocking state of things on the *Justitia:* 'carelessness and neglect in supplying the convicts with the means of washing themselves; their blankets and bedding were dirty; they were insufficiently supplied with shirts and clothing; and their persons were loaded with dirt and infested with vermin'. When Henry Mayhew visited the hulks in the 1850s, he noted approvingly that conditions were much improved from the 'horrible filth' of several years before. He spoke to a long-serving warder who remembered prisoners' shirts 'when hung out on the rigging, so black with vermin that the linen positively appeared to have been sprinkled over with pepper'.[13]

Kimpton queued with his fellow convicts to stow their hammocks away by 6am, then they sat down to breakfast. Each man had his own tin to eat from, which he cleaned himself. The meal consisted of a hunk of bread weighing approximately 12 ounces, served with oatmeal gruel. Captain Williams wrote that the prisoners hated the gruel, which they compared unfavourably to what had been served up in Millbank, 'and a very lamentable waste is occasioned by the large quantities being thrown overboard from their positive rejection of it....'

In their defence, it has to be admitted that it would have been difficult to enjoy even the most sumptuous breakfast on the *Justitia* because of the all-pervading smell of sewage. If the washing facilities on board were poor, the lavatories were even worse. Although flush toilets had been invented, they had not been introduced to the hulks. The sewage was just dumped over the side. As the Williams report put it: 'Where the *Justitia* is placed, there is a considerable deposit of mud, which is described by the Surgeon as emitting very unpleasant, if not deleterious, effluvia in hot weather'.[14]

The men were rowed ashore to start their day's work at the Royal Arsenal at half past seven. The heavy manual labour included such tasks as moving timber, cleaning guns, scraping rust from shot, and plenty of digging. By this time Kimpton had probably ceased to be bothered by the crowds of sightseers who flocked to stare at the toiling convicts and their gun-toting guards. He would also have become accustomed to the clamour of the rifle and artillery practice. Back in October 1847 one of the guns had burst, causing shells to fall right onto the deck of the *Justitia*.[15] Kimpton may also have had to get used to hostility from his fellow convicts once word got round that he was an ex-policeman. Previously, the enforced isolation of Springfield and Millbank would have protected him against this. The worst-case scenario would have been if he had helped to send down a friend of a friend of someone else on the ship. Kimpton probably had to grit his teeth and endure constant small acts of bullying or having his food tampered with, the warders unwilling to interfere.

At this time in the history of the hulks, both convicts and members of the public used the same lavatories at Woolwich. This was a weak link in the security, as it provided an opportunity for civilian clothes to be smuggled in and used for escape attempts. Tobacco, food and alcoholic drink were also passed to the prisoners by these means.

The interior of a convict hulk, with tables laid for dinner

Whatever job Thomas Kimpton was assigned to that February day, we can be sure that it would have been exhausting, and he certainly looked forward to the hour's break at midday. The weary men downed tools and went inside sheds on shore where their dinner awaited. This was the main meal of the day, and like the breakfast it was not inspiring. Kimpton usually sat down to a dinner of meat, potatoes and bread. On Mondays, Wednesdays and Fridays a pint of soup was added, but the meat ration was reduced accordingly to five ounces.

The convicts were not allowed to have food brought in from outside. Their diet was not only dull but positively unhealthy. The Williams report of 1847 examined 600 prisoners and found that nearly half of them had scurvy. This is caused by a lack of Vitamin C, and its symptoms include skin lesions and bleeding into the muscles and joints. Teeth become loose, and eating can be difficult and painful. Scurvy can be fatal if left untreated. Over a hundred years before this, the British naval surgeon James Lind had proved that citrus fruit was an effective cure, and from 1795 the Royal Navy provided a daily ration of lime or lemon juice to all its men. There is some evidence that vegetables were grown on allotments at Woolwich and added to the thrice-weekly soup given to the convicts, but clearly not in sufficient quantities to provide them with essential vitamins and minerals.

After the dinner hour, it was back to work until 4pm (5pm in summer) when the men queued to board the boats and return to the *Justitia*. Their rowers were also convicts, and there was much competition for this prestige job. On getting back to the ship, the men did their best to wash off the day's grime before sitting down to supper at 4.45pm. It was bread and gruel again, the same fare as at breakfast.

There was a chapel on board the hulk, and during the evening the prisoners assembled there for a service. Later, those who had difficulty reading and writing attended lessons. As we have seen with regard to Millbank, the authorities were keen to raise levels of literacy amongst the convicts. Those who could already read were allowed to borrow volumes from the onboard library. Perhaps Kimpton spent that February evening clutching a book in his blistered and calloused hands. Unfortunately, it's unlikely that he would have been able to immerse himself in the latest bestseller from Dickens. That outspoken author was banned after criticising the prison system, and novels in general were not thought to be suitable fare for the convicts. Mayhew observed some years later that the library shelves on the hulks chiefly contained improving works including *Recreations in Physical Geography* and *Easy lessons in Mechanics*.

At 7.30pm Kimpton lined up with the other men to retrieve their hammocks from the storage cupboards. Half an hour later they were all in bed. Did he lie there thinking of Ellen and their seven children and wondering what they were doing? It may have been many weeks since he had seen a friend or relative. Visits were normally allowed once every three months, on Sunday afternoons, and probably took place on shore.

That same morning, less than five miles west of the *Justitia,* William Parsons made his way towards Christ Church in Whitechapel. Whilst Kimpton and Hickton were a sorry sight with their prison uniforms and shaven heads, their former sergeant had taken particular care to look his best that day. He was about to get married again. His new bride was Ann Mary Secker, known as Annie, daughter of John Secker, a brickmaker. The ceremony was carried out by William Stone, and the bridegroom's 21 year-old half-sister Harriet was one of the witnesses. According to the marriage certificate, both bride and groom were living at 24 Union Street, Whitechapel.

At that time weddings had to take place between 8am and noon. Whilst Hickton and Kimpton were eating prison fare at midday, the new Mr and Mrs Parsons had probably adjourned to a pub for the wedding breakfast. As he knocked back more than a few beers and accepted the congratulations of fellow-drinkers, did Parsons spare a thought for his unfortunate ex-colleagues? We do not know whether his daughter Maria, now approaching her third birthday, was present that day. It seems unlikely that he had much contact with her now.

She continued to be looked after by her Rawlings grandparents at the Fairlop Oak in Barkingside, while her father turned his thoughts to starting a new life. He had ambitions that would soon take him far away from the crowded streets of East London.

CHAPTER 11

'Shouting in his sleep, crying "Murder, Murder!"'

The following month Isaac Hickton tried once more to win his freedom. This time the petition was written from his own point of view rather than that of his parents.[1] We know his reading and writing skills were limited, so sympathetic prison staff probably assisted him. And this time, rather than submitting his plea to the Home Secretary, he went straight to the top. Dated 16th March 1849, it was addressed 'To the Queen's Most Excellent Majesty'.

Hickton wrote that he was 'deeply penitent', and again stressed that there had been no criminal intent: 'Your petitioner when he took the false oath did so in part from fear – in order to keep his situation – fully believing he should lose it if he did not screen his Sergeant in the Police'. His previous good record was also emphasised: 'up to the time of this offence [he] always bore the best of characters and upon that account was highly recommended and actively employed as a policeman'.

The main gist of the petition was that Hickton's health, both mentally and physically, was deteriorating. The stress of his situation was overwhelming. He 'has scarcely had rest day or night from fretting over his sentence and prospect of removal to a foreign land without expectation of health and strength to get a living...' On top of that, his eyesight was 'greatly impaired'. This condition, like the scurvy affecting the convicts on board the hulks, was probably caused by vitamin deficiency. A diet lacking in Vitamin A can lead to the cornea becoming opaque and ulcerated. Night blindness occurs, and eventually sight may be lost altogether.

Hickton rounded it off by pleading not for an out-and-out pardon, but a commutation of his sentence to a short imprisonment instead of transportation. He attached an outspoken letter on his behalf from the prison chaplain, Charles West, who wrote that 'No convict can have behaved better or in my conscientious opinion deserves - and I may say requires - commutation of sentence'. The economic value of convict labour was always carefully calculated by the authorities. We have seen that Hickton had, unusually, not been sent to the 'public works' at Woolwich along with Kimpton. Charles West suggested it would be a waste of public money to transport Hickton, as he would be a burden rather than a productive worker:

> I do not believe he will weather the passage to Australia, and should he do that I fear he would do no good either for himself or others...I fully expect that should he be sent abroad even with the boon of an exile's prospect he will fret himself to death – he being of such a nervous delicate temper of mind and

body that we have only by very great attention to his case kept him from despondency and despair.

West argues that by remaining in England, on the other hand, Hickton would have a future:

....whereas if his sentence be mercifully commuted to a further short imprisonment here or elsewhere he would return home to assist his aged father in the cultivation of some land in his possession and regain his station in society.

This proves that not all Victorian prison staff were as severe and uncaring as the popular image would have it. Charles West was probably one of many in the system who were willing to do their utmost to help in difficult cases.

Incidentally, the petition shows that Hickton's father Joseph was by this time no longer a poverty-stricken framework knitter. Perhaps Sergeant George Hardy had, after all, kept his promise to share the reward money for Isaac's capture. By whatever means, Hickton senior had now set himself up as a market gardener, and appears as such in later Derby trade directories and census returns. He may also have been helped out by sympathetic friends and neighbours.

This new petition was received on 20th March 1849. Although addressed to the Queen, it would still have been dealt with in the first case by the Commissioners and Home Secretary. Just three days later, the decision was made. Hickton's sentence was reduced to two years' imprisonment, which meant he would be freed in the middle of July.[2] We can well imagine his feelings of delight and relief when the long-awaited news came through. There was a downside, however. Instead of spending the final four months of his sentence at Northampton, Hickton was moved back to Chelmsford's Springfield Gaol. He must have greatly missed his congenial job in the prison kitchen, and the company of the sympathetic chaplain. Also, Northampton was not far from Derby, so his parents would not have found it difficult to visit him when allowed. But at least Hickton was now able to count down the days until his release. He would also have been allowed the morale-boosting privilege of growing his hair long again in preparation for his return to civilian life.

Meanwhile, back on the convict hulk, there was no such hope of reprieve for Thomas Kimpton. In April 1849 he would have heard news of Richard Loder. The absconding overseer had been on the run for eleven months, and had made short work of the stolen £750. When only 12 shillings and sixpence (62½p) remained in his pockets, Loder decided it was time to give himself up. He walked into Westminster's King Street Police Station and asked Inspector Charles Otway, whom he had known for sixteen years, to take him into custody. There is more than a touch of Uriah Heep, the classic hypocrite from *David Copperfield*, in Loder's protestation that the theft had brought him nothing but misery. He told the Inspector that 'he had wandered all over the country in wretchedness and despair'.[3] Loder pleaded guilty at the Old Bailey later that same month, but if he thought his ostentatious penitence would afford him a lighter punishment he was to be proved wrong. Loder was sentenced to seven years' transportation, so most likely spent some time back on a convict hulk. We can imagine the uproarious scene when the one-time overseer returned as a chained prisoner.

Two months later, the *Justitia* and the hospital ship the *Unité* were again hit by cholera. On 10th June an 18 year-old convict named Vullalove became ill, and died just ten hours later. The following day a fellow-prisoner named Williams, aged 24, fell ill. Two days later he breathed his last, and one of the warders also succumbed. Mr Bligh, assistant surgeon of the *Unité,* reported gloomily to the *Times* on 18th July that during this outbreak 'the disease was in a very severe form, and there were very few recoveries'. In his opinion, the reason the *Justitia* and the *Unité* were affected was because they 'were directly within the unwholesome influence of Plumstead marshes'. His colleague George Henry Dobbs contented himself with saying that the cholera 'undoubtedly arose from a generally prevailing atmospheric cause which no human being knew of'.

The authorities moved quickly. Once more, the *Justitia* was to be abandoned. There had been no cases of cholera on board the hulk *Warrior,* moored a mile upstream. On the morning of 15th June, 160 convicts were moved from the *Warrior* by watermen's steamers to Nine Elms and then onto a train. Their destination was Portsmouth, where they were to live on the hulks there and work in the dockyard.[4] The following day they were joined by two-thirds of the inmates of the stricken *Justitia*. The remaining third, including Thomas Kimpton, took the short journey to their new berths on the *Warrior.*

The *Warrior* lay opposite Woolwich Dockyard, and housed nearly 500 convicts.[5] Some were given similar work to that carried out at the Arsenal, while others cleaned out ships and loaded and unloaded cargoes. If his first quarterly report, or 'muster', on the *Warrior* is anything to go by, Thomas Kimpton seems to have got on better there than on the *Justitia*. His conduct was rated as Very Good.[6] Other prisoners whose names appeared on the same page include John Palmer aged 23, sentenced to seven years' transportation for stealing a sieve of gooseberries, and Edward Oliver, a 26 year-old found guilty of 'stealing a pair of boat oars the property of Her Majesty'.

The Warrior convict hulk

Meanwhile, the burial ground at Millbank Prison was also filling up with cholera victims. Again the nonplussed authorities tried some desperate measures, such as supplying every inmate with a daily half-pint of Barclay and Perkins beer.[7] This may have helped morale if nothing else. Half a pint per day was not enough to replace completely the drinking water which we now know was the true cause of the outbreak.

During the summer of 1849 the cholera was killing up to two thousand people a week throughout the country. It is an intestinal infection which causes severe diarrhoea. Dehydration then sets in, and this can swiftly lead to multiple organ failure. Fear gripped Dagenham in August as the dreaded disease swept through the parish. The little police station in Bull Street was not spared. Sergeant Thomas Pearson fell ill, and was to die on 23rd August. The following day Richard Flavell, a Dagenham labourer, succumbed after just two days' illness. Day after day, more victims were interred in Dagenham churchyard. In August and September 1848 there had been just seven burials. During the same two months in 1849 the total was 34.

Elsewhere in Essex, on Saturday 14th July the day of freedom dawned for Isaac Hickton. It was exactly two years since he and Kimpton had stood before Mr Baron Parke to hear the devastating sentence. If his own clothes had been located they would have been returned to him. Otherwise, new ones would have been provided, but were not at all popular as they were made in-house and easily recognizable.

Joseph and Elizabeth Hickton may have travelled to Chelmsford to greet their son when he stepped outside Springfield's gatehouse. Hickton returned to his home town of Derby, where he took up residence with his parents and younger brother Henry in the Hockbrook Fields area. Isaac Hickton may have stepped off the conveyor belt of Victorian justice, but others were lined up to take his place. Hickton's cell would probably have been used to house one of the new batch of 41 prisoners brought in to be tried at the Essex Summer Assizes. The proceedings began two days later, on Monday 16th July.

Now that Hickton was free, John Kimpton made a fresh appeal to the authorities on his son's behalf. Once more Charles Gore, the Hendon MP, was keen to assist. On 4th October 1849 he wrote to the Home Secretary, Sir George Grey, urging that the pair should be treated equally. 'I am induced to request you as to be so kind as to take into favourable consideration the case of Kimpton and to pardon him also, as I am not aware that there was any distinction between his offence and that for which Hickton was convicted, and I am assured that his conduct during his confinement has been good'.[8]

Herbert Voules, Superintendent of the hulks, forwarded the muster reports to the Home Office. Kimpton's behaviour had been rated 'good' on six occasions, plus one 'very good' and a single 'indifferent'. These were confirmed by the Governor of the *Warrior,* Henry Masterman, who commented approvingly that 'with the exception of a trifling offence against the Rules when first received, his conduct has been very good on board the hulks....this prisoner was 18 months at *Justitia,* where he had one indifferent muster, received here 16th June last, conduct very good since admission'.

Sir George Grey acted with caution, however. He could see that Hickton might have been considered a special case because of his chequered medical history. Grey wrote that 'Hickton's sentence was commuted partly on the grounds of health, rendering him unfit for transportation. I would like to have Mr Mayne's opinion before anything further is done in Kimpton's case'.

Before making a recommendation, Rowan and Mayne decided to speak to Superintendents Marquard and Pearce, who had been closely involved with the Clark murder enquiry from the outset. The question of Hickton's poor health was not discussed. Instead, the men concentrated on whether Kimpton deserved a heavier punishment than his colleague. On 24th October Mayne reported the result of the meeting. It was one that would gladden the hearts of Kimpton's supporters. Mayne's conclusion was that 'there is no reason to believe that the prisoner Kimpton was more criminal than Hickton who was tried with him and upon whom the same sentence of transportation was passed'. Now that Hickton had been freed, it followed that it was time for Kimpton's sentence to be commuted.

Rowan and Mayne had also to consider public opinion. The storm of negative publicity following George Clark's murder had, as we have seen, put the very existence of the Metropolitan Police under question. How would the release of Kimpton be viewed in the wider world? The Commissioners eventually decided that there was no need to worry. They did 'not apprehend that this mitigation of the punishment would have any bad effects upon the Police'. So the way was clear for the Home Secretary to recommend the Queen to grant a free pardon, which would allow for Kimpton's immediate release. .

Meanwhile, at Windsor Castle, the 30 year-old Queen Victoria had fallen ill. She was not, however, a victim of the cholera epidemic. On 28th October 1849 the Royal Physician, James Clark, issued a statement: 'The Queen has had an attack of chicken-pox. The disease was not attended with any untoward symptom, and although still suffering from the effects of the eruption, Her Majesty may be considered convalescent'.

At this stage in her life Victoria was normally in very robust health. She was positively impatient when it came to any illness, whether it affected herself or those around her. So on 30th October she was probably far from amused to be forced to stay at Windsor while her husband Prince Albert and their two eldest children travelled to the City of London for the opening of the new Coal Exchange. Victoria was also three months pregnant with her seventh child Prince Arthur. Yet she didn't let illness get in the way of dealing with the interminable pile of red despatch boxes full of documents needing her attention. With so much paperwork to be tackled, the Queen probably hardly glanced at the wording of Thomas Kimpton's pardon that day before signing it.[9]

Kimpton was summoned and given the good news. Having been in captivity since March 1847, a total of two years seven months, he was now able to turn his back on the hated hulks and rejoin his wife and family in Bethnal Green.

If Kimpton harboured any thoughts of confronting William Parsons, the cause of his awful ordeal, he was to be too late. Just ten days before Kimpton's pardon was granted, Parsons and his new wife Annie had left the country.[10] The man dubbed by Joan Lock[11] as 'the slippery Parsons' had now pulled off yet another escape. Before joining the police force, Parsons had been a miller, and now decided to follow his trade once more but this time in a remote part of the British Empire. He arranged to be indentured to the Hudson's Bay Company for five years, running a saw mill in the vast Canadian wilderness.

Parsons and Annie left Gravesend on 20th October 1849 on board the ship the *Norman Morison*. This was the first ever voyage to Victoria, British Columbia, by a Hudson's Bay Company vessel, and Annie was one of only three female passengers. The ship rounded Cape Horn on 11th January 1850. As William Parsons travelled northwards off the western coast of South America, unknown to him back in Barkingside his little daughter Maria was fighting for her life. After a three-week struggle against measles and typhoid, she died. She was buried on 23rd January in the churchyard at Barkingside, where her young mother had been laid to rest just over three years previously.

The *Norman Morison* sailed at last into Fort Victoria on 24th March. Most of the emigrants were set to work on various farms in the area. Parsons knuckled down to take charge of his mill, and showed a capacity for enterprise and hard work. He constructed a bridge over the millstream, and built and operated a grist mill on the opposite bank.[12] Before very long his previous life must have been a distant memory.

A group of Dagenham officers outside the 1851 police station. The photograph dates from the early 20th century

Back in London, that year of 1850 brought death to the founding father of the Metropolitan Police. In the evening of Saturday 29th June, four years to the day since George Clark went on duty for the final time, Sir Robert Peel was riding his horse along Constitution Hill when it suddenly shied. Peel was thrown from the horse, which then fell on him leaving him unconscious with severe back and shoulder injuries. The Queen's physician Sir James Clark happened to be passing, and helped move the stricken man to his home in nearby Whitehall Gardens. Three days later, on Tuesday 2nd July, Peel died aged just 62. The same year also saw the retirement of Sir Charles Rowan, accelerated by ill-health. He and Mayne had worked harmoniously as joint Commissioners for twenty-one years. Rowan was replaced by Captain William Hay, but unfortunately Hay and Mayne were to clash almost from the outset.

The major event of the following year, 1851, was the Great Exhibition in London's Hyde Park. Crowds flocked to it from all over the world. If George Clark had been alive to see it, he would have been proud of the fact that the splendid Crystal Palace which housed the exhibition had been designed by a man from his own part of the world. Its creator, Joseph Paxton, was a native of Milton Bryant, the neighbouring village to Battlesden. The son of a tenant farmer, Paxton began his illustrious career on the Battlesden estate of the Page-Turners. The Great Exhibition, incidentally, provided the opportunity for a public relations coup for the Metropolitan Police. A temporary Division X was formed to deal with crowd control, and foreign visitors were greatly impressed by the smooth running of the event.

Back in Dagenham, the police had by this time moved out of the rented house that had served them for over ten years. A new, purpose-built station was provided for them further north along Bull Street[13] towards the Four Wants. It was a big investment in terms of both buildings and manpower. The officers must have found it palatial compared with the old premises, being 'a substantial brick and slate building containing 9 rooms exclusive of 2 cells, 2-stall stable, 2 water closets, 3 coal vaults, 2 dung pens with a yard at the rear'.[14]

The new building had been built on a plot of freehold land costing £100, and the police took possession in March 1851. The census of that year shows six policemen living there. The sergeant was 30 year-old Frederick Stratford, a Londoner born in Blackfriars. He was joined by constables Henry Gayler from Hertfordshire, Yorkshireman Edward Gray, George Dew from Dorset, Harry Lugg from Hampshire and Charles Honeybourn from Harefield in Middlesex. Three other constables, William Pearson, John Nicholls and Joshua Hitchman, lived elsewhere in Dagenham.

No doubt the murder was still a frequent topic of conversation at the newly-built Dagenham police station. Any newcomer would have been shown Clark's grave on the south side of the parish churchyard. Each must have harboured the thought that maybe he would be the one eventually to solve the murder. The church itself underwent extensive restoration a few years after Clark's death. According to the 1851 Kelly's Directory, its interior 'has recently been repaired, and a new gallery and organ erected'.

In April 1852 the George Clark murder case suddenly came to the forefront once again when the police were given the name of yet another suspect. PC Kirby of P Division, which was centred in Camberwell, had been speaking to a Mrs Croper of 41 London Road, who told him 'it was a pity the two policemen should have suffered innocently'. She implicated her own son-in-law, who she said was named Kenrick and used to have a business as a barber in the Dagenham area. Apparently, 'while in a state of excitement he had been heard to make remarks relative to the murder of Clark, stating he had kicked the B___r .' When Superintendent John Lund heard this and directed further enquiries to be made, Mrs Croper flatly refused to say anything more, 'stating that she being so near a relative, and that the consequence to him (Kenrick) might be of such serious import, that she could not be seen in the matter'. Lund reported that he had been told this Kenrick was 'a drunken dissolute fellow…'

Dagenham's Sergeant Frederick Stratford soon had the opportunity to become involved in the investigation. Had the mysterious Kenrick really lived and worked in the Dagenham area as his mother-in-law had stated? If so, where was he now? Stratford and the Ilford senior officer, 35 year-old Inspector Henry Procter, set to work. However, on 26th April 1852 Procter was forced to report to his superintendent that the search had been unsuccessful. 'We cannot find any trace of such a person and I think that it is quite certain that he never kept a shop (as a barber) in the above neighbourhood'. He went on to say that they had made careful enquiries at Dagenham, Rainham, Hornchurch, Romford, Beacontree Heath, Chadwell, Ilford & Barking 'and no such person is known at those places'.

Several months later, on 31st July 1852, there was a change of personnel at the head of K Division. Superintendent Cort Henry Marquard retired aged 48 after seven years in charge, on the grounds that he had 'become unfit for further duty'. He was awarded a pension of £150 per annum. Marquard's replacement was 38 year-old Wiltshireman Daniel Howie, who had previously been an Inspector in the N Division before serving for six years in the Royal Household.

William Parsons had chosen to try his luck in Canada, but on the other side of the world there were even greater opportunities for emigrants to make their fortune. In 1851 the first major discovery of gold took place in Victoria, Australia. The following year, a letter to the *Essex Standard* declared that 'The other day a piece weighing 27lb 8oz of pure gold was picked up within a few hundred yards of where I am now writing, and is being exhibited at 1s per head. Many men that I have known as common labourers have now their thousand or more pounds; and what is more satisfactory is, that every man may make his pound's worth a day, merely with a tin dish and a spade'.[15]

Many could not resist the lure of this Australian gold, and left England in droves to try their luck. Others stayed behind, and continued to follow a more traditional route to riches, that of smuggling. In July 1852 dramatic scenes took place on the Dagenham marshes. A constable named William Miles spotted two men and a boy leading three heavily-laden carts along a track at midnight. He recognized them as members of a Barking family named Lee. They told him the wagons only contained potatoes, but Miles was suspicious and insisted they went with him to the police station. On the way, one of the men and the boy ran off, but Miles managed to keep the other man with him. The carts were found to contain packages of tobacco stitched up in canvas. When his fellow-constable Charles Honeybourn made a further search in the marshes, he found more packages hidden in a cornfield. The tobacco weighed about four tons, and it was estimated that the duty on it alone would amount to £1,280. The *Times* declared that 'The conduct of Miles in the transaction was praiseworthy and intrepid in the highest degree. To arrest, single-handed, on so lonely a beat, three persons with so valuable a freightage, was an act of no uncommon daring'.[16] To underline his bravery, the newspaper reminded readers that the swoop took place 'where it will be remembered that another constable of the same division was mysteriously murdered a few years since'. The would-be smugglers were tried and convicted before the Ilford magistrates. The two men, who worked as straw carters and jobbers at Choats, Barking, were fined the huge sum of £100 each, while the lad was set free, adjudged to have acted under the influence of the others. William Miles, the officer who had captured them, resigned from the force in September of the same year and settled down to the rather calmer occupation of a market gardener in his native town of Epsom with his wife Kezia and their children.

That same year, 1852, saw the death from cancer of Sir Charles Rowan, who had retired from the post of joint Commissioner two years before. The *Times* reported that he had passed away on 8th May, 'after a protracted illness, probably superinduced by mental and bodily exertions in the discharge of

Colney Hatch Asylum, 1851

important public duties'. It described his distinguished military career, then looked back at the part he played in setting up and running the Metropolitan police, an organization now, incidentally, praised by the *Times* as being 'efficient and popular'.

During the five months that the Great Exhibition had been open the previous year, there had been eight million visitors. Many, like the Queen herself, returned time and time again to marvel at the spectacle. One person who was most certainly not among them was Abia Butfoy. As we have seen, it was only by a stroke of luck that Butfoy had escaped prosecution in the aftermath of the Clark inquest. He had afterwards been compelled to give evidence against his colleagues Kimpton and Hickton. Butfoy left Dagenham and moved with his wife Elizabeth and their children to Cross Street in his native Bethnal Green. He returned to his previous occupation of weaver. It did not offer the standard of living he had been used to as a police officer. In 1848 Hector Gavin described Bethnal Green weavers thus: 'Their earnings are very small and very precarious, and their habits are commonly intemperate'.[17]

The year 1849 saw the birth of Butfoy's youngest child John in March, to be followed in September by the tragic death of the baby's three year-old brother Charles. On 17th January 1851 Butfoy was taken away from home and admitted to Bethnal Green Workhouse 'as a lunatic'. Perhaps there was a genetic predisposition to mental illness within the Butfoy family. Abia's cousin Emma had died in August 1841 aged 18 at the Weaver's Arms in Spitalfields, where her father was landlord. According to the death certificate, poor Emma 'poisoned herself in a temporary state of insanity'.

After six months' confinement in the workhouse, 41 year-old Butfoy became only the second patient to be admitted to the huge newly-opened Colney Hatch Pauper Lunatic Asylum, in Friern Barnet in Middlesex. The foundation stone had been laid by Prince Albert in May 1849. The asylum was officially opened on 1st July 1851, just two months after the Crystal Palace, and as a building was almost as astounding as Paxton's masterpiece. [18] It was the largest of its kind in Europe, built to house 12,000 inmates, and had more than six miles (9km) of corridors or wards.

The *Times* reporter attending the opening of the asylum wrote approvingly: 'we noticed with pleasure that the greatest regard was paid to the comfort and well-being of the wretched inmates'.[19] Yet the description is uncomfortably close to that of a model Victorian prison. There was an exercise hall, cells, workshops, and the thoughtful touch of windows at the ends of the galleries 'so that the patients in their walks may avoid the dreary aspect of a blank wall'.

Unlike prisoners, then, Butfoy was allowed the privilege of gazing at the world outside the walls, but he had no hope at all of recovery and a return to normal life. A report on his condition while at the asylum makes grim reading.[20] He was 'suffering from mania, delusions and Incipient General Paralysis'. This indicates that at some stage in his life, possibly during his spell as a soldier, Butfoy had contracted syphilis. This was widespread in Victorian times, and there was no effective cure. The centuries-old remedy of mercury could help relieve the sores which appeared in the early stages, but it was of no use when the disease progressed to the stage of tertiary syphilis. This often did not happen until many years had passed after the initial infection, but the effects were devastating. They could include neurosyphilis, an infection of the brain which the Victorians referred to as General Paralysis of the Insane, and which Butfoy was unfortunate enough to suffer from. The assessment of his condition goes on to say that 'The Paralysis shows itself in the unsteadiness of his gait, tremor of his tongue and the peculiar mouthing of his words. His health appears weak and his appetite is bad. He is unwilling to enter into conversation. Face bloated, flesh flabby'. To cap all this, Butfoy was also prone to occasional epileptic fits.

The damage to the brain by neurosyphilis causes dementia, muscle weakness and on occasion total paralysis. For the final two years or so of his life Butfoy lay on a water bed in the asylum's infirmary, severely disabled in mind and body. The water bed would have helped prevent bed sores and ulcers, and the report on his condition states that his life was 'much prolonged by the comforts he received'. We have already seen that some of the staff attending to Isaac Hickton in Northampton Gaol were extremely sympathetic and went out of their way to help him. The example of Butfoy is further evidence that the system contained some very enlightened individuals.

The report goes on to mention Butfoy's connection with the George Clark case: 'He is suspected and reported to have been engaged in the murder of a Policeman some three years since in Essex, since which time his mind has been more or less affected. He was put on trial for the crime, but for want of evidence, acquitted'. This gives us an indication of how many inaccuracies were circulated regarding the Clark case, for as we have seen Butfoy was never put on trial for the murder.

Yet as he lay on the water bed, Abia Butfoy's thoughts kept returning time and time again to the terrible death of his fellow-constable. Like Isaac Hickton in his cell, he was subject to unremitting mental agony. This was the man who had rounded on his colleague Kimpton when Clark's body was discovered.

Kimpton had been unwilling to approach the corpse, and Butfoy had accused him of being 'a pretty cow-hearted sort of policeman'. Now, it seems, Butfoy's own thoughts while waking and sleeping were constantly haunted by the dreadful scene. The report paints a pitiful picture of his situation, bringing to mind Lady Macbeth's sleepwalking scene. 'He has many delusions, rambles much in his conversation and talks incoherently generally in his soliloquies bringing in the expression, Murder – intimating that his mind is much engaged with the subject – during the night he is frequently restless – shouting in his sleep crying 'Murder, Murder'. On 7th July 1853 Butfoy's suffering was finally brought to an end. He died at the asylum, aged only 43, the cause of death being given as 'Chronic changes of brain'. He was laid to rest in the asylum burial ground four days later. [21] The service was carried out by the chaplain Henry Murray.

Back at Scotland Yard, the year 1855 saw the death of the joint Commissioner Captain William Hay. Richard Mayne was now in sole charge, and his increasingly autocratic style earned him the nickname of 'King Mayne'. In 1856 an act of Parliament was passed which forced every borough and county to set up a local professional police force. The voluntary system was now consigned to history.

Many of the people George Clark had come to know during his brief stay in Dagenham were gradually joining him in eternal rest in the village churchyard. At Eastbrookend, Mrs Sarah Stone of Huntings House died on 5th November 1852 at the age of 85, and was buried eight days later. It had been her uncle William Ford whose legacy had founded the school for Dagenham boys and girls. In her own will, Sarah supplemented this by leaving £200 to be invested for the purpose of giving Christmas dinners to the schoolchildren.

Things were also changing elsewhere in Dagenham. The Fanshawes, squires of the parish, were no longer at the family seat of Parsloes Manor. The Reverend Thomas Lewis Fanshawe was entitled to live at Parsloes for life at a rent of just 5 shillings per year, but he now decided to economise by residing in the vicarage and letting out the manor.[22] One of his tenants was none other than Lord Chief Justice Thomas Denman, who had presided over the abortive trial of William Parsons in 1848. It would be a remarkable coincidence if Lord Denman had been living at Parsloes at the actual time of the trial, but it appears that he took the lease some time afterwards. The census of 1851 records a large Denman household at Parsloes, including the 72 year-old judge and his son Richard, a barrister. The following year brought sadness to the family with the death of Lord Denman's wife

Theodosia Ann on 28th June 1852. She was buried in Dagenham parish churchyard along with her granddaughter, also named Theodosia, who had died earlier the same month. The Denmans did not stay at Parsloes for much longer after these sad events.

Parsloes Manor falling into decay. It was demolished in 1925

After the departure from Dagenham of the Lord Chief Justice and his family, John Gaspard Fanshawe, a son of the vicar, moved into Parsloes. He only remained there for a short time, however, leaving in 1855. John Gaspard was the last member of the Fanshawe family to live in the house. His father, who had conducted George Clark's burial service back in 1846, suffered a mental breakdown and resigned his post in 1857. He had been Vicar of Dagenham for the grand total of 41 years. On 5th March 1858, he passed away at Kingsbury in West London. Twelve days later, a mournful crowd of ex-parishioners followed the funeral procession as it wound its way from the old family mansion. Over two hundred local children lined the approach to the parish church.[23] The coffin of Thomas Lewis Fanshawe was then laid to rest in the family vault alongside many generations of his ancestors. He was succeeded as vicar by the Reverend Robert Bewick.

By this time, the dramatic events of summer 1846 were probably fading from view. The murder would not have been completely forgotten by any means, but after such a long interval the chances of a breakthrough seemed remote. Twelve harvests had come and gone in the cornfield where George Clark's body had lain. James Parfey Collier himself, who farmed the land, would himself be dead within a few months at the age of 52. He was laid to rest near Clark on the south side of Dagenham churchyard. Yet against all expectations, a sensational event was about to occur that would bring the Clark murder back into national prominence once again.

A view of Eastbrookend in the 1920s. The houses on the right stand close to the site of George Blewitt's cottage. Thomas Waters Brittain's farmhouse can be seen in the centre middle distance

CHAPTER 12

'It is my duty, my man'

The summer of 1858 was a scorcher. It brought back memories of the sweltering heat at the time of George Clark's murder twelve years before. On 9th July, the *Essex Standard* reported that 'rain has been much wanted by the crops in this neighbourhood, and vegetation generally has suffered from the continued drought'. The hay harvest would have been well under way on Thursday 24th June, when a group of men strode into one of farmer Samuel Seabrook's fields in Dagenham. They headed purposefully towards a smock-frocked labourer. The spokesman for the group, a man in his mid-40s with dark brown hair, blue eyes and a pockmarked face, asked whether his name was George Blewitt? Yes, it was, agreed the farm worker. His questioner, who was not in uniform, announced that he was a police officer. He said he had a warrant for Blewitt's arrest in connection with the murder of George Clark, based on evidence supplied by a Mrs Mary Ann Smith. It seems that this was not a complete surprise to George Blewitt. His cool response was: 'Very well, I am quite willing to go anywhere with you, for I am quite sure that she cannot say anything to hurt me'. Under the astonished gaze of his fellow-workers, Blewitt was then handcuffed and driven off in a horse and cart to Ilford Gaol.

The seeds for this episode had been sown almost a year before. Middle-aged Mary Ann Smith lived in Workhouse Lane, to the north-west of Dagenham Village, with her husband Francis, a farm servant. In August 1857 Mrs Smith told her neighbours, Jane Noble and Jane Palmer, both wives of agricultural labourers, that she knew the truth about the murder of George Clark. She confided to them that Clark was killed after confronting a gang of men stealing corn from a barn belonging to Thomas Waters Brittain at Eastbrookend Old Hall. One of the murderers was, she said, her former husband William Page, now deceased, and another was George Blewitt, who lived very close to Mr Brittain's farm. She also implicated Ralph Page, of Thorntons Farm, who apparently had been waiting in his own barn that night to receive the spoils.

This was not the kind of story to remain under wraps for long, and Blewitt and one of his sons appeared at Mrs Smith's door one Sunday morning demanding to know 'what I meant by spreading these reports about him'. The tale also reached the ears of Dagenham's police sergeant Frederick Stratford. Back in 1852, as we have seen, Stratford had spent a lot of time in vain pursuit of the man Kenrick whose mother-in-law had accused him of Clark's murder. So he was probably not expecting much when he called on

Mrs Smith to follow up the rumour. It was the first of three or four lengthy visits to her cottage. The sergeant's reports of what she had to say were impressive enough to send Detective Inspector Jonathan Whicher hot-foot down to Dagenham.

Camberwell-born Whicher had shown an aptitude for plain-clothes work soon after joining the force in 1837, and on the formation of the Detective Branch in 1842 he was appointed one of the first six Detective Sergeants. Whicher had been promoted to Inspector in 1856, and in an age when detectives were celebrities his was the biggest name of them all. Some years later, he was portrayed as Sergeant Cuff in Wilkie Collins' novel *the Moonstone*. Collins describes Cuff as 'dressed all in decent black, with a white cravat round his neck. His face was as sharp as a hatchet, and the skin of it was as yellow and dry and withered as an autumn leaf. His eyes, of a steely light grey, had a very disconcerting trick, when they encountered your eyes, of looking as if they expected something more from you than you were aware of yourself'. *The Official encyclopaedia of Scotland Yard* says: 'Known to friends and colleagues as Jack, he was also regarded as "The Prince of Detectives"; a man who never made a blunder'.[1] We have seen that Whicher had worked on the original investigation into Clark's murder twelve years before, and with his meticulous nature he must have been eager to be involved in the resumption of the case, especially as Mrs Smith implicated someone whom Whicher had suspected back in 1846.

Whicher and Stratford passed on the results of their questioning to Sir Richard Mayne, who authorized bringing the case to the attention of the magistrates. Soon a warrant had been issued for the detention of Blewitt, the only member of the alleged gang whose whereabouts were known. Seizing his man in Mr Seabrook's field must have been one of the easier arrests in Whicher's long career. Blewitt was not the kind of quarry that needed to be patiently hunted down amidst the London throng. Instead, he had been at work as normal, and was willing to co-operate rather than becoming violent or attempting an escape.

On Monday 28th June George Blewitt was taken out of Ilford Gaol and brought into the adjoining court house.[2] The crowd of press and public craned their necks for a glimpse of the man in the dock. The *Essex Standard* reporter described Blewitt sympathetically as 'a labouring man about 50 years of age, middle height, has an open face, and very healthy appearance, and is known to be a man of great nerve'.[3] Blewitt must have looked good for his age, for he was in fact 60 years old. He had been baptized in 1798 in Hornchurch,[4] an adjacent parish to Dagenham. Blewitt did not appear in his

Sunday best before the magistrates. Instead, he wore his working dress of a long faded blue⁵ smock-frock.

Blewitt was represented by Charles Joseph Rawlings, of Market Place, Romford, whose brother Benjamin had appeared for William Parsons during the perjury scandal all those years before. The newspapers noted that 'no legal gentleman appeared for the Crown'. Whicher must have been accustomed to having to conduct prosecutions himself, as the police authorities were unwilling to part with money for legal services. It is a measure of the perceived importance of the perjury trial of Kimpton and Hickton back in 1847 that a whole raft of barristers had been employed to bring the case against them.

For three of the witnesses now brought forward to testify, it was merely a case of repeating the evidence given at the inquest and the subsequent prosecutions of the policemen. The only one of George Clark's colleagues to be called was John Farnes. He recounted what he knew about the night of Clark's disappearance, the discovery of his body four days later, and the inquest hearings which followed. William Page, who as a child had been the first to come upon the murdered man in the cornfield, now described the event yet again. By this time Page was a 24 year-old excavator living in Bethnal Green. Joseph Collin was next to step forward. He gave lengthy evidence about the state of Clark's corpse and the various wounds upon it. After giving up medicine due to ill-health, Collin had studied at St John's College, Cambridge, and had then taken Holy Orders. He was now vicar of Strethall in Essex, although actually living in the neighbouring parish of Elmdon.

The first surprise was provided by a witness who, like so many labourers in those days before the introduction of old age pensions, was unable to support himself because of age or infirmity and forced to enter the Romford Workhouse. This was Thomas Archer. On the night of the murder he had been working in the stables at Wants Farm, and had told the inquest jury that he did not see Clark at all. Archer now admitted that this was untrue. Between midnight and 1 o'clock he had noticed Clark passing by, heading towards Brittain's Farm at Eastbrookend. Archer's silence in 1846 meant that the last known sighting of the policeman had hitherto been his meeting with Luke White in Tanyard Lane at 10.30pm. According to the new statement, Clark was walking his beat as usual over an hour and a half later than this. Archer gave no explanation for withholding this crucial piece of information at the original inquest. Perhaps he had been frightened of suspicion falling on him as the last person to see Clark alive.

Eastbrookend Old Hall, shortly before its demolition in the 1950s

Next, a completely new witness was summoned. This was 74 year-old widower Thomas Waters Brittain. He had not been called to give evidence in 1846, but had been a member of the inquest jury. He was descended from the Waters family, which had farmed at Eastbrookend for many years. His grandfather Thomas Waters had died after falling from his horse in 1778, leaving two daughters. The elder girl, Sarah, later married Robert Brittain. The family had long played a leading role in Dagenham's affairs. Thomas Waters Brittain served as a churchwarden from 1845 to 1860, and at the time of the Blewitt hearing he was involved in an action against the Romford brewers Ind Coope. They were accused of polluting the River Rom, which is known as the Beam as it passes through Dagenham on its way to the Thames. According to the Dagenham Vestry minutes, the river was in a 'filthy and putrid' state.

In 1858 Thomas Waters Brittain was still living at Eastbrookend Old Hall, and farming nearly 200 acres. Brittain told the magistrates that at the time of the murder George Blewitt worked for him as a horse keeper, and lived in a cottage 'near my farm gate, about 200 yards from my barn'. He added that Blewitt and his family had continued to live there until two or three years after the murder.

Brittain then spoke about the night of 29th June 1846. He had been to London, and returned home at about 9 o'clock. There was corn in his barn at the time, some of it dressed. (Dressing is the process of removing dirt, small stones and weed seeds, then grading the corn ready for market.) 'The keys', he added, 'I had or should have had in my house'.

Blewitt's composure wavered for the first time while his ex-employer was speaking. It was noticed that 'during the examination of Mr Brittain the prisoner became very uneasy, and breathed with difficulty'. Brittain was not questioned for very long, and on his departure from the bar all eyes turned to the witness whose revelations had set the whole sequence of events in motion.

Mary Ann Smith said she had lived in Dagenham 42 years, and at the time of the murder was married to her second husband, William Page, a farm labourer. They were approaching their tenth wedding anniversary, having been married at Havering-atte-Bower, north of Romford, on 21st August 1836. Like the Blewitts, the Pages lived in a cottage on George Clark's beat. It was in fact the first habitation passed by Clark as he walked from the Four Wants towards Eastbrookend. Mary Ann and Page were childless. Her first marriage to a man named John Brown had produced a daughter Mary Ann, who in 1846 was nineteen years old and living with her mother and stepfather.

Mary Ann Smith then told the magistrates and the hushed galleries about the night of the murder. Her sworn depositions survive in the National Archives and are signed with a cross .[6] Mrs Smith may have been illiterate, as would be expected given her humble station in life, but her evidence, especially the vivid dialogue, conveys a powerful sense of immediacy.

Shortly after parting with Sergeant Parsons at the Four Wants at the beginning of his duty that evening, Clark had passed her house and stopped to speak to her. William Page was not at home, and his wife was keen to chat to Clark. She began by telling him he seemed happy. 'Yes, Madam, I am' he replied. She said she envied him, and proceeded to pour out her troubles into his sympathetic ear. 'I am in danger of my life, and so is my child, from my husband; he is such a violent man'. She begged Clark to help her. 'If you meet my husband you might tell him, for his good, he is a bad man'. She told the court that 'I said this because I knew Clark was a good man'. She then became frightened and told Clark to go away, 'as I did not wish my husband to see him talking to me, as he was so jealous'.

When an enraged William Page came home some time later, it was clear that Clark had done what Mary Ann had asked, and had given Page some advice about how his behaviour must be jeopardizing his immortal soul. Page was beside himself with fury. 'He was cursing and swearing about the _____ policeman and speaking about his soul, and said, 'I wonder what the _____ does he know about my soul?'

Page then revealed to his wife that he and others planned to steal some sacks of corn from the barn of his employer Brittain, whom he nicknamed 'Old Tom'. Page then made dark threats against Clark. 'I dare say he knows a great deal about souls, I will soul him if he interferes with me, old George says he will, and if he interferes with us tonight we will stab the bugger down to the ground'. 'Old George' was Blewitt.

In the meantime an unsuspecting Clark walked up to the boundary with Romford and then retraced his steps. Mary Ann told the magistrates that shortly before ten o'clock the policeman passed their house on his way back to the Four Wants, and called out 'Good night'. She said that she and Page 'went to bed about 10 o'clock; about eleven I saw my husband dressing himself, I said to him you told me you was not going out'. Page's mood had not improved. He accused his wife of lying awake watching him, 'and for that you shall go with me'. He insisted she get up and dress. Twelve year-old William Blewitt, one of George's numerous sons, then appeared at the door and called out 'Come, Billy, get up'. Mary Ann's daughter was at home that night, but she was apparently asleep and they did not disturb her.

The husband and wife left their cottage with the lad and took the ten-minute walk along the Eastbrookend Road or across the fields to George Blewitt's house. They entered to find Blewitt sitting in a chair and not at all pleased to see Mary Ann. He asked 'What is up now Billy, you did not ought to have brought her with you'. Page explained that 'She is bloody uneasy to know what we are up to'. He then turned to his wife and threatened her with: 'If you get saying anything about what you see and hear you will be bloody well served out'. Blewitt resigned himself to her presence, telling her 'As you are here missus you may as well come and look out'.

According to the deposition, George Chalk, Ned Wood and Thomas Page were also there. The name Thomas Page has been underlined, and someone has written 'Ralph?' in the margin. The newspaper reports of Mrs Smith's statement name Ralph Page as one of the conspirators, so it seems that the name Thomas may have been written in error. According to Mary Ann, a man named Edward or Ned Willcocks was also involved in planning the theft but did not actually appear that night.

At about midnight they prepared to leave. Ralph Page presumably then walked to his barn at Thornton's Farm to prepare to receive the booty. The other five, the four men and one woman, left via the back door of Blewitt's cottage and through his garden. Blewitt and William Page led the way, while George Chalk and Ned Wood followed. Mrs Smith didn't remember them carrying anything. Within a couple of minutes they had reached their destination. Blewitt opened one of the doors of the barn using duplicate keys. The men then went inside, leaving Mary Ann to stand guard. Very shortly afterwards, she noticed Clark approaching. He must have checked out the farmhouse and then walked quietly round the side of the barn. Evidently Mrs Smith, who was as we have seen on friendly terms with Clark, didn't try to warn him of the danger he was in while she had the chance. Her husband's threats to her had clearly had their effect. She turned round to the barn door and called out 'Bill, here is a policeman'. The gang inside stopped what they were doing and looked at one another, seemingly taken by surprise. One of them then came out. It was William Page, and he carried a loading stick. This would have been a formidable weapon. The *Oxford English Dictionary* defines a 'loading' or 'loaded' stick as being weighted, especially with lead. We have seen that both Page and Blewitt worked for 'Old Tom' Brittain. It would not, therefore, have been unusual for them to be in the barn at that time of night. Not far away, at Wants Farm, Thomas Archer was at that moment busy getting horses ready for the early-morning journey to market. Other labourers were employed as night watchmen. Page could have tried to bluff his way through by telling Clark they were there for a legitimate reason. Instead, he appears to have been spoiling for a fight.

This view of Brittain's farm clearly shows the large barn behind the farmhouse

Page said 'Who told you to watch us?' and Clark retorted 'It is my duty my man'. Page shouted to George Blewitt 'Here is that Bugger watching us, come out!' He then rushed up to Clark and attacked him with the loaded stick. Clark immediately drew out his cutlass and their weapons clashed. The policeman quickly gained the upper hand and Page called out to the others for help. Mrs Smith told the court that at this point 'I rushed on to my husband and pulled him with my main strength, as I was pulling my husband he said now you b.... b...... if you don't get out of my way I will serve you as we mean to serve him'.

The other three emerged. Like Page, they had seized farm implements that had been lying about in the barn. One of them had a pitchfork, and used it to try to disarm Clark by trapping the blade of the cutlass between the prongs. Clark was surrounded, and Mrs Smith declared 'I am quite sure that the prisoner George Blewitt is the second man that struck the policeman'.

She then fled back to Blewitt's cottage. 'I saw all 4 of the men mentioned, before I left, driving the policeman before them'. Mrs Alice Blewitt and her seventeen year-old son Henry were there. Mary Ann then went home and waited for her husband to return. Her daughter was apparently still asleep and ignorant of what was going on. Page came home between two and three o'clock. He told his wife that after they had knocked Clark down and murdered him they carried him away to the spot where he would eventually be found. One of the gang, sixteen year-old George Chalk, then beat in Clark's skull with the heel of his boot.

There was a lot of cleaning up to be done, and Page's first thought was to destroy his clothes. Mrs Smith said 'He had a fire made up and had them burnt, his flannel jacket was splashed with blood round the collar where it was not covered by his smock frock...., before my husband's frock was burnt it was besmeared very much with blood and also his trowsers'.

It was now time for Page to leave for work, so he donned a new set of clothes and exited the house. A day or two afterwards, he brought a pitchfork home and burnt the woodwork. It was probably cut badly. According to his wife, he said 'I am going to have a handle put in this fork, it is the fork that done the deed'.

Clark's body, as we have heard, was discovered four days later. The day afterwards, Saturday 4th July, the Pages went shopping in Romford. They met George Blewitt there, and the trio walked home together. It was the day of the first inquest hearing. The Pages and Blewitt may have even mingled with the crowds of sightseers eagerly flocking to Eastbrookend to see the murder scene for themselves. According to Mary Ann, there was a fleeting tinge of regret as Blewitt and Page talked about what had happened. 'Blewitt said to my husband Who would have thought of seeing him there Billy. My husband said No, I did not think of seeing him, well my husband said We bloody well served him out – George Blewitt said 'Well we did'.'

Both were worried that Mary Ann might tell what she knew. Blewitt said 'You must not say anything about it mistress'. Page then growled 'if she does I will bloody well serve her out'. He turned round as if to strike her, and Blewitt intervened to try to pacify him. 'Don't do that Billy,' he said, 'for that will make it worse'. Page then threatened his wife with: 'Mind now you say nothing about it, if you do I will serve you the same'. Blewitt tried another approach, asking: 'How shall we manage this so it is not found out, can't you tell her something Billy to keep her from saying anything about it?' Page declared: 'I will tell her her brother Billy was there and she won't then say anything about you'.

Page then spoke about a person who was clearly very upset about Clark's death: 'It is that poor girl I am thinking about George. I would not care a f….. if it had not been for her that is all through your old woman getting her in on her coming home from Romford'. This is the first sign of a softer side to Page's nature. Whoever the young lady was, and her identity is currently a mystery, her distress clearly affected Page. Many local girls must have been interested in Clark. He would have been an exciting outsider, someone with a smart uniform rather than the usual smock frock. He had a friendly manner, was willing to help people in difficulty, and must have had a wealth of stories to tell concerning the year he had spent in London.

The trio eventually reached Blewitt's gate. He went in, while the Pages walked on. Suddenly they heard Blewitt calling them. 'We both went back and the prisoner said again Don't let her say a word Billy as it turned out so bad, we then bade him good night and went home'.

One of the Ilford magistrates then asked Mrs Smith why she had not spoken out earlier. She replied: 'I did not mention this before for I was afraid I thought I should get locked up myself. I am sincerely sorry I did not divulge in my husband's lifetime, it has troubled me very much'.

She then burst into tears. The proceedings now drew to a close. Blewitt was taken back to his prison cell, and a further hearing was set for the following Monday.

On the afternoon of Saturday 26th June, two days after George Blewitt's arrest, a Brentwood tradesman named Stephen Westwood Brown[7] penned a letter to Richard Mayne. He wrote that 'The reports of the discovery of the murderers of Police Constable Clark has[sic] caused considerable excitement here'. Brown enclosed a statement made to him that very day by a local bill-sticker named Thomas Hunnikin, 'which I forward to you hoping that it may be a link in the chain of evidence that will lead to the conviction of the murderers'. Hunnikin, it seems, believed that he, and not Luke White, had been the last person to see George Clark alive.

Hunnikin stated that at the time of the murder he lived in Dagenham, and was employed by farmer Samuel Seabrook as a night watchman. On the 29th June 1846 Hunnikin worked from 6 o'clock at night until 7 the following morning. He remembered meeting Clark: 'About 12 o'clock at night Clark was with me in a shed where turnips were washed. We had some bread & cheese together'. According to his statement, Hunnikin then went off on his round, telling Clark he would return in about an hour. However, a heavy thunderstorm came on and Hunnikin decided to go home to his clay cottage for a while. He wanted to be with his wife, 'fearing she would be alarmed at the storm'. It was two hours before Hunnikin returned to the spot where he and Clark had parted. 'I waited a considerable time ($\frac{1}{2}$ hour or 20 minutes) and he did not appear'. Hunnikin revealed that he knew Clark well. 'Clark was a religiously disposed man and we often had a chat on these matters'. Hunnikin then went on to say that Clark had told him: 'I have called on the various cottages in the neighbourhood and I have conversed with them and have given them tracts and I am on very good terms with them'. Hunnikin explained that his beat as a night watchman was about a mile from the murder scene. He heard no noise or cries for help.

Hunnikin then stated that the night previous to the death of Clark he had seen three men who aroused his suspicions. 'I got into the shed – the dog I had with me ran out and barked and they made off'. A few nights before this, he had seen some men stealing potatoes from one of Mr Seabrook's fields. 'I fired a gun and they made off'. Hunnikin then mentioned that Sergeant Parsons had passed by on horseback at about 10 o'clock on the night of the murder. Parsons asked him 'have you seen any of my men here tonight?' According to Hunnikin, 'he had never spoken to me before. I thought it very singular that he should not have done so'. Finally, Hunnikin asked to see George Blewitt in case he could identify him.

What are we to make of Hunnikin's statement? Perhaps he was another attention-seeker like Elizabeth Dodd, and concocted the whole story. Or maybe he had taken one drink too many with his friends, did not really know what he was saying and had to play along when the authorities were alerted. Yet Hunnikin appears to have been a man of some respectability. He had lived in Brentwood for at least eleven years with his wife Susannah (née

Meadows) and several children. On the death certificate of his infant daughter Susannah in 1847 he is described as a baker, and he later earned his living as a bill-sticker. Perhaps Stephen Westwood Brown, the stationer who witnessed the statement, was his employer.

There is plenty of convincing detail in Hunnikin's account. Samuel Seabrook owned and ran Sermons Farm, situated in Frizlands Lane. It was on Clark's beat, so a night-watchman there in the summer of 1846 would certainly have met him. The clay cottage mentioned by Hunnikin could have been the one nearby in what later became Marston Avenue. The times given by Hunnikin tie in with Thomas Archer's statement that he saw Clark passing the Four Wants 'between twelve and one'. The scene of Clark and Hunnikin in the turnip shed, sitting on the floor munching their bread and cheese, backs against the large troughs in which vegetables were washed, is a pleasing one and does seem to ring true. It is odd that Hunnikin didn't come forward during the initial investigation. He must surely have been questioned due to his job as night watchman. Perhaps like Archer he had been fearful of coming under suspicion if he admitted to being the last person to see Clark alive.

Unfortunately there is a major stumbling-block in Hunnikin's evidence. Nowhere else is there *any* mention of a thunderstorm between midnight and 2am on the night of Clark's murder. It is inconceivable that this would have been overlooked had it been the backdrop to such a dramatic event. The likelihood is that Hunnikin did know Clark, but that the meeting in the turnip shed happened on a different night. His tale was not followed up. When Inspector Whicher was shown the letter, he replied that 'I don't think there is anything in the statement to assist the present enquiry'.

As we have seen, Mary Ann Smith implicated several other men besides George Blewitt, so why was he the only one to be charged? Respecting William Page, the answer is simple. In October 1847 he had been driving a horse and cart in Whitechapel when the animal was frightened by a railway train and bolted. Page was thrown out and crushed beneath the wheels. He was taken to the London Hospital, where he lingered for five days before dying on 21st October. He was 33 years old. His step-daughter Mary Ann had made her escape from his household three months earlier by marrying a man named John Allsopp. On her wedding day she was three months pregnant with her daughter Caroline. Mary Ann senior didn't remain a widow for very long after Page's untimely death. On 6th August 1848 at Dagenham Parish Church she married widower Francis Smith. At the time of the 1851 census the couple were living at 14 Bull Street, in Dagenham Village, and afterwards moved, as we have seen, to the cottage in Workhouse Lane.

Ned Wood, another of the alleged gang, was also dead by the time Mrs Smith's story was made public. He had committed suicide aged 52 on Wednesday 27th July 1853 in a granary at Cooper's Farm, Dagenham. Charles C. Lewis was brought back to preside over the inquest, and a verdict of 'Temporary Derangement' was returned. The *Essex Standard* gives the particulars. 'Deceased, who for some time past had been in a deranged state of mind, which had incapacitated him for work, had lately been in the habit of sleeping in the granary; and on the afternoon in question the door being found fastened inside, was broken open, when the poor man was discovered suspended by a handkerchief, quite dead'.[8] (Handkerchieves, incidentally, were large enough at this time to be used by farm labourers for shielding the back of their necks against the sun as they toiled in the fields.) Ned Wood was buried in Dagenham parish churchyard, where George Clark had been laid to rest seven years before.

George Chalk, as we have seen, was only sixteen when the murder took place. He was the son of a farmer from Barking named William Chalk and his wife Louisa (née Smith). At the baby's christening at Dagenham on 2nd May 1830, there seems to have been a mix-up over his name. It was entered as John William in the register, but in 1838 a signed declaration was added by his godfather John Hawkins Chalk stating that he had named the child George William. When George was only four, he and his younger brother Henry were orphaned when their parents died within four months of each other. George was then taken in by Thomas Bell, a farmer and butcher living in Crown Street in Dagenham. The 1841 census records Thomas Bell aged 60, Mary Ann Bell aged 50, and eleven year-old George Chalk.

The boy must have been quite a handful. He attended William Ford School, but in June 1842 the headmaster complained to the trustees that 'the boy Chalk's conduct still continues so bad that he requests for the good order and better regulations of the school that he be dismissed'.[9] George Chalk's guardian Thomas Bell died in November 1847, and by the time of the 1851 census the lad had left Dagenham altogether. When police were following up Mary Ann Smith's statement seven years later, they were told that Chalk had emigrated to Australia.

Ralph Page, who was incidentally no relation to William Page, was also no longer alive. It will be remembered that when he died in 1847 rumours flew about the district that he had taken an overdose of laudanum. He had attracted suspicion because he had been inside his barn at Thornton's Farm during the night of the murder. According to a *Chelmsford Chronicle* report on Mrs Smith's allegations, Jonathan Whicher 'at the time suspected one of the persons now implicated'. It is likely that Ralph Page was this suspect.

George Blewitt appeared at the second hearing on Monday July 5th, and was again dressed in the blue smock frock. He stood throughout the hearing, which lasted several hours.[10] Blewitt certainly lived up to his reputation as 'a man of great nerve', appearing unconcerned in the face of a charge which could bring him to the gallows. He was described as 'seldom betraying more interest in the narrative of Mrs Smith than a mere casual observer, except perhaps occasionally, when the witness touched upon personal subjects, a deep flush might be observed on his ruddy countenance, which however quickly subsided, and he resumed the same stolid demeanour, almost indifference, which characterised his conduct on the previous occasion'.

It had been an easy arrest for Inspector Whicher, but making the charge stick was a different matter. He was forced to tell the magistrates that he could not at that stage bring forward evidence to corroborate Mrs Smith's story. If they would grant another remand, however, he was optimistic, telling them that 'he had that morning received information from Sergeant Stratford, which he thought would lead to the discovery of some persons connected with the prisoner at the time of the commission of the crime'.

The evidence previously given by Mrs Smith was read out. From time to time she interrupted the recital with comments such as 'That's true', 'Quite right', and 'Yes'. Reporters noticed that this 'caused some amusement' in the courtroom. Whereas Blewitt aroused admiration for his 'fine, open countenance and vigorous frame' and 'calm and collected demeanour', his accuser was becoming something of a figure of fun. When her statement had finished, she added 'I assure you that it is true. It has troubled me very much and I could not keep it to myself any longer. I was obliged to tell the truth, to let the world know who had done the deed'.

Blewitt's defence lawyer Mr Tindal Atkinson then moved into action. His objective was not to provide positive evidence in favour of Blewitt. It would in any case have been well-nigh impossible to establish an alibi, as the crime had been committed at night and twelve years before. Instead, the aim was to demolish Mrs Smith's evidence. He began by claiming that parts of Mrs Smith's statement should not be admitted. What relevance, he asked, did the account of the conversation between Mrs Smith and Clark, followed by William Page's anger at Clark, have to the case against George Blewitt? The Clerk of the Court, Mr Clifton, agreed with this, and 'after some conversation, the objectionable portion was expunged'.

With this success under his belt, the defence counsel then proceeded to cross-examine Mrs Smith. Had she been drinking, he wondered, when she first told her neighbour the tale? She replied firmly that 'We had been drinking

¹/₂ a pint of beer a piece and no more'. Mrs Smith was asked to confirm that she had spoken to an Eliza Woolmer. She said that she had: 'I know a person named Eliza Woolmer. I have at times talked to her'. The defence had evidently tracked down Mrs Woolmer, who lived at the hamlet of Five Elms, near Beacontree Heath, with her husband Isaac, a farm bailiff, and their children. What had emerged from their questioning provided Mr Atkinson with an opportunity to throw doubts on Mary Ann Smith's motivation, her reliability as a witness and even her sanity. Mrs Smith naively agreed that 'My neighbours sometimes have said that I wander in my mind. Sometimes they say there is something that troubles me'.

She confirmed that she had told Mrs Woolmer she had searched a box belonging to her husband William Page and found it contained two pounds ten shillings. On his death, she declared, 'I afterwards went to the box and found the money was gone. I said I did not know what had become of it unless my husband had lent it to the prisoner Blewitt or his wife'.

Mrs Smith was then encouraged to reveal more about Page. She asserted that he had been an habitual criminal. 'My husband was travelling night after night, the same as the police'. She spoke about some of the crimes she suspected Page to have been involved with. 'I told Mrs Woolmer that my husband had informed me that he had shot at old Jacky Bearblock and caught his hat'. John Bearblock, incidentally, was the Hornchurch squire who had alerted Superintendent Nicholas Pearce to the story of William Roots and the bloodstained clothes, and who had at the same time mentioned Ralph Page's death in connection with the Clark case. Mrs Smith then accused her husband of bringing home seven sacks of stolen potatoes: 'He shot them out into the kitchen'.

She agreed that she had also blamed William Page for setting fire to the premises of Anthony Vince at Whybridge Farm in South Hornchurch. The questioning then took a bizarre turn. Had she told Mrs Woolmer that a fire engine had appeared in her room? Mrs Smith replied that the fire at Vince's farm must have caused her to dream of seeing a fire engine, which she thought at the time was real.

The defence then asked her if it was true that she was being haunted by another manifestation, this time none other than the ghost of William Page. Mrs Smith agreed that despite being dead and buried for eleven years, her unsavoury spouse had not stopped tormenting her. Eyebrows must have been raised around the courtroom as she gave details of the visitations: 'I have seen my husband's apparition with my eyes open. I have also seen him 3 times in a dream. I saw him in 3 different cottages when I was awake and getting up. He was dressed in a green smock frock on, and a flannel jacket. I saw him as plain as I see you now'. She declared that this did not come as a surprise, as 'My husband told me in the hospital that if I said anything he would rise from the grave and crush me'.[11] She had not sought advice from a clergyman.

What was more, Page seemed to have supernatural allies. Mrs Smith confirmed that she had told Mrs Woolmer: 'You can be happy, I can't, if I sit down to have a meal of victuals a devil comes and taps under my chair'. Because of the sinister threats Page had made before his death, 'I have really believed that the visitations were through the devil from my husband'. This unsettling experience had occurred to her five or six times, the last occasion being just the previous week.

The defence barrister then quoted another of Mrs Smith's neighbours, Sophia March, the wife of farm worker Robert March, in an attempt to demonstrate that her account of the events on the night of the murder had not been consistent. This time, though, she denied intentionally changing her story: 'I don't think I ever told her that I did not go in to the prisoner's cottage that night. I will not swear I did not....I possibly might have said that I went under an apple tree and did not go into the prisoner's cottage. If I did it is a mistake. I did not tell Mrs March that they took the corn out of the barn and when they saw Clark they took it back again'.

The defence had, it seems, also spoken to Mrs Smith's own daughter, Mary Ann Allsopp, and found out that Mrs Smith had gone to her house to talk about Clark's death. The mother became flustered on being questioned about this: 'I have not asked her to say she knew all about the murder. There was some little conversation between us but I don't know what it was'. Eventually, she conceded that she had visited Mrs Allsopp and they had spoken about the crime. 'It was after I had seen the police. It was not at their wish that I went to see my daughter. I now remember asking my daughter if she knew any thing about it, to tell me'.

Had Mrs Smith given William Page an alibi in 1846? She admitted that 'I might possibly have said that my husband was in bed the whole night of the 29th June when the murder was committed for the sake of screening him'. It was then put to Mrs Smith that far from trying to pull Page away from Clark, she had actually held Clark's head while Page cut his throat. She vehemently denied this, and exclaimed, 'If I had committed the murder I would tell the truth; right is right, but wrong is no man's right'.

The questioning then reverted to the subject of the £2 10s that had disappeared from Page's box. This now emerged as a possible motive for her accusations against Blewitt, especially as Page had not left her any money. Mrs Smith told the court that Blewitt and his son came to see her one Sunday morning after word of her allegations had got around. He greeted her with: 'Well Mrs Smith you know what I have come for'. She agreed that she had mentioned the missing money to Blewitt, and had rounded on him with the words: 'When Bill died you never gave me a half penny but your brother John gave me a shilling…Had you a given me one I don't know where the harm would have been'. The defence barrister then declared that Mrs Smith had threatened Blewitt with: 'As it is it may cost you pounds' and 'If it had not been for the money I should not have said anything about it and I wish now I had never said anything about it'. She vehemently denied uttering these words.

Mrs Smith's reliability as a witness was now looking distinctly shaky. The *Essex Standard*[12] reported that the lengthy questioning was intended 'to show that she was suffering under some mental hallucinations, and the strange manner in which she replied to many of the questions put to her tended very much to strengthen the suggestion'. Moreover, she was very hard of hearing, and obviously rather naïve and uneducated. Once again, she declared she was full of remorse for keeping quiet for so long. 'I hid the secret, and I am truly sorry. I was in fear, and I would not have done so for £5000 if I had known what troubles I should have encountered'.

Mr Atkinson ended by telling the Bench that there was no substance to the case against his client. 'If this were a mere case of summary jurisdiction, I should say the magistrates would not pull a feather out of a sparrow's wing upon such evidence as this…it is a mere case of suspicion, and this poor man ought not to be kept in gaol'.

Blewitt was, however, remanded in custody a further five days, until Saturday 10th July. The *Chelmsford Chronicle* reported an emotional scene as he was led away. 'Two of the daughters of the accused were in court during the proceedings, standing close by his side, and on hearing the decision of the magistrates they burst into tears and affectionately embraced their parent, whose unhappy position they seemed greatly to deplore. The prisoner however seemed but slightly affected, and calmly shook hands and bade them 'keep up their spirits' as he was being removed by the officers of the gaol'.

Three days later, on Thursday 8th July, The *Times* printed a letter about the case from 'An inhabitant of the neighbourhood'. The correspondent made a scathing attack on the incompetence of the police investigation. 'I think you will agree with me, Sir, that the fact that there should be so many persons resident in the neighbourhood implicated, as appears by Mrs Smith's statement, in the murder, and that some of them should have continued to reside there until the present time unsuspected, does not reflect much credit upon the manner in which the police prosecuted their investigation'. The writer recommended that the other officers on duty that night should be traced and questioned, 'with reference to Mrs Smith's statement, which may bring facts to their minds which at the time they thought little of, and they may be able to explain how he could have got to the field where he was found without the clearest evidence of a mortal struggle having taken place, when he was attacked, it seems, at a barn, a very considerable distance from the spot'.

Interestingly, this anonymous letter-writer then mentioned the feeling in Dagenham that Parsons having been proved to be not on duty 'led to the belief at the time that Parsons desired the deceased to go to the spot for the purpose of murdering him'. He then declared that the lack of a prosecuting counsel was further proof of the apathy that had shown itself throughout the case: 'The remark made by the Bench, that they observed with some surprise that the Police Commissioners had not instructed any counsel to attend, is perhaps indicative of the manner in which the authorities, unless urged on through the press, will conduct the renewed investigation...'

The correspondent then criticised the practice of sending lone officers out on long beats in rural areas: 'the men have allotted to them such wide and distant beats that they are not only unable to protect themselves, but can afford very little protection to the property of the inhabitants'.

It was now a race against time for Jonathan Whicher and his team. This latest remand of five days could be the last, and it was essential that they come up with concrete evidence to support Mrs Smith's story. Once more, just as in the summer of 1846, detectives descended on Dagenham. On the morning of Friday 9th July Whicher and his younger detective colleague, 35 year-old Lincolnshire-born Creasy Robertson, toured Dagenham making house-to-house enquiries. The *Times* evidently had a source within the detective force, and it reported that the mood was optimistic. On 10th July it told its readers that 'from important information they have received during the last few days in the village and its outskirts they fully expect to bring forward two witnesses who can give corroborative evidence in connexion with this tragical affair'.

The *Times* also reported that Daniel Howie, Superintendent of K Division, was also at the sharp end of the investigation. This proves what a high-profile case the Dagenham Murder was, and how much the reputation of K Division would be enhanced by a successful prosecution. Howie joined the hunt for potential witnesses in Dagenham itself and in other parts of Essex. In particular, he was out 'to obtain some testimony relative to a woman who, it is alleged, washed the clothes of the man Chalk after the perpetration of the fearful tragedy'. George Chalk's only brother Henry, a farrier, had settled down in nearby Chadwell Heath with his Dagenham-born wife Elizabeth and their children. It is likely that he was tracked down and questioned about his brother, but perhaps could give no important information.

Jonathan Whicher's notes on the Constance Kent case in 1860, in which a sixteen year-old girl was accused of killing her half-brother, survive in the file on the murder at the National Archives.[13] Unfortunately we have no surviving memoir of his thinking in the Clark case. Edward Willcocks, the man accused by Mrs Smith of helping to plan the theft of Mr Brittain's corn, was living nearby in Rush Green.[14] It is not recorded whether he was interviewed by Whicher.

The *Times* also pointed out that other newspapers had wrongly dismissed Mrs Smith's story of a throat-cutting murder. 'It has been stated that the throat of the deceased was not cut; but, on the contrary, the neck exhibited two mortal wounds, which the medical gentleman (who was examined on Monday week, and gave testimony at the coroner's inquest in July 1846) stated on oath nearly separated the head from the trunk. The stock which the deceased wore was completely cut through, as the surgeon said, by a double-edged knife or dirk'.

The *Times* confidently told its readers that: 'The investigation will be resumed this morning, when evidence of an important character will be brought forward which will, in all probability, implicate other persons not yet in custody'.

At 10am that day, Saturday July 10th, Blewitt was brought into court once more. He was described in the *Chelmsford Chronicle* as seeming 'somewhat altered in his features, but his general demeanour was calm and collected'. Jonathan Whicher was asked whether he could produce more evidence or witnesses, and to general dismay was forced to reply in the negative: 'The rumours that were in circulation last week were unfounded. If they had been true they would have been highly important in the case'. The magistrates then announced that they were sending the case to the next Essex Assizes, which were opening at the Shire Hall in Chelmsford in eleven days' time. The charge was read out, and Blewitt replied 'I am not guilty of it'. He was then led away. The strain was beginning to show, as the *Essex Standard* reported that he 'for the first time betrayed some emotion, and staggered as he retired'.

Jonathan Whicher immediately sat down to report that day's proceedings to the Commissioners. He stressed the short period of time remaining before

A public hanging above the Springfield Gaol gatehouse in 1829

the start of the Assizes, and pleaded: 'I beg respectfully to suggest to Sir Richard Mayne that legal aid be obtained to prosecute in this case'. This time, his wish was granted, and the Solicitor to the Treasury was given charge of the prosecution.

George Blewitt was moved from Ilford to Springfield Gaol, which as we have seen had been at various times a place of confinement for Kimpton, Hickton and Parsons. Unlike the three disgraced officers, though, Blewitt was facing the death penalty. In those days, execution could follow within weeks of a guilty verdict. The husband and wife Frederick and Maria Manning were hanged above the gatehouse of Horsemonger Lane Gaol within three weeks of being convicted of murder in 1849. As he walked through the gate house at Springfield, did Blewitt glance up at the flat roof above, where executions were carried out? In August 1848 38 year-old Mary May had been hanged there for the murder of her brother William Constable, watched by an enthusiastic crowd over three thousand strong.

George Blewitt was the only prisoner accused of murder among the 16 cases on the gaol calendar. The others were chiefly theft, assault and arson. There were two women on the list. Jane Dawson was accused of stealing a plate, a dinner knife and two calico shirts at Stansted Mountfitchet. Mary Barker, a twenty year-old servant, was charged with concealing the birth of her child at Clavering. The standard of literacy of each defendant was given. According to this, Blewitt could read imperfectly but not write.

Blewitt's case was put before the Grand Jury on the morning of Wednesday 24th July 1858. He was now represented by Mr Serjeant Parry.[15] This hearing was, as we have seen, the preliminary to the actual trial, which would be held before the 12-man Petty Jury later during the same Assizes. The indictment was read out. The charge was that Blewitt 'feloniously wilfully and of his malice aforethought did kill and murder one George Clark against the peace of our said Lady the Queen her Crown and Dignity'. The Grand Jury consisted of 23 men, all prominent Essex property holders, headed by the Honourable Frederick Petre. In addressing them, the judge, Sir James Shaw Willes, stressed that Mrs Smith's evidence was uncorroborated. He told them: 'If you think that the petty jury may convict upon the evidence of Mrs Smith – then I think you ought to bring in a bill, but if you do not think a conviction can take place, then I think you should withdraw it'.

The Grand Jury hearing was not held in open court but in a separate room, as had happened when Parsons, Kimpton and Hickton had cases heard in their absence in Spring 1847. The prosecution witnesses came into the room one by one to give their evidence, unaccompanied by counsel. They were

Farnes, Thomas Archer, William Page, Joseph Collin, Brittain, Mary Ann Smith, Jonathan Whicher and an Inspector Alexander Thomson. Eventually, at about half past one, the members of the Grand Jury filed back into court. They announced that they had reached a decision of 'No Bill' against Blewitt, meaning that the case would not be brought to trial. This was written on the back of the indictment. The judge asked whether any further charge would be brought, and 'Mr Poland, who had been instructed for the prosecution, informed his Lordship that there was no probability of any other bill being preferred against the prisoner'. Blewitt had to wait a further two hours until the Grand Jury had finished considering that day's cases, and then was allowed to leave as a free man.

On ordering Blewitt's release, Mr Justice Willes said that he thought the Ilford magistrates had been right to send the case for trial,[16] and also that in his opinion the Grand Jury 'had exercised a sound discretion in not finding the bill'.

As we have seen, Mary Ann Smith had named George Chalk, only 16 years old in 1846, as one of the murderers. He was rumoured to have emigrated to Australia, but we have no evidence of enquiries being made there about his whereabouts. It was impossible to communicate rapidly between Britain and Australia at that time. Letters travelled by sea and took two months to arrive.[17] If Whicher had written to the police forces of the various Australian states, he might easily have waited almost five months for the replies. As we have seen, however, time was of the essence in the prosecution of Blewitt.

The Australian police made more use of plain-clothes detectives than in England, so if they had been asked to look for Chalk, it is possible that he may have been tracked down. In 1844, for example, ten per cent of the police manpower of Victoria were plain-clothes, and by 1862 there were 42 detectives spread throughout the colony. Many Metropolitan Police officers moved to Australia – in 1853 alone, 54 were sent to Victoria.[18]

Towards the end of that year of 1858, however, Frederick Standish, Chief Commissioner of Police for Melbourne, Victoria, saw a report in the *Sunday Times* newspaper about the Clark murder. He wrote to Sir Richard Mayne, declaring that 'there is residing in this Colony a person named Henry Chalk, who, about 15 months ago, was heard to state that he knew the Constable who was murdered on the occasion in question, and he further said that the parties in the murder must have been disturbed in the act of removing from the barn that is alluded to, a quantity of smuggled tobacco'.

This must have seemed promising, especially as this man was 'supposed to have been born in the neighbourhood of Romford'. He was described as 'about 50 years of age, 5ft 10 in high, full face, stout build (rather corpulent), fair hair (turning grey), eyes grey, whiskers grey and cut square'. Like Abel Magwitch from Dickens's *Great Expectations*, Henry Chalk seems to have been a convict made good. Standish goes on to say that 'Appearances lead to the belief that he was transported from England. He is an illiterate man, and can neither read nor write, but is possessed of a great deal of property; having been long resident in the Colonies (Australian). He is married, and has four children, the eldest about twenty or twenty-one years of age'.

The letter arrived in England on the RMS *Columbian* in February 1859. Richard Mayne passed it on to Jonathan Whicher, but the detective soon spotted major discrepancies in the account. Whicher's reply pointed out that the suspect named by Mrs Smith was George, not Henry. He went on to write that "Chalk' was then (in 1846) about 18[sic] years of age, consequently his age would now be about 30. I do not think therefore that the man alluded to can be the same person'. Finally, he noted wearily that 'if he were actually the same person alluded to by the woman 'Page' there is not sufficient evidence against him to warrant his apprehension'.

It seems from the tone of Whicher's letter that the arrest and prosecution of Blewitt had been a last throw of the dice. Perhaps the police were now losing hope of ever bringing the murderers of George Clark to justice.

This photograph shows the loneliness of the Eastbrookend beat.
Eastbrookend Farm is just visible in the distance

CHAPTER 13

'Let's Clark him!'

Back in the summer of 1858, when the arrest of George Blewitt brought George Clark's murder into the spotlight once more, a police constable by the name of Coleman began working at Dagenham. He was 28 years old, and like Clark had previously been stationed at Stepney. Coleman had also had first-hand experience of the perils of the job, having been injured dealing with a disturbance on the notorious Ratcliffe Highway. On arriving at Dagenham he was given Clark's old beat at Eastbrookend, and as he trod those lonely roads he must surely have thought of the tragic fate of his predecessor.

It was the evening of Sunday 10th October 1858, three months after the collapse of the prosecution of Blewitt. At ten o'clock Coleman and a fellow constable left the police station in Bull Street to begin their night duty. As this was the winter season, with the sun rising later, their shift began and ended an hour after Clark's had done. The pair walked together to the Four Wants junction, where they separated. Coleman had not gone far from the Wants when he became aware of voices. He took no notice and walked on. Suddenly he was surrounded by three men who had jumped out from a ditch. One of the gang shouted 'Let's Clark him!' and blows and kicks were rained on the hapless officer. He tried to get away, but was overpowered. According to the *Chelmsford Chronicle* Coleman was 'subjected to most cruel treatment, the villains striking him in every part of his body, kicking him about the head and face, [and] jumping upon his body...In the conflict, Coleman's cutlass and lamp were taken from him, and his uniform almost destroyed'. The gang then dragged their victim to a pond by the roadside, and threw him in, leaving him for dead. Luckily for Coleman the water level in the pond was unusually low, otherwise he would certainly have drowned. Eventually he regained consciousness. The *Times* told its readers that 'the poor fellow managed to extricate himself from the mud and filth and crawl into the road, and ultimately, with assistance, to reach the station; though almost in a dying state'.[1]

The inhabitants of Dagenham were said to be in 'a state of terror' at this new atrocity. It beggared belief that another police officer had come so close to losing his life just 'the length of a field' from where George Clark's body had been found back in 1846. In a further bizarre echo of the Clark case, there was speculation that Coleman may have been singled out for a revenge attack. It was reported that a few weeks previously he secured the conviction of some Dagenham men for stealing corn from their employer.[2] It was hoped that Coleman would be able to identify his assailants. However, it seems that no-one was ever charged. Coleman's attackers, like Clark's, were never brought to justice. There is no mention of the incident in the Police Orders. Coleman doesn't appear to have been awarded any compensation. Neither was he invalided out of the force, although he was no longer at Dagenham at the time of the 1861 census. Let's hope he had a more uneventful time during the rest of his police career.

It seems that after 1858 the search for Clark's murderers was scaled down. If there were any more enquiries, they have not been recorded. The people involved in the case returned to their day-to-day lives. Let us now look at what happened to them in the years that followed.

Clark's fiancée, Elizabeth How

First of all, what of Elizabeth, bereft of her husband-to-be just days before their wedding? We know that immediately after Clark's murder she was interviewed by detectives in Bedfordshire, but it is not recorded whether she was working in the London area during the time Clark was at Arbour Square and Dagenham. Five years later, in 1851, Elizabeth was employed as a general servant in the household of stockbroker Thomas Upton at Sydenham in Kent, a town rapidly becoming absorbed into the London suburbs. Later that decade Sydenham was the site of the relocation, with considerable enlargement, of the Crystal Palace which had housed the Great Exhibition of 1851. Just a few days into the new year of 1857, over a decade after the tragic loss of Clark, the 31 year-old Elizabeth married William Beal in St Bartholomew's Church at Sydenham. On the marriage certificate she was described as a dressmaker. Her husband was 32 and a native of Ridgmount in Bedfordshire. By 1861 the couple were living in Wells Road in Sydenham with their two children, Emily and Arthur John. William was now a general dealer. Another son, Walter, was born to them in 1866. The family later moved the short distance to Beckenham, where William became a market gardener. On 5th September 1880 Elizabeth died at her home, 26 Sommerville Road. She was 54 years old and had suffered from ovarian disease.

George Clark's parents

James Clark lived to the age of 61. His death from inflammation of the bladder took place on 29th June 1862, the sixteenth anniversary of his son's murder. Charlotte Clark outlived her son by 33 years. She died in September 1879 aged 77, the cause being given as 'softening of the brain'. The couple are both buried in Battlesden churchyard.

George Clark's sister Mary in old age with her son George Tearle

Clark's sisters

George's two surviving sisters, Ann and Mary, both lived into the twentieth century. Ann married Thomas Hollingsworth and they and their family settled in South London. At one time they lived in Peabody Buildings in Stamford Street, Southwark. Their home was in Block D, which by a strange twist of fate was at one time inhabited by Mary Ann Nichols, who later became the first victim of Jack the Ripper.[3] Ann's final home was in Beckenham, where she died in 1910. Elizabeth How's descendants lived nearby, so it is likely that the two families remained in touch over the years.

George Clark's younger sister Mary became the wife of Jabez Tearle in October 1862, just a few months after the death of her father. During her marriage Mary resided in her native county, but after being widowed she went to live with her daughter in Pitsea in Essex. Mary died there in 1932, and her body was then taken back to Hockliffe in Bedfordshire for burial alongside her husband.

Clark's cousin William Markham

Just over a year after his cousin's murder, in August 1847, William Markham married Rebecca Rawlings at St Mary's Church, Paddington. The couple lived in Bexley, where William worked as a market gardener. Their first child, George, doubtless named as a tribute to Clark, was born in September 1848. Three more boys and two daughters followed. Two of the sons died of tuberculosis when only in their twenties. William himself passed away on 9th August 1878 aged 69.

CLARK'S POLICE COLLEAGUES

We have seen that Abia Butfoy died in Colney Hatch Asylum in July 1853. Unfortunately, details of the later life of Clark's room-mate Jonas Stevens are unknown. But what was the fate of the other officers?

Isaac Hickton

On his release from prison, Hickton returned to Derby and resumed his previous occupation as a currier. He remained single until the age of 62, in 1876, when he married 52 year-old widow Eliza May at the parish church of St Peter in Derby. At the time of the 1881 census Isaac was living with Eliza and her daughter Carrie, and was working as a 'railway labourer in screw shop'. Hickton died four years later of bronchitis, aged 71.

Thomas Kimpton

Kimpton settled in Bethnal Green with his wife Ellen Maria and their family after being freed from the hulks in late 1849. They had two further children, Louisa in August 1851 followed by Martha Jane three years later. On 11th August 1858 Ellen died at 3 Parliament Street. She was 44 years old, and had suffered from the chronic lung condition pthisis, which usually indicates tuberculosis. Three years later, at the time of the 1861 census, Thomas and his two youngest daughters were living at 26 Luke Street in Shoreditch, the home of 45 year-old grocer Thomas Winmill. Winmill had been born into a well-known Dagenham farming family, so he and Kimpton doubtless met during the latter's time as a police constable there.[4]   Two years later, on 5th June 1863, Thomas Kimpton died at 11 Kings Head Square in Shoreditch. He was 49 years old, and the cause of death was 'pleura pneumonia'. Seven years later, at the time of the 1871 census, his 19 year-old daughter Louisa was listed among the inmates of the Shoreditch workhouse. Were the repercussions of the George Clark murder now affecting the second generation of this unfortunate family?

John Farnes

After being dismissed from the police force in 1847, Farnes, his wife Ann and their children settled in London's East End. When the 1851 census was taken, the family were living in Emma Street, Bethnal Green, and John was working as a dock labourer.

Sutton Isacke, the youngest brother of Ann Farnes, joined the Mormons (the Church of Jesus Christ of Latter-Day Saints) in 1850, and persuaded his sister to be baptized in April of that year. Her children followed suit, but John Farnes at first refused to be converted. He did, though, allow his home to be used as a meeting-place for Mormon missionaries visiting London. These included Brigham Young Jnr. His father, Brigham Young, was the second President of the Mormon Church and the man who established the Mormon community at Salt Lake City in Utah. Five of the Farnes children emigrated to Utah. Eventually John and Ann Farnes, with their remaining two children, Matilda and Jane, plus an adopted son, decided to make the voyage too. They booked a passage on the Amazon, which left from the London Docks on 4th June 1863. Six weeks later they sailed into New York and the most perilous part of their journey began. They took a cattle truck via Canada to St Joseph, Missouri. Here they took a steamboat on the river to the point where the wagon trail began. With a wagon and oxen they began the weary trek to Utah. There is an account of what happened next from the pen of Matilda Farnes:

John Farnes and his wife Ann

When we reached the Three Crossings of the Sweetwater River, I saw father was very ill. He walked with lagging steps and pallid face all day, yet never a word of complaint. At last, in mid-afternoon, a part of the company had drawn up at a small stream to rest and be refreshed. Ill and weary myself, almost to the point of exhaustion, I fell asleep immediately. When I awakened, which I did suddenly, as if some hand had touched me, my first anxiety was for father. I looked around for him, but he was nowhere to be seen. The banks of the stream were covered with growths of small shrubs, and running towards these I called again and again.

At last in despair I dropped to my knees and as if in answer to my prayer I saw like a phantom my father emerge from the growth of tree, leaning on a stick and carrying in his hand a twig from which hung two very small fish. He staggered as he came, trying to smile at my fright. He looked very old and tired, yet on going back to camp, insisted on putting up the tent. During the process he fell to the ground three times. That night (September 17th 1863) he died, and was buried next morning before we broke camp. He was wrapped in canvas with only a broken box to mark his grave. Oh, the agony of leaving him by the wayside.

The following morning John's son Ebenezer, who was on his way from Utah with supplies for the emigrants, met the advance company who abruptly told him that his father had died in the night. John's widow and children eventually completed the gruelling journey. Ann set up home with her son George and his family in Logan, Utah. She died at the age of 87 on 23rd July 1891.[5]

William Parsons

As we have seen, ex-Sergeant Parsons had also made his way to North America, running a watermill in British Columbia for the Hudson's Bay Company. When his five-year contract ended, Parsons bought some nearby land by a bridge and built a large wooden public house and hotel there. The diary of Robert Melrose, another Hudson's Bay Company settler, mentions that on Friday 13th July 1855 'Mr Parson opened his Public House with a grand spree'.[6] Somehow Parsons had overlooked purchasing a liquor licence, and did so the following year after paying a fine of £2.10s. The pub was a success, and Parsons became a well-known figure in the area.

A photograph said to be of William Parsons and his wife Annie while they were running Parson's Bridge Hotel. This picture has remained at the hotel until the present day

The bridge still bears his name, but what was once the Parson's Bridge Hotel is now called the Six Mile Pub. It is the oldest public house in British Columbia still operating today.[7]

In spite of the success of the business, after some years Parsons made the decision to leave. He travelled to the Columbia River area in the USA, where he found work as a millstone cutter. His wife Annie remained behind to run the hotel. Parsons had appeared in the local police court several times over the years on wife-beating charges, so Annie may not have been too sorry about his departure. When news came through that Parsons had died in Washington State, his widow promptly married again. The date was 11th July 1878, and her new husband was William Gray, a carpenter, who had been a fellow-passenger on the *Norman Morison* back in 1849. Annie died in December 1908 at the grand age of 94.

Jonathan and Maria Rawlings

William Parsons' original parents-in-law Jonathan and Maria Rawlings continued to live at the Fairlop Oak public house in Barkingside. Jonathan died there of apoplexy 31st August 1861 aged 73 and was buried at Barkingside's Holy Trinity church on 5th September. His widow joined him thirteen years later, after her death from 'decay of nature' aged 85.

Julia Parsons

Julia, who had maintained such a spirited defence of her brother William Parsons throughout the Clark inquest, married Devon-born James Lane in Whitechapel in February 1850. Her husband worked as a porter in an auctioneer's warehouse. The couple and their four children lived firstly in Soho, before moving back to Julia's mother's home in Whitechapel. Julia died from cancer of the uterus in 1891, aged 65.

THE POLICE COMMISSIONERS

Richard Mayne

We have already seen that Charles Rowan died in May 1852. His fellow-Commissioner Richard Mayne's career as Metropolitan Police Commissioner lasted very nearly forty years, an astonishing achievement. He was still in office when he died aged 79 on Boxing Day 1868 at his London home, 80 Chester Square. Mayne's reputation had suffered in later years. He suffered criticism, for example, after the so-called 'Fenian outrage'. Irish revolutionaries trying to spring two colleagues from Clerkenwell House of Detention exploded over 500lbs of gunpowder and killed six people, including two children. The police were seen as slow to react to rumours of the impending attack. The Commissioner's autocratic style had also given him the nickname of 'King' Mayne.

Mayne insisted in his will that 'my funeral may be conducted in the quietest and most economic a manner suitable to my condition in life and that a plain tablet or grave stone alone be put up in the churchyard wherein I may be buried'.[8] His estate was valued at under £5000.

Mayne was buried 30th December 1868 at Kensal Green Cemetery. An account of his funeral from the *Times* shows that his instructions were followed to the letter. Only three carriages followed the hearse. 'The Duke and Duchess of Sutherland, Miss Burdett Coutts, and many other persons of distinction wished their carriages to follow as a mark of respect, but the offers were declined by Lady Mayne and family, as it was the particular request of Sir Richard that the funeral should be conducted in the plainest manner'.[9] His widow Georgiana was awarded a Civil List pension of £150 per annum.[10]

THE DETECTIVES

Let's now look at the later careers of the various members of the Detective Branch who worked on the George Clark case.

Edward Kendell

Kendell, the Cornishman who worked so hard in his ultimately fruitless search for the murderers of George Clark, took part in the successful pursuit of the husband and wife murderers Frederick and Maria Manning in 1849. He was awarded a bonus of £8 for his work on this case.[11] The following year Kendell was involved in an investigation that was to transform his own life.

Towards the end of September 1850 a brutal murder took place in a quiet Surrey village, shocking the nation as much as the Clark case had done four years previously. Burglars entered Frimley Vicarage and shot George Edward Hollest, the Perpetual Curate. His wife Caroline was pinned to the floor with a pistol at her head but survived without injury. The *Times* reported on 8th October 1850 that 'Sergeant Kendall *[sic]* of the London detective force is actively engaged in investigating the affair on the spot'. The efforts of Kendell and the local Surrey police officers proved successful, and two men were hanged for the killing.

Early the following year Kendell was promoted to Inspector of G Division during the sick leave of Inspector Gray. He moved into bachelor lodgings in Spencer Street in Clerkenwell, but maintained a friendship with Caroline Hollest, widow of the murdered clergyman. On 16th October 1852, aged 37, he married 42 year-old Caroline at St Botolph's Church in Bishopsgate in the City of London.

Kendell was to play no part in the reopening of the Clark murder case on George Blewitt's arrest in 1858. In January 1854, fifteen months after his marriage, he had been forced to retire from the police force due to ill-health. Kendell was described as suffering from 'incipient phthisis' and awarded a pension of £108 per annum. Ten years later, on 23rd February 1864, Kendell made his will at his home, 11 Gresham Place in Brixton. One of the witnesses was Jonathan Whicher, then living in nearby Wandsworth. They were close in age, and eighteen years previously they had been the first detective sergeants sent to Dagenham after Clark's body was found. On 30th March, five weeks after making his will, Kendell died at home aged just 48. The death certificate reveals that he succumbed to phthisis, the lung disease that had led to his retirement. When Kendell's will was proved 13th May the same year his estate was valued at under £200. All was bequeathed to his 'beloved wife' Caroline, the sole executrix.

Frederick Shaw

Shaw worked for another ten years after the murder of Clark, retiring on 13th May 1856 on the grounds of cerebral disease. He was 48 years old, and was awarded a pension of £133 per annum. Four years previously, he too had been promoted to the rank of Inspector. Shaw remained in London after his retirement, and at the time of the 1861 census was living with his wife Eliza and their children at Ponsonby Place in Westminster.

Edward Langley

Langley too was involved in the Manning case – in fact he was on the scene when Frederick Manning was captured while in bed in his lodgings in Jersey.[12] Unlike his colleagues, Kendell and Shaw, Langley was never promoted. When he retired on 3rd March 1856, due to chronic rheumatism, he had served just under 11 years as a Detective Sergeant. Langley was awarded a pension of £72 per year, and continued to live at 22 Crown Street, Westminster, with his wife Hannah and their children. At the time of the 1861 census he was supplementing his pension by undertaking private work as an 'enquiry agent'.

Henry Smith

Smith remained in the force until 1863, when he retired at the age of 51 due to 'infirmity of the body arising from vertigo'. He had served for 26 years and was awarded a pension of £72 15s 9d per annum. By the time of the 1871 census he was living in Warwick Street, Westminster, and working as a debt collector. Ten years later Smith and his wife Eliza had left London, having retired to Eliza's home village of Puddletown in Dorset.

Nicholas Pearce

Superintendent Pearce, who played such a major part in the hunt for the murderers of George Clark, was in retirement far away from Dagenham when George Blewitt was arrested in 1858. Pearce had left the force at the age of 55 on the grounds of ill health in November 1855, after 30 years' service. He and his wife Eliza Lucille left their London home of 21 Great Russell Street, near the British Museum, and settled in the Cornish village of Gerrans. This was close to Pearce's birthplace of St Anthony Roseland – which was also, incidentally, the village where his detective colleague Edward Kendell had been born in 1815. Pearce, sadly, was not to enjoy a long retirement amidst the spectacular Cornish scenery. On 15th December 1858 he died at Mount View Cottage in Gerrans. According to the death certificate, Pearce had suffered kidney disease for six years. Other contributory factors were given as 'paralysis and epilepsy'. He was buried in Falmouth. When his will was proved the following year, his estate, valued at less than £200, was left entirely to his 'beloved wife'.[13]

Jonathan Whicher

Whicher, the 'Prince of Detectives', was faced with his most well-known case two years after the collapse of his prosecution of George Blewitt. It was the 1860 murder of 4 year-old Francis Savile Kent at Road House in Wiltshire. Whicher suspected 16 year-old Constance Kent, the victim's half-sister. He had her arrested and charged, but the case was thrown out due to insufficient evidence. Douglas Browne, in *The Rise of Scotland Yard,* suggests this arrest was 'quick work' and that Whicher had admitted later that he was counting on Constance Kent breaking down. 'There he was mistaken; she was not the sort to break down; and once he had discovered this, Whicher must have feared that his throw had failed'.[14] Whicher has the reputation of being a careful and painstaking investigator, not the type to make rash decisions, but his approach to the Kent murder echoes his perhaps rather precipitate arrest of George Blewitt in 1858.

In 1862, Scotland Yard received a request from Czar Alexander II for help in setting up an English-style police force in Warsaw, which was at that time part of the Russian empire. Jonathan Whicher and Chief Superintendent Robert Walker were selected to make the journey.[15]   Two years later, on 18th March 1864, Whicher left the Metropolitan Police aged 49 due to 'congestion of the brain'. He had served for 26 years, and was awarded a pension of £133 6s 8d per annum. It was rumoured that he had been forced to resign after losing the backing of Richard Mayne in the aftermath of the Constance Kent case.[16] However, Whicher himself denied this in a letter to a newspaper several years later.   Ironically in April 1865, just a year after Whicher's resignation, Constance appeared before the magistrates at Bow Street to confess that she had indeed killed her small half-brother. Whicher, now vindicated, continued to carry out private enquiry work. He was, for example, instrumental in proving that the Titchborne Claimant, widely believed to be the long-lost heir to a fortune, was in fact a fraudster called Arthur Orton.

On 21st August 1866, Whicher married a widow named Charlotte Piper at St Margaret's Church, Westminster. His address at the time was 63 Page Street, and he was still there when he made his will in 1875. By 1881 Whicher and Charlotte were living at 1 Cumberland Villas, Lavender Hill, Wandsworth with their niece Amy Gray. On 29th June of that year, the 35th anniversary of the murder of George Clark (it is extraordinary how the date recurs throughout this story) Jonathan Whicher died at home aged 69. According to the death certificate, he died of 'gastritis and ulcer of stomach 7 days, perforation of stomach 12 hours.'

The obituaries were generous. The *Daily News* of 1st July 1881 proclaimed that Whicher 'will be remembered as one of the leading inspectors of the Detective Department at Scotland Yard; and from his intimate connection with many celebrated criminal cases'. The *Police Guardian* of the same date described him as 'a man who, in his day, achieved considerable eminence'. It says that he 'was regarded by Sir Richard Mayne as one of the most capable officers in the force'.

Whicher's estate was valued at £1500. One of the executors of his will was his protégé Superintendent Adolphus Frederick Williamson, who was also bequeathed £100. Whicher was clearly especially proud of his watches. He specifically mentions his 'large Gold watch by Granthony [numbered] 3538 together with the Gold watch Chain and Seal attached' and 'my Gold Geneva watch [numbered] 7546 by Muller Geneva'. He also bequeaths 'my Blood Stone Signet Ring with the monogram thereon'. Charlotte Whicher moved to Saunders Road, Notting Hill with her niece Amy Gray. She survived her

Joseph Collin, the surgeon who carried out Clark's post-mortem, photographed (on the extreme left) with his sisters in the garden of their home 'the Colony' at Elmdon, Essex, c.1870

husband only eighteen months, dying on 19th January 1883. Once again her husband's colleague Adolphus Williamson was pressed into service as executor of her will.

Creasy Robertson

In 1858, Detective Sergeant Robertson had worked in Dagenham with Jonathan Whicher seeking supporting evidence for the allegations against George Blewitt. Robertson had been a bricklayer before joining the police force in 1844. His life came to a tragic end only six years after the Blewitt investigation. On 4th July 1864, aged 42, he committed suicide at 61 Millbank St, Westminster where he lived with his wife Eliza and their children. He was found unconscious with his throat cut with a razor, and died within minutes.

Frederick Stratford

Sergeant Stratford had been in charge of the Dagenham station in 1858, and was the first to interview Mary Ann Smith and pass on her story to Inspector Whicher. Stratford retired from the police at the age of 56 on 18th July 1876 on the grounds of being 'unfit for further service'. He and his wife Elizabeth moved to the nearby parish of Hornchurch, where he took up a new career as Registrar of Births, Deaths and Marriages. He was also the School Attendance Officer.[17] In October 1878, at the occasion of the re-opening of Dagenham parish church after its restoration, Stratford was presented with a 'handsome clock, in ebony frame' which had an inscription praising the 'efficient and conscientious manner' in which he had carried out his duties as Dagenham's sergeant for nearly thirty years.[18] Stratford died unexpectedly on 14th August 1886 aged 66. An obituary in the *Essex Times* on 21st August tells us that Stratford 'was of a kindly disposition, quiet and unobtrusive, and was held in very general esteem, and his somewhat sudden death will be regretted by all who knew him'. He was buried in the churchyard of St Andrew's, Hornchurch. His memorial stone, an obelisk surmounted by an urn, is a more elaborate version of the one to George Clark. Stratford's wife Elizabeth survived him by almost a quarter of a century, dying in 1909 at the age of 86.

THE SURGEON

Joseph Collin

The surgeon Joseph Collin, who subsequently changed careers and became vicar of Strethall in Essex, set up home with his two unmarried sisters in the neighbouring village of Elmdon. Their house was punningly nicknamed the

Colony. On 30th April 1900 he died at Elmdon at the age of 87. In his will he was generous to his servants, leaving each of them two pounds for every year or part of year they had been working for him.

THE CORONER

Charles Carne Lewis

Like Richard Mayne, Charles Carne Lewis never retired. When he died at Brentwood of a 'cerebral effusion' on 26th July 1882 aged 75 he had held the post of Coroner for South Essex for 48 years. During his final 16 years Lewis had been assisted by his eldest son, also Charles C. Lewis, who eventually succeeded him as Coroner. John W. Laskin remembered Lewis as 'Tall, thin and straight, remarkably well dressed, always wore a boxer [a tall hat, presumably very shiny] in which you could see your face, with about four inches of perfectly white pocket handkerchief hanging from his breast pocket. A man of very fine presence, quite the leading man of the town. No-one ever did anything without first consulting Coroner Lewis'.[19]

Lewis had made his will on 20th December 1880. He bequeathed to his son Charles 'my law books and the large seal I usually wear and which he has often expressed a wish to have'. Another son, Edwin, was given his watch and chain. Lewis, like Richard Mayne, did not want a grand funeral. He declared that 'I desire to be buried as inexpensively as possible at Ingatestone by the side of my late very dear wife'. However, when he was laid to rest five days after his death, the whole county turned out to mourn. The funeral procession from Brentwood through Mountnessing to Ingatestone was 'some 400 or 500 yards in length' according to the *Essex Times*. It wrote of Lewis that 'hardly any man in the county of Essex was better or more widely known, and wherever he was known he was liked and esteemed'.

'A FRIEND IN YOUTH'

Mary Ann Jones and her sampler

Among the friends made by George Clark during his all-too-brief stay in Dagenham was a young woman of his own age named Mary Ann Jones. She was brought up in Folly House, which was one of the few buildings in Green Lane, the road which connected Dagenham with Ilford. By the mid 19th-century Folly House was not the genteel residence the name might suggest. It accommodated several families. Mary Ann's father was an agricultural labourer, and for most of her life Mary Ann worked as a servant in various households. She was employed at Valentines Mansion in Ilford at the time of the 1841 census. Ten years later Mary Ann is found as a servant in the household of Charles Graves, a silk merchant of Cranbrook Road, also in Ilford. She never married. Did she perhaps regard George Clark as more than a friend?

His death must have affected Mary Ann a great deal, for later in her life she worked a cross-stitch sampler in tribute to him. Its design is in the style of the schoolroom samplers so widespread in Victorian times, and the wording is as follows:

The top reads:

M A Jones Friend in Youth Ilford

Prepare / To Meet Thy God / For We Must All Needs Die

The centre panel seems to represent the memorial obelisk in Dagenham churchyard, complete with a small urn shape on top. The words echo those on the memorial:

The Sacred Memory / Of George Clark / The Dagenham / Policeman Who Was / Barbarously Murdered Mangled / And Cruly [sic] Entreated / By Some Unknown / Person in The Above / Parish Of Essex / 29 Or 30 Of June / Aged 20 years 1846 / Seek Ye The Lord

The left hand panel:

They Hid / Him in / The Corn / Feild [sic] / Not A / Friend Was / Standing / By To Wipe / Away The / Sorrowing / Tear And / Hear His / Mournful / Cry

The right-hand panel:

The Eye / Of God / Watch / Over Him / While / Slain Upon / The Ground / Jesus / Standing / Ready To / Place On / Him The / Crown

At the bottom of each side panel are three shapes which seem to be heaps of earth around the base of the memorial.

The bottom panel (its position suggests these words are spoken by Clark from the grave):

Weep Not For Me My Dearest Friends / Which You On Earth Remain The Lord Of / All Protect You Now Until We Meet Again

Mary Ann eventually moved back to Folly House. She appeared there in the 1881 census, but by that time she did not have long to live. She died 13th September 1881 at the age of 56 after an asthma attack, and was buried at St

Mary's Church, Ilford, three days later. The death certificate gives her occupation as 'formerly a cook'. The sampler was passed down via one of her sisters and is still in the family's possession.

'A FORGOTTEN HERO'

Let us leave for a while the later lives of those involved in the Clark case, and turn to the re-appearance of the story in the *Police Review* magazine at the end of the nineteenth century. An article on murders of Metropolitan Police officers appeared in the *Review* in 1898 but made no mention of George Clark's name. It prompted a response in a subsequent issue by a writer using the pen-name 'Refero'. His article of 2nd December 1898 was headed 'A forgotten hero'. It began by lamenting the fact that Clark's death seemed to have vanished from memory: 'the crime, possibly owing to the lapse of time since its committal, in 1846, coupled with the fact of its having occurred almost at the boundary of, but just within the Metropolitan Police District, seems to have been entirely forgotten, with the exception of the area of the K Div[ision]...I feel sure that it will prove of great interest to Police Officers of the Metropolis, and I desire to bring before them the record of a brave young Constable, who so long ago, in the performance of his duty, was 'Faithful even unto death'.

He goes on to describe the murder in these terms:

> The PC was patrolling his beat at East Brook End, Dagenham, which was, and is still, a very lonely spot, when he met with three or four men who were stealing corn from a field, and although the odds were greatly against him, he arrested one of them, upon which he was overpowered, knocked down, and his brains beaten out with a garden fork...the suspected murderers, whose names I am unable to furnish, were arrested, and committed for trial at Chelmsford Assizes, but all were acquitted, owing to insufficient evidence.

It is interesting to note that 'Refero' treats it as an established fact that Clark was killed by the corn-stealers. He then gives the source of his information:

> Although 52 years have passed since that awful tragedy, an old gentleman, who actually was one of the jurymen at the Coroner's inquest, died in the village as recently as the 30th of September last; and I was assured by him some few months ago, that all the suspected murderers died by violent means, so that although they escaped the hangman's rope, stern Nemesis overtook them.

The elderly man can be identified as Edward John West, a saddler, who died aged 87 on 30th September 1898 and was buried in Dagenham parish churchyard five days later. In 1903 his descendants founded the Dagenham funeral company of West & Coe that is still in business today. Edward John's great-great-great grandson Jeremy West, the present director of the firm, describes his ancestor as 'a knowledgeable man of law, and in many cases was called upon as an overseer – a term used in those days meaning to rectify decisions made at court cases'.[20]

'DAGENHAM'S CRIME OF YEARS GONE BY'

We now move into the twentieth century. A hundred years and two world wars had passed since the death of Clark. His murder was brought back into the public consciousness by a lecture given by local historian Cyril J. Hart, which took place early in 1949 at Rectory Library in Dagenham. Although it dealt with the general history of crime in the Dagenham area, the Clark case was clearly the main topic of Hart's talk. It was reported in a local newspaper under the headline 'Policeman's battered body at Wantz Corner: Dagenham's crime of years gone by'.[21] The article declared that one of the 'biggest stories in 1846 would have been the first murder in England of a policeman, when the battered body of PC George Clark…was found in a ditch at Four Wantz'.[22]

This report indicates that over the passage of time the stories handed down locally must have led to a degree of confusion between the separate attacks on Clark in 1846 and Coleman twelve years later. We have seen that it was PC Coleman, not Clark, who was ambushed near the Four Wantz and thrown into a ditch, although by great good fortune he managed to escape with his life. Hart's belief that Clark was the first murdered police officer in England is also incorrect. According to the Metropolitan Police Book of Remembrance, two were killed in 1830 alone, only a year after the force was set up.[23] Constable Joseph Grantham was kicked in the head on 29th June attempting to arrest a drunken man at a disturbance in Somers Town, and PC John Long was later stabbed to death on challenging three suspected burglars at night in Gray's Inn Lane. Murders may also have happened in other police forces around the country.

The report of Hart's talk also gives the widely-held opinion that the first Dagenham police station was situated over a corner shop at the junction of Bull Street and Crown Street. We have seen that in fact the police took up residence in an old cottage in Bull Street, rented from a widow named Hannah Wade.

THE SUSPECTED MURDERERS

Was Edward John West correct when he asserted that the alleged gang lost their lives 'by violent means'? We have already seen that William Page died after being run over by a cart in Whitechapel in 1847, and that Ned Wood committed suicide in 1853. These dramatic events would certainly bear out the truth of his statement. But what of the others accused by Mary Ann Smith?

George Blewitt

Thomas Waters Brittain told the magistrates in 1858 that George Blewitt had remained in his employment at Eastbrookend for two or three years after Clark's murder. By the time of the 1851 census Blewitt and his family had moved the short distance northwards to Rush Green, in the neighbouring parish of Romford. George Blewitt lived another thirteen years after his failed prosecution for the murder of Clark. On 19th May 1871 he died of apoplexy at his home at the age of 73. His funeral service was held four days later at St Edward's Church in Romford, followed by burial in the parochial cemetery at Main Road. Blewitt's widow Alice survived him by ten years. Her financial circumstances were not good, judging by the number of times her name appears in the books of two Dagenham charities, the Uphill and the William Ford foundations.

Ned Willcocks, alleged by Mrs Smith to have helped plan the corn theft, was a near neighbour of the Blewitts at Rush Green. He lived to be 84, dying of bronchitis in the Romford Union Workhouse in 1888. He was buried in Crow Lane Cemetery in Romford.

George Chalk

When Edward John West declared in the 1890s that 'stern Nemesis overtook them' he must have had no idea that the final alleged murderer was still very much alive, and had done rather well in life. This was George Chalk, who had been only 16 years old when Clark was killed. We have seen that at the time of Blewitt's arrest in 1858 it was said that Chalk 'was supposed to have gone to Australia'. Enquiries were made there, but with no success. Yet the rumours were true. George Chalk was in fact living quite openly in the state of Victoria, under his real name.

The Australian gold rush of the early 1850s has already been mentioned. Chalk, then a bachelor aged 22, was one of the many adventurous individuals willing to try their luck. He raised the necessary £31 for a passage on the

1100-ton clipper ship *John Melhuish,* and set sail from the London Docks on 29th November 1852. The vessel was described as 'one of the fastest afloat, and offers a most excellent opportunity to passengers and shippers desirous of speed…and fitted throughout with every recent improvement expressly for passengers'. Chalk was booked to land at Sydney, but seems to have left the ship at Port Phillip, Melbourne, in January 1853. The following year he married 21 year-old Londoner Jane Flannery at St Peter's Church in the North-East Melbourne suburb of Collingwood. Chalk was at that time described as a baker, but when his daughter Annie Amelia was baptized in 1860 the family were living in the gold rush town of Lamplough, near Avoca, in Victoria. During late 1859 and early 1860 a township had sprung up there virtually overnight, including hotels, billiard rooms, schools and churches. As soon as the gold ran out, the miners left just as quickly for the next promising location.

George Chalk eventually became the father of ten children. He lived for another 64 years after the murder of Clark. He died aged 83 at 145 Napier Street, Melbourne on 21st August 1910. It seems that he may have suffered a fall, judging by the official cause of death, 'fractured femur and cerebral thrombosis'. Chalk's wife Jane also reached the age of 83, passing away at the Covent of the Little Sisters of the Poor in the Melbourne suburb of Northcote on 12th August 1915. The couple are both buried in Melbourne General Cemetery.

So we have seen that for some people there was a return to their former lives after the dreadful murder of George Clark. Others, however, were put on a path that led them to the other side of the world.

A modern view of the Cross Keys

Dagenham parish churchyard, autumn 1996. The memorial to George Clark is in the foreground

CHAPTER 14

'He haunts that road, you know'

John Peter Shawcross wrote in the early years of the twentieth century that 'In a few years Dagenham will lose its rural individuality, and be drawn into the relentless vortex of Greater London, and the fields, lanes, woodlands, and green swards will disappear never to return'.[1] His prophecy was to be proved right. If Clark were to stroll around the village today, he would have great difficulty recognizing it. Most of old Dagenham was razed to the ground in the 1960s and early 1970s. An archaeological survey carried out on the last row of cottages in Church Street before their demolition revealed that they were much older than originally thought.[2]

Clark would look in vain for the little Bull Street chapel where he had worshipped. A new Methodist chapel was erected on the opposite side of the road in the 1880s, and the original building became known as the Village Mission Hall. It was described by Jack West (a descendant of the Edward John West who was a juror at the Clark inquest) as 'a very simple square brick building…It continued as an independent chapel by attracting sincere and devout Christian folk…After many years they reformed themselves and started the New Free Church in Charlotte Road'.[3] After this, the old chapel was used for Spiritualist meetings, and local children nicknamed it the 'Spooks' Church'. It can be seen in early 20th-century photographs of Bull Street, but was demolished as part of the village redevelopment.

One building Clark would certainly recognize is the Cross Keys Inn, where the second and subsequent inquest hearings took place. It was completely restored in 1952, but came under threat in October 1993 when its owners Bass Taverns put it up for sale, declaring 'it no longer fits in with our portfolio of pubs'. It remained empty for some time, and when fire swept through the building in 1995 the outlook appeared grim. Fortunately, however, the deterioration was eventually halted. The 15th century building has now been renovated and is a thriving pub once more.

Just along the road from the Cross Keys is another structure that would have been familiar to Clark. This is Dagenham's Old Vicarage, inscribed with the date 1665. By the end of the 1970s the building had become so expensive to maintain that the church authorities decided to sell it to a freighting company as offices. It was intended to build another vicarage in the grounds, but this was frustrated by a planned road scheme. When Deryck Spratley took up his post as Dagenham's Vicar in 1982 he was accommodated in the vicarage of St George's Church a mile away in Rogers Road. When Graham Gittings arrived as the new vicar of St George's to find his vicarage already occupied, he was given a flat in Ibscott Close, a modern housing development near the parish churchyard. By the end of 1983 the situation had not changed, and more than five hundred people signed a petition calling for action.[4] They even took their case to the Supreme Head of the Church of England. The *Barking Advertiser* of 9th December reported that 'churchgoers are writing to the Queen in a legal wrangle that has left them without a resident vicar for the past four years'. The situation was eventually resolved with the building of a new vicarage in Church Lane for the Rev. Spratley and his family.

There is a small building adjacent to the church that Clark would also recognize if he were to pass by today. It was opened as a school by the Reverend Fanshawe in 1835 with the aid of grants from the government and the National Society, and later became the parish office. At the time of writing (2005) it is hoped to obtain a Lottery grant to restore it for use as a heritage and educational centre. Dagenham's other early school, William Ford in Church Elm Lane, was demolished in 1975 and replaced by a new building in nearby Ford Road.

The Parish Church

Another structure that would be familiar to Clark is, of course, the parish church of St Peter & St Paul. However, it too has undergone many changes since Clark's funeral service that stormy Sunday afternoon of July 1846. The interior of the church was restored in 1878 at a cost of £860. This involved lowering the nave, and there must have been great excitement when the skeleton of a man in armour and the jawbone and teeth of a horse were discovered underneath. A report in the *Essex Times* sums up the work. 'The unsightly old gallery has been removed, and a neat one substituted at the west end of the building, the chancel has been heightened…a large and handsome memorial window has been placed at the eastern end, in commemoration of the Fanshawe family'.[5] Another alteration occurred in 1921. The wooden spire on the church tower was deemed to be unsafe, and the local firm of West & Coe (who were at that time still carpenters as well as undertakers) were called in to remove it.

The Parish Churchyard

The churchyard is unexpectedly large. In spring its mass of bluebells is a delight. George Clark's grave is surrounded by other stones resounding with the names of the community amongst whom he lived for such a brief time in that summer of 1846. Some, like the Fanshawe family, squires of the parish, lie in vaults within the church itself. At the re-opening in 1878, John Fanshawe made a speech in which he said that 'His family had been resident in the parish for 300 years, and it was only natural that all their interests centred in the place which he might call their home'. Yet even the Fanshawes have now left Dagenham. Their ancestral home, Parsloes Manor, was a ruin by 1900, and was eventually demolished in 1925. In the 1960s, however, the Fanshawes generously donated the family portraits to Valence House Museum in Dagenham.[6]

At the other end of the social scale, some of those involved in the Clark case have been interred in the churchyard with no memorials to mark their resting place. One of these is the conscience-stricken (or possibly deluded) Mary Ann Smith, who denounced George Blewitt in 1858. She died in February 1882. Two others are Luke White and Thomas Archer, who were among the last to see Clark alive on the fatal night. Both men died in Romford Workhouse, and were buried at their home village in unmarked graves.[7]

George Clark's beat today

Having strolled around what is now left of Dagenham Village in the early 21st century, George Clark might decide to have a look at what changes have occurred along the roads that made up his beat. He would find much of the route unrecognizable. Walking from his police station north towards the Four Wants (incidentally, the spelling is now Wantz), Clark would soon find himself crossing a bridge which takes the road over a railway line. This line was laid down in 1854 for the London, Tilbury & Southend Railway, although trains did not stop here until 1886. The station is now known as Dagenham East.

Approaching the Wantz junction, Clark would look in vain on the right-hand side of Rainham Road South for Rose Cottage, formerly the home of his colleague Thomas Kimpton. This was demolished in 1961 to make way for a road widening scheme. The *Dagenham Post* of 15th March of that year wrote that 'The house, which withstood a delayed action bomb and rockets during the war, could not stop the hand of the planners and is now in the last stages of its long life'. It was described as a 'quaint old timbered house, originally two cottages' and had apparently been home to fifteen families since its construction in 1787. A petrol station now stands on the site.

The Four Wantz junction itself, once so lonely, is now a busy and built-up area. Its farmhouse and outbuildings – where Thomas Kimpton stopped on horseback on the fatal night to ask Thomas Archer 'Have you seen my mate?' – were demolished in the 1940s. The farmland is now occupied by an industrial estate.[8] Clark might not be altogether pleased to see a large public house named the Eastbrook on the south-east corner of the junction.

The Four Wantz junction, pictured in 2005

Taking the road north of the Four Wantz (formerly Tanyard Lane, now Rainham Road North) George Clark would see on the right-hand side a building he recognized. This is Woodlands, once known as Scrimpshires, a late 18th-century flat-roofed house of three storeys. It was purchased by Dagenham Council in 1954 and is now used as a hostel for teenage girls. The farmhouses Clark knew as he strode along Frizlands Lane have now all disappeared, to be replaced by housing. Hunters Hall Farm in Oxlow Lane, where the first inquest hearing was held in July 1846, has also been pulled down.

On going east from the Four Wantz and heading towards Eastbrookend, the first cottage that Clark might look for would be the home of Mary Ann Page. Here she had supposedly implored Clark to urge her husband to mend his ways just hours before the murder. A disused petrol station now occupies the site, which lies opposite Eastbrook Comprehensive School.

Striding further along what is now known as Dagenham Road, Clark would see once again a landscape of open fields and wide vistas. In contrast to much of the rest of Dagenham, this area still retains a rural atmosphere. It was used for gravel extraction in the 20th century and some of the resulting pits became landfill sites. Others have been turned into fishing lakes. The *Angling Times* of 31st August 1983 was full of praise for the way the Bowlers Angling Society had transformed one of these ex-gravel pits, now named Tom Thumb Lake. That same year, a proposal to put an 18-hole golf course over the land met with opposition from local environmental groups, and the plan was eventually dropped.[9] The London Wildlife Trust identified Eastbrookend as a key wildlife site, and the decision was made to develop the area as a country park. An undulating landscape was formed on what had been very flat terrain. More than 50,000 small trees were planted, and a series of interconnecting footpaths were constructed. After three years of work, the Eastbrookend Country Park was eventually opened in June 1995. Several years later, an award-winning visitor facility was built, to be called the Millennium Centre.

Eastbrookend Country Park today

Very close to the Millennium Centre stands the Farmhouse Tavern. In Clark's day this was Eastbrookend Farm, the smart new residence of Mrs Rebecca Mihill. She died in 1872, and eventually the farm passed into the hands of the Gay family. The building was extended westwards in the early 20th century by farmer W.J. Gay who had a large family of ten children. Mary Gay, his granddaughter, remembered that 'During World War II the army commandeered the billiard room (a wooden structure outside). Ten soldiers of the Royal Artillery were billeted there manning a sound detector for aircraft (the forerunner of radar) in a meadow behind the farmhouse'.[10] The Gay family left in 1945, and in November 1947 the building became a public house.

The lane on the right by the Farmhouse Tavern, called the Chase, still leads to Hooks Hall Farm, as it did in Clark's time.[11] During World War Two Alfred Garrett, a builder, moved to the farm with his wife and four sons and set up a riding centre there.[12] It is still used for this purpose today. In 1914 a cemetery was laid out just west of Hooks Hall by the local firm of undertakers West & Coe.[13] It is now run by the local authority.

Returning to Dagenham Road and walking further along his former beat, Clark would quickly note the disappearance of Eastbrookend Old Hall. According to Mrs Smith, this had been where Clark had confronted the corn-stealers. Thomas Waters Brittain had continued to live there during the remainder of his long life. He died on his 85th birthday, 25th February 1869, and was buried in the parish churchyard alongside his Waters and Brittain ancestors on 4th March. The farm was then occupied by George Edward Litchfield Currie, who was a prominent figure in local affairs, becoming the first Dagenham member of the Essex County Council.[14] Currie died in July 1896 aged 57 and was buried in Dagenham parish churchyard on 11th July. His widow Elizabeth carried on the farm. She eventually retired to Eastern Road, Romford, and died aged 90 in October 1931.

The neighbouring farm cottage occupied by George Blewitt and his family in 1846 is no longer standing. Walking further along Dagenham Road, Clark would recognize Huntings, where Mrs Sarah Stone had lived in 1846. It is now called the Bell House.[15] After the death of Mrs Stone, it was occupied by Joseph Sutton, a wealthy retired sailmaker from Bankside in Southwark. He died at Eastbrook End on 6th July 1873.[16]

In 1846 Clark would not of course have walked as far as Thorntons Farm, which lay north of Eastbrookend in the direction of Romford. Nevertheless, it is important to his story, as his body was found nearby. By the early twentieth century this Tudor farmhouse was in poor condition and was home to the Saunders family, who worked for local farmer Mr Parrish. It was

Huntings, now known as the Bell House

demolished in the 1940s, and the site is now occupied by sheltered housing for senior citizens. However, the trees seen in the 1864 watercolour by Thomas Dibdin (opposite page) still remain, and the lane which once led to the farm has become Thorntons Farm Avenue.

The cornfield where Clark was found on that July evening is now within the grounds of Barking College, founded in 1962. The actual spot where his body lay is now beneath a car park.

The Clark murder in local legend

Does Clark still walk that lonely beat 160 years on? A lady who grew up in Dagenham remembers that her father, born before the First World War, always used to say 'He haunts that road, you know'. Closer to our own time, the apparition of a broad-shouldered figure wearing a cape was reportedly seen several times during the 1970s and 1980s. The ghost is said to have walked from the direction of Eastbrookend towards the Four Wantz junction and then turned into Rainham Road North, which was once Tanyard Lane.

Right up to its demolition in the 1940s, there were stories that Thorntons Farm was haunted by the apparition of a headless man. Interestingly, this legend links with the following experience, which happened to a child in the 1960s. It occurred in Hooks Hall Drive, part of a housing development built at Eastbrookend after World War Two.

Barking College car park. This covers the site of the cornfield where Clark's body was found

Our house was near fields where farm crops like cabbages and onions were grown…the fields were sold for sand and gravel to be extracted. Large earth moving equipment was brought in and the topsoil scraped off into huge mounds…One night, I believe it was summer, I woke up out of a deep sleep and was immediately aware that something was very wrong. I opened my eyes and saw, standing just beside my bed, a tall, dark figure. To me it seemed very tall and although the room was dark I had no trouble making out the shape as it seemed to be outlined against the surrounding darkness and more black.

The figure was wearing some kind of shoulder cape, I focused on the head and shoulders as I was still thinking it was a real someone standing there, so I cannot recall if there were any other details on the clothes. As I looked I became aware of a feeling of immense evil, I don't know of any other way to describe it, and that where the head and face should be there was nothing, just a deeper blackness. I was so terrified I just shut my eyes tight and pulled the blankets over my head. I lay there until light, not daring to look again or even to move or make a sound…For some reason I told no-one about this encounter for a long time. Firstly I think I knew I would not be believed and it all put down to a bad dream while I know only too well I was wide awake. Secondly, in some part of my mind I was terrified that by talking or even thinking about what had happened, it would come back. In fact I have spent most of my life deliberately not thinking about my experience.

At the time I knew absolutely nothing about the story of George Clark or of his murder. It was many years later that I first heard the stories, but knew very few details. So I made no connection with my childhood experience until a few years ago, when I saw an article …describing how a memorial to him was going to be put up in the Fels Field, in what is now Eastbrookend Country Park. This is where the sand and gravel were extracted many years ago and the park is on the landfill site. As far as I could tell from the map with the article, the memorial was in the fields not far from our former house. If you were to ask me if I think I saw George Clark that night, I would have to say yes, definitely. If I was pressed for an explanation, I can only say that perhaps the work disturbed some memory and I was the unwitting recipient of the haunt.

I have found this really hard to write about. I cannot really describe how terrified I was at the time or how I used to huddle in bed, not daring to open my eyes in case I saw it again....I can still recall every detail, especially the total blackness where the head should have been but wasn't.

Another local legend about Clark is the belief that he was buried upright. This was reported by a curate at Dagenham Parish Church in the 1970s, and was later supported by a man who, like his father and grandfather before him, had worked as a gravedigger there. According to the legend, it was apparently a Victorian custom that a police officer should stand on duty at all times, even in death.[17]

POLICE STATIONS ASSOCIATED WITH CLARK

Arbour Square

Arbour Square, where George Clark began his police career, was remodelled in the 1920s. In 1944, a century after Clark had lived and worked there, it suffered extensive damage from a V1 flying bomb. An unflappable officer entered Adolf Hitler's name into the visitors' book, which had survived unscathed. In 1999 the station was closed. It was planned to convert the property into luxury flats, but a nasty surprise awaited the developers early in 2005. The building was taken over by about twenty squatters who then added insult to injury by hoisting a skull and crossbones in place of the Union Flag. The *Daily Mail* reported that 'the building in which the Kray twins were once held is now the scene of late-night parties' and a police source told the paper that 'It is all very embarrassing because they're probably using our old showers and cooking in the canteen'.[18]

Dagenham Police Station

As we have seen, the old cottage in Bull Street used as a police station in George Clark's day was replaced in 1851 by a purpose-built station further north along the same road (now known as Rainham Road South.) There is an early 20th-century photograph of a group of officers standing proudly outside. Dagenham was then still a small rural community, but the building of the giant Becontree Estate after World War One meant the population mushroomed to over 100,000 by the 1930s. Inevitably this had an impact on many services, including the police, and in February 1931 a local councillor named Bale told a council meeting that he thought 'the number of police in the district was utterly inadequate'.[19]

Later that decade the councillors campaigned again, this time concentrating on the woeful facilities of the building itself. It may have been state of the art in early Victorian times, but almost 90 years later its shortcomings were obvious. In 1939 the *Evening Standard* ran the eye-catching headline 'Police get lumbago by changing in cells'. The article went on: 'When a constable at Dagenham police station wants to change his clothes he goes into a cell or retires to a bicycle shed. Dagenham Council include this among complaints they are making to the Commissioner of the Metropolitan Police about the lack of facilities at the station. They say that policemen doing a spell of station duty are usually taken ill with lumbago because of the draughtiness of the building'.[20]

Cllr A.E. Gibbs also complained that if officers were called for special duty, there was often no room for them inside the station, and they overflowed into the street. The Commissioner, Sir Philip Game, was horrified that the complaints had appeared in the Press before being referred to him, and he traded words with the Dagenham councillors. The spat was reported in the *Evening News* under the headline *"War"* over a police station.[21]

It was to be another twenty years after this before the police eventually left the old building for good. Their new station was built further north along Rainham Road South. The old 1850 building was put up for auction and was purchased for £8,600 by Dagenham bookmaker Mark Lane. Back in 1946 Lane had left the army and become an illegal bookmaker, taking bets outside the Beacon pub in Oxlow Lane. He was soon able to employ a chain of 'bookies' runners', and on average had a runner in court twice every week.

The Dagenham Police Station of 1851, during its time as a betting shop

When the 1960 Betting and Gaming Act made off-track betting legal, Mark Lane's business moved from strength to strength, and eventually took over the Joe Coral group. At the time of Lane's death in 1975 his company had 600 betting shops as well as West End casinos.[22] When he bought the old police station, he joked that he had already paid for it twice over in fines.

The new Dagenham Police Station took 18 months to build and was opened in December 1961. According to the District Three staff magazine, the new building boasted improved staff areas and 'Another new idea is the Finger Print Room – a little room set aside for this purpose and fitted with a little sink for the "customers" to wash their "dabs" afterwards'. The building was extensively renovated in 2004/5. George Clark would of course have walked past the site on his way to the start of his beat at the Four Wants. New police recruits to Dagenham were as a matter of course taken to Clark's grave until well over a century after his murder,[23] but the custom now seems to have been discontinued.[24]

OTHER POLICE OFFICERS ASSOCIATED WITH DAGENHAM WHO MET UNTIMELY DEATHS

We have already seen that the attack on Constable Coleman in September 1858 is sometimes confused with the Clark case in local folklore. There are also two other murders which are occasionally mixed up with the killing of George Clark.

Inspector Thomas Simmonds, 1885

Nearly forty years after George Clark, the Dagenham force again found themselves involved in the investigation of the murder of a police officer which made headlines across the country. The dead man was Inspector Thomas Simmonds of the Essex Constabulary, who had previously been awarded the Order of Merit for 'the bravery he displayed in a midnight contest with a burglar in the London Road, Romford'.[25]

The tragic sequence of events began in the early evening of Tuesday 20th January 1885. Inspector Simmons and Constable Alfred Marden, in a horse and trap, were pursuing three men from Rainham Railway Station in the direction of Dagenham. They recognized one of the trio as David Dredge, a well-known thief. The officers caught up with them by the sewage farm at the River Beam, not far from the border between Hornchurch and Dagenham. As he lay on his deathbed Simmonds described what happened next. 'I pulled up and said 'Where are you chaps going to?' They said 'Home', and I said 'Let us look at you', and got out of the cart at the same side as they were, and when about six or eight yards off I think one of them – a tall man, six feet or so, no whiskers, little moustache, and I think fresh or sallow complexion – turned quickly round with a revolver in his hand, and fired at me, saying 'Take that!' I believe the words were. I felt a blow in the abdomen.'

Although wounded, Simmons tried to follow the gang, but they bolted across the fields towards Dagenham.[26] The stricken Inspector was taken to Dagenham police station, then to his own house, where he died four days later. He was buried on 27th January at Romford's Crow Lane Cemetery. Newspaper coverage of his funeral and the pursuit of the killers jostled for space with the fall of Khartoum and the fate of General Gordon. Local men were soon being questioned, and this is perhaps why the circumstances surrounding the murder of Inspector Simmonds have occasionally been confused with the George Clark case.

Eventually an East Londoner named James Lee was convicted of the killing of Simmonds and executed at Chelmsford on 18th May 1885. Another suspect was hanged for a different crime the following year.[27] The *Essex Times* paid tribute to Simmonds in terms that could also be applied to George Clark: 'In a word he loved his work too well. Had he been less brave and had he cared less for the interests of the public he would still have been carrying out the duties of his office'.

Constable George Gutteridge, September 1927

Dagenham also has an association with yet another brutal murder of a police officer that shocked the nation. At 3 o'clock on a September morning in 1927, 38 year-old PC George Gutteridge of the Essex force was on foot patrol in a country road in Stapleford Abbotts when a Morris Cowley car came towards him. He stopped the vehicle, and was questioning the two occupants when one of them produced a pistol and fired at the officer's face. As Gutteridge lay on the ground, he was shot through each of his eyes. The gunman must have feared a superstition that the last image the eye sees is imprinted on the retina, helping to pinpoint the killers. The car had been stolen from Dr Edmund Lovell at Billericay, and was later found abandoned in London. Two men were soon arrested, convicted of the killing and hanged the following year. George Gutteridge's wife Rose and children Muriel and Alfred eventually settled in Dagenham. During World War Two, Muriel worked as a postwoman in Dagenham, and she later lived with her husband John Alexander in Ford Road. Because of the Gutteridge family's close links with Dagenham, it is sometimes said that the murdered policeman is buried there, but in fact he was interred at Great Warley near Brentwood.

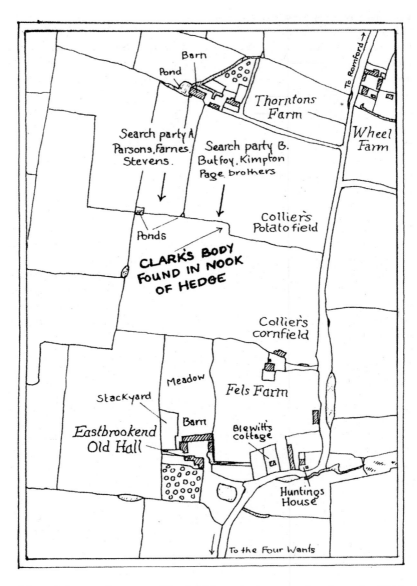

Map of the murder scene. The field boundaries are taken from the 1844 tithe map of Dagenham

CHAPTER 15

Weighing up the evidence

The unsolved murder of George Clark – a 'truly mysterious affair', as the *Times* described it back in 1846 – has become embedded in the folklore of Dagenham and the surrounding areas. The case has much in common with the legend of Jack the Ripper not very far away in London's East End. Both feature particularly brutal killings, with numerous suspects and motives, yet with no-one ever brought to justice. At this distance in time, after almost 160 years, is it possible to reach a solution in the Clark case? It's now time to take a look at the most popular theories.

Mistaken identity?

For

First of all, let's consider whether Clark was not the intended victim, but just happened to be in the wrong place at the wrong time. In the early days of the enquiry, as we have seen, this was certainly the favoured theory. Clark had only been in the area for six weeks, was just turned twenty years old, and had 'inoffensive manners'. Surely such a man could not have been targeted. After all, the attack had taken place at night, and the appearance of a police officer of the time, in the distinctive uniform and top hat, could be anyone when seen in silhouette.

Clark had taken over Abia Butfoy's beat, and when Butfoy told the first inquest hearing about the threats made to him by William Walker, it seemed an open and shut case. The *Essex Herald* reporter wrote that Butfoy gave 'such evidence as will, no doubt, lead to the apprehension of the guilty parties', and Coroner Lewis agreed. Perhaps Clark and Butfoy were approximately the same height and build. Butfoy had been a police officer since 1837, and had doubtless been threatened quite a few times through the years. Early in his career, when stationed at Arbour Square, he was viciously beaten, kicked into the gutter and only rescued from further injury by the timely arrival of a colleague.[1] Yet it seems that the incident with Walker really frightened Butfoy. Sergeant Parsons, too, had been subjected to threats from the Romford brothers James and Thomas Young, leading to their house being raided shortly after Clark's murder.

Against

Yet there are arguments against the mistaken identity theory. It was thoroughly investigated at the outset by the combined talents of the Detective Force, but the Walkers and the Youngs must have had strong alibis as they were never charged. We must remember that Amos Walker insisted on speaking out publicly at the second inquest hearing. He admitted that he and his brother William had had several run-ins with the police over stolen goods, but denied that they were capable of murder. This hardly seems the action of a guilty man.

Also, given that Butfoy and Clark may have looked superficially similar, in other respects they were poles apart. Butfoy was born and bred in Bethnal Green, while Clark was from rural Bedfordshire, so their accents would have been totally different. We know that Butfoy had been in the Dagenham force for six years, so it's likely that a man such as Walker would have encountered him many times and be able to recognize his voice. Finally, we must remember that the confrontation between Walker and Butfoy happened in Workhouse Lane, near Dagenham Village, and nowhere near Eastbrookend. It occurred in March 1846, nearly four months before the murder. Would Walker really have waited so long before getting his revenge?

Enemies from Clark's time in Stepney?

For

Clark, as we have seen, spent eleven months at the K Division headquarters in Arbour Square, Stepney, before being sent to Dagenham. Could his murder have been a revenge attack connected with his time there? Perhaps a gang came to Dagenham with the express purpose of assassinating Clark, then returned to the East End immediately afterwards and melted away into the underworld, never to be traced. It was well known that officers patrolling areas such as the Ratcliffe Highway near the docks occasionally had to face some desperately violent characters. Maybe Clark had incurred their wrath by securing arrests or convictions. Was his name put forward for the Dagenham vacancy because he faced danger by remaining in Stepney?

Against

Unfortunately no information has as yet emerged to back up this theory. The crime reports in the *Daily News* and the *Morning Chronicle* have been examined from June 1845 through to the following May, but there is no mention of Clark's name at all. It seems highly unlikely, therefore, that he was involved in any major prosecutions during his time at Arbour Square. If Clark was known to have been threatened in Stepney, this would surely have been reported to the investigating detectives, who would have pursued it. Of course this explanation for the killing cannot be completely ruled out, but it awaits concrete evidence.

Smugglers?

For

Many people at the time put the blame for the crime firmly on smugglers. Clark, it was said, had caught them in the act, tried to arrest them, and paid with his life. As we have seen, the *Times* reported soon after the killing that 'some hint very strongly the probability of the real murderers being smugglers infesting Barking and the surrounding villages, Dagenham only lying two miles from the desolate Essex bank of the Thames, and being well adapted for smuggling transactions'.[2] It is said that a community of so-called 'Marshmen' lived in remote huts near the river, making a living from gathering reeds and concealing contraband.

As we have seen in the previous chapter, Henry Chalk, although far away in Australia, echoed this theory when he asserted that Clark was killed after interrupting a gang taking smuggled tobacco from a barn. There can be no doubt that smuggling was widespread in this part of Essex at the time. People living in Dagenham Village and looking out from their upper windows could watch the sails of vessels gliding along the Thames. Craft from every corner of the world went past on their way to the great port of London. The little inlets and channels along the marshy bank would have provided ideal hiding places for barrels of brandy or packages of tobacco rowed ashore under cover of darkness from passing ships. Just west of Dagenham was Barking, the busiest fishing port in the country at that time. Barking's large fleet worked in the North Sea. Fish was not always their only cargo, though, as local historian Fred Brand described in his short story a *Barking Rose*, set in 1838:

> It might happen that, at suitable periods, a Dutch port could even be entered, or communication had with a foreign vessel at night. Then would follow the loading-up, not of cod and turbot, but of sacks filled with such merchandise as the British Government had thought fit to impose an excise duty on.[3]

The *Times* of 1st October 1812 reports a case of watermen accused of stealing a cargo of silk and ostrich feathers. The plan apparently was to take the goods ashore at Dagenham Breach. We have noticed that in 1852 the resourceful PC William Miles, treading the beat John Farnes had patrolled back in 1846, seized the huge haul of four tons of tobacco being transported across the marshes.

A great deal of money could be made by evading duty payable on tobacco. *Douglas Jerrold's Weekly Newspaper* of 8th August 1846 stated that duty charged on tobacco is 900%, and declared 'It seems a farce to talk of the ascendancy of free trade principle, when the only luxury of the labouring man is subject to so enormous a tax'. Official figures showed that over 2,600,000 lbs of tobacco were smuggled into London in 1843 alone.

Against

The chief argument against this theory comes from the pen of Commissioner Richard Mayne himself. In his note on an anonymous letter which put the blame on smugglers, he wrote that 'The enquiry as to smugglers was carefully made in the first occurrence of suspicion immediately after the murder, but no grounds whatever could be obtained to support such'.[4] It is clear that the involvement of smugglers, together with the mistaken identity theory, were the two most obvious lines of enquiry in the early days after Clark's death. The detectives carried out a thorough investigation but were unable to find any firm evidence at all to back up the cloud of speculation.

Another point that must be made is that Clark's beat was nowhere near the marshes and the river. It was his colleague John Farnes who had the unenviable job of patrolling what was known as the Lower Road, or the Gores, at the edge of the Thames.

The corn stealing gang?

For

Let's now consider Mary Ann Smith's story that Clark was murdered by the local gang of George Blewitt, George Chalk, Ned Wood and William Page, who planned to deliver stolen sacks of corn to Ralph Page at Thorntons Farm. As we have seen in the previous chapter, at least one of the jurors at the Clark inquest, Edward John West, believed in this theory. Over half a century after the crime, he told the *Police Review* journalist that 'all the suspected murderers died by violent means, so that although they escaped the hangman's rope, stern Nemesis overtook them'.[5] William Page certainly met an untimely end only a year after the murder, crushed beneath the wheels of a wagon, and it is odd that Ned Wood should have killed himself in a granary, of all places. Ralph Page reportedly left his daughter's wedding party in order to take a fatal dose of laudanum. A horror story might depict justice being done as they are lured to their deaths one by one by the ghastly apparition of their victim!

Looking back at reports in the *Times* shortly after Clark's death, we note that the murderers were thought to know the area well, having left the body 'in a nook as far away as possible from the three farms nearby'. The same newspaper also mentions more than once that a 'notorious gang' was said to exist in 'the immediate vicinity' of the murder – that is, at Eastbrookend. Admittedly, it doesn't mention William Page and Blewitt by name, but in such a sparsely-populated area it is very possible that they and their cronies are being referred to. There is also a strong but unsubstantiated rumour that one of the alleged murderers named by Mrs Smith made a deathbed confession.

Contemporary maps confirm the route Mrs Smith says was taken by the gang from Blewitt's house to the back door of the barn, bypassing the farmhouse itself. We can also see the approach Clark would have taken from the other direction, that of the main road. The very vividness of Mrs Smith's story also counts in its favour. Her description of the conversation between the Pages and George Blewitt on their way home from the Romford shopping trip is remarkably detailed, as is her account of how Page returned after the murder and burnt his clothes: 'his flannel jacket was splashed with blood round the collar where it was not covered by his smock frock'. If Mrs Smith invented all this, she must have been an excellent storyteller.

The timings given by Mrs Smith fit in with what is known of Clark's movements. He parted from Parsons at the Four Wants at about 9.20pm, meaning he would have reached her house around ten minutes later. During the chat that followed, she persuaded Clark to reprimand her husband William Page. Clark continued on his way, encountered Page and spoke to him, reached the limit of his beat at Eastbrookend, turned back and passed the Page household again just before ten o'clock, calling out 'Good night' as he did so. This ties in nicely with the sighting of Clark by Luke White in Tanyard Lane at about 10.30pm. He was now heading for Miller's Corner and his rendezvous with Isaac Hickton. Clark would have reached the spot about ten minutes later. Yet the two officers did not see each other. Why?

Hickton told the inquest he waited there for about twenty minutes but didn't see Clark. Hickton didn't mention raising the alarm at that time. He did say there was singing and noise coming from the nearby farmhouse. It was the time of the hay harvest, so perhaps Farmer Miller was ensuring his workers had plenty of food and beer after their long day in the fields. It's possible that Clark joined the revelry for a while, thus missing his appointment, but this seems highly unlikely. As we have seen, staunch Methodists such as Clark would have disapproved of alcoholic drink. Besides, given what we know of his sense of duty, he doesn't seem the type to attend a party when he ought to have been pounding his beat.

We know Clark was alive after midnight, as Thomas Archer saw him around that time at the Four Wants. Hickton stated that he reached the meeting-point at Miller's Corner at 11.15pm, so the most likely reason for him not meeting Clark is also the simplest. Clark probably reached the spot about half an hour before Hickton, waited for some time and then decided to carry on with his beat as he had a schedule to stick to. There was no report to pass on, so maybe it wasn't regarded as an important meeting.

When Archer saw Clark pass by Wants Farm just after midnight, the officer was heading 'straight to Mr Brittain's'. This was the third time that night that Clark had tramped this portion of his beat. He was due to return to the Wants by 1am for his rendezvous with Parsons, when he would collect the report and pass it on to Hickton at their next meeting. Mrs Smith says the gang left Blewitt's house just after midnight to walk the short distance to Brittain's barn. As they did so, Clark could have been striding from the Four Wants, past Page's cottage, and towards the fatal confrontation.

Clark would have reached Brittain's at about twenty minutes past midnight. Either it was his normal practice to check out the barn, or he noticed something that aroused his suspicions. He walked the 200 yards from the farm gate, then round the side of the barn only to come face to face with Mary Ann Page standing guard at the corner. Perhaps the thieves had a horse and cart ready to transport their booty to Thorntons Farm. Instead, it bore a live cargo. Clark had been battered unconscious by the loaded stick, and pitchfork, and appeared to be dead. He was tipped out of the cart into the cornfield and fell on to his back on the ground. He may have regained consciousness and reached out to try to get up, only to grab some corn in his right hand. One of the attackers had a double-edged knife. Could this have been 16 year-old George Chalk? Chalk was an orphan who had been brought up by his guardian Thomas Bell, a butcher. He would have been well skilled in using such a knife to slaughter animals. William Page told his wife that Chalk ground Clark's skull with the heel of his boot. This would account for the gaping hole that astonished the surgeon Charles Butler, who noted that there was 'not a particle of brain left in it'. Shards of the victim's skull were left embedded in the ground. The medical evidence left no doubt that Clark must have been lying on his back when his throat was cut. This explains the lack of blood on the front of his shirt. John Farnes had also reported that 'The blood was in one place, just where the head was lying'.

This entire explanation was in fact offered by the *Morning Chronicle* just three days after the body was discovered. It had asked: 'how is it that he was found in a spot so remote from the beaten track? This can only be accounted for on the supposition that he was first rendered insensible by a heavy blow, inflicted whilst on his beat, and afterwards removed to the spot where the murder was completed – a suspicion which would involve the participation of more than one party'.[6] As we know, Clark was due to meet Parsons at the Four Wants at 1pm and 3pm. When Parsons claimed he had seen Clark as usual at 1o'clock, Clark was in fact already dead. By trying to cover up his own absence from duty that night, Parsons unwittingly sabotaged the investigation by leading the detectives to believe Clark was killed later than was actually the case.

We have seen that in his summing-up, the coroner emphasised that the vicious injuries inflicted upon Clark surely pointed to revenge as the prime motive. The personal hatred William Page – clearly a volatile man – bore for Clark might account for the ferocity of the attack. We are told that Page was overpowered by Clark and had to call out for help. This may have affected his male ego and increased his hatred for Clark. By urging Clark to warn her husband about his behaviour, Mary Ann herself set off the chain of circumstances that would lead to the policeman's death. She admitted in 1858 that she may have covered up for Page by providing him with an alibi at the time, which indicates that he was subjected to questioning, either as part of a general house-to-house survey of the Eastbrookend area or perhaps because he was seen as a possible suspect.

Although the journalists and lawyers poured scorn on Mrs Smith's claims to have seen her husband's ghost, and to have felt the Devil tapping her chair, these would have been accepted without question by many of the inhabitants of the parish. Many country folk at the time were very superstitious. In the same summer as Clark was murdered, a policeman was dismissed from the Birmingham force because he refused to go down a lane which was on his beat, where he had seen his uncle's ghost.[7] The memories of Nellie Reader, who grew up at Beacontree Heath in the early years of the 20th century, contain several references to the supernatural.[8] She said it was well known that two women living on the Heath were witches, and recounted that a friend of her father met the Devil one day at Purfleet, a Thames-side town not far from Dagenham. Nellie and other Dagenham folk were also convinced that a long-dead member of the Fanshawe family haunted the lane leading to Parsloes Manor.

The *Essex Herald* reports that in September 1858, just two months after Blewitt's prosecution, a 75 year-old woman named Mrs Mole of the Essex village of East Thorpe was denounced as a witch by her neighbours the Brazier family. Apparently she had bewitched their pig into climbing a cherry tree and helping itself to fruit from the top boughs. A 200-strong crowd gathered near her cottage, eagerly awaiting the arrival of a witch doctor from Hadleigh. Unfortunately, what happened next is not recorded.

Even sophisticated Londoners were convinced that supernatural forces were at work. In September 1858 Sarah McDonald, aged 32, of Bethnal Green, was brought before the magistrates at Worship Street charged with obtaining the sum of 14s 6d (72^1/$_2$p) under the pretext of practising witchcraft. Mary Anne Gable, wife of a Stepney coppersmith, explained that she had believed she was cursed, and she and her daughter decided to seek Mrs McDonald's help. The prosecuting counsel, Mr D'Eyncourt, asked a local PC named Horton 'Are there many persons who believe in this woman's power?' The answer was 'A great number'.[9]

It was not just the uneducated classes who believed in the paranormal. The spiritualism movement was introduced to England from America in the early 1850s, and in 1851 the Ghost Club was formed by Cambridge University undergraduates. Ronald Pearsall writes that 'spirit circles were an amusing way to spend the long winter evenings'. He also says that 'Table-turning was a parlour amusement for Queen Victoria and Prince Albert.'[10]

Let's now turn to the renowned Jonathan Whicher, the 'Prince of Detectives'. He was, as we have seen, convinced of the truth of Mrs Smith's story, and his thinking, as far as we know, was firmly based on rational deduction rather than the supernatural. In 1858 he had been a police officer for over twenty years. Whicher is described in the *Official Encyclopaedia of Scotland Yard,* by Martin Fido and Keith Skinner, as 'a man who never made a blunder…his deliberate contemplative manner seems to have impressed most acquaintances as a mark of shrewdness and caution'. Whicher's method of working is summed up as 'painstaking investigation, repeatedly interviewing possible witnesses and carefully noting all possible evidence. If his manner was slow and deliberative, this reflects his true ability as the first great Metropolitan detective whose genius was, indeed, more perspiration than inspiration'.[11]

Unfortunately no notes have survived to give us an insight into Jonathan Whicher's approach to the Clark case. We are told that Mrs Smith's evidence served to confirm some of the initial suspicions he had had back in 1846, and that he personally marched into Mr Seabrook's field to arrest George Blewitt in 1858. Whicher went on to tell the Ilford magistrates that he was certain of being able to produce a raft of witnesses in time for the Grand Jury hearing at the Essex Assizes. Presumably Whicher and Sergeant Stratford had questioned local people and found some who initially backed up Mrs Smith's story. If these witnesses had come forward at the Assizes, the case against Blewitt might have held up. Did they pull out at the last moment through fear? Had they been threatened or blackmailed?

We are told that Jonathan Whicher had suspected one of the men named by Mrs Smith when he worked on the case back in 1846. It seems likely that this person was Ralph Page. The police were certainly very interested in him. We have John Bearblock's letter to Superintendent Pearce, with the cryptic postscript 'Ralph Page died on Wednesday last under great suspicion of death by laudanum'. Superintendent Marquard attended the inquest on Page, and reported that 'the deceased had made no allusion to the murder of PC Clark'.

After Ralph Page's death, much was made by his defenders of the fact that he was left permanently disabled and in continuous pain after a fall. He was, however, fit enough to take part in the election brawl at Romford a few days before his decease. Yet this might all be irrelevant, as Mrs Smith does not accuse Page of direct involvement in the killing of Clark. According to her, he was waiting in his barn at Thorntons Farm to receive the stolen sacks of corn. Ralph Page was not a poor man. On his death he left £600. If he was worried, as he claimed, about the possibility of his corn being stolen, it is odd that he didn't pay a night-watchman a shilling or so to keep guard throughout the night. We know that Thomas Hunnikin performed this office for Samuel Seabrook not far away at Sermons Farm. If Page was indeed a permanent invalid, then surely he would have been far better off in his own bed than sleeping on sacks of wheat in a draughty barn.

Looking at the statements made by Ralph and Elizabeth Page at the inquest, it seems that they were intent on turning attention away from themselves and towards the police. One example of this is Ralph Page reporting his conversations with Kimpton and Parsons two days before the body was found. Kimpton had apparently said 'I think he will be found in one of the cornfields', but that same afternoon Parsons told Page the Eastbrookend cornfields had been searched. This all must have seemed highly suspicious, bearing in mind that Clark was lying dead not very far away. Also, we must not forget that Mrs Page was reportedly up in her kitchen all night. Perhaps her role was to provide food and drink for the conspirators?

Against

Mrs Smith's evidence was never positively *disproved*, but there was no corroboration of her story at the time, or hard evidence to back it up. No newspaper report exists of corn stolen that night from Eastbrookend Old Hall or anything out of the ordinary there. An absolute silence existed at night then, unlike today's constant hum of traffic. A fight outside the barn must have caused a lot of noise, with weapons clashing and men shouting. Thomas Waters Brittain himself was at home, having arrived back from London at 9pm. Neither he nor his household appear to have heard anything.

If they had, he would surely have mentioned it at the prosecution of Blewitt.

We have noted that Ralph Page left the tidy sum of £600, so he had no financial motive for being involved in the theft of his neighbour's corn. Page's farm was certainly not failing. He was closely related to the Ford and Stone families, both well known for their philanthropy in Dagenham. Certainly Thomas Waters Brittain made a spirited defence of Page in his letter to the *Chelmsford Chronicle* in 1847, describing him as 'a respectable farmer and neighbour', while the Romford chemist James Macarthy stressed Page's 'harmless and kindly disposition'.

Also, the juror Edward John West's statement that 'all the suspected murderers died by violent means', obviously does not apply to George Blewitt, who died in his own bed aged 73 after suffering a stroke. West was not to know that George Chalk, far away in Australia, would live on into the twentieth century.

Another important argument against Mrs Smith's story is that it was generally assumed that Clark had encountered the killers at the spot where he was found. There were reportedly signs of 'a desperate struggle', and John Farnes told the inquest that 'The corn in the fields was very much trodden down just in the place where the body was'. Mrs Smith did not claim to be an eyewitness to the murder itself, having left the scene while the men were fighting outside Brittain's barn. According to the newspapers, (but not, incidentally, confirmed in the original depositions), Mrs Smith alleged that her husband told her that the gang 'knocked Clark down and murdered him' and then 'carried him away to the spot where he was found'. Many have found it difficult to reconcile this statement with the evidence of an apparent fight to the death in the cornfield itself, and of course the medical opinion was certain that the fatal neck wounds were inflicted on Clark at the spot where he was found.

Earlier in this chapter, we noted that there was no evidence of Clark being involved in any prosecutions during his time in Stepney that could have led to him being targeted in a revenge attack. Similarly, during his short time at Dagenham he is not recorded as thwarting any crimes. This makes it harder to justify anyone having a grudge against him.

Let us now turn to the chief witness, Mary Ann Smith. What do we know of her background? At her marriage in 1848 to Francis Smith at Dagenham parish church, she stated that her father was a labourer named Henry Roach, but her baptism has not yet been traced. Mary Ann married her first husband, John Brown, on 28th January 1827 at Shenfield in Essex. A licence was issued the previous day, and reveals that the bride was a minor and that she married with the consent of guardians. It states that she was illegitimate and that both her mother and her reputed father were still alive [12]. The newlywed couple's daughter Mary Ann Brown was baptized at the same church just over four months later. Mary Ann next appears in the records as marrying William Page on 21st August 1836 at Havering-atte-Bower. She is described as Mary Ann Brown, 'Spinster'. So what has happened to John Brown in the meantime? His death and burial have not been traced. Was Mary Ann a widow, or a bigamist, or was her marriage to John Brown found to be invalid? [13] If so, why did she keep the name Brown at all?

It is more important to examine how she appeared to people at the time. Did she seem reliable? The disparaging way she is described in the newspapers, as causing 'some amusement' in the courtroom – uneducated, rather deaf, fond of making interruptions, and of course firmly believing in ghostly fire engines and tapping devils – would seem to indicate that she was not taken totally seriously. Mrs Smith described seeing her husband's apparition 'when I was awake and getting up'. This is in fact a well-known medical phenomenon. Some people's dreams continue for a while after they have woken up. [14] They see figures in the room with them, which seem solid and absolutely real.

We must also bear in mind the attention-seeker Elizabeth Dodd, who sent the detectives off on a wild goose chase with her story about seeing the man with a large knife on the night of Clark's murder. Perhaps she and Mrs Smith had a lot in common. Also, Mrs Smith herself admitted in court that some of her neighbours spoke out against her, calling her 'a bad woman'.

Was it Clark's fellow officers as a group?

For

This theory has always had its supporters in the Dagenham area. Bill Potter, for example, who as a boy early in the 20th century worked as a bird-scarer in the fields at Eastbrookend, was certain that 'his mates did him in'. [15] In the 1960s the *Essex Countryside* magazine printed a selection of essays on the Clark case written by 15 year-olds from a Basildon school. Without exception, they put the blame on the Dagenham police. [16] It appeals to human nature to see those in power humbled and shown to have feet of clay. The Dagenham officers were known to have lied about certain things, so people have felt justified in wondering what more they had to hide.

It must be said that Clark did possess characteristics which would have made it difficult for him to fit into the group. First and foremost was his attitude towards religion. He was a devoted worshipper at the Ebenezer Chapel and enthusiastic tract distributor, even when on police duty. The coroner, Charles

Carne Lewis, was quick to pick up on this, asking Jonas Stevens whether Clark was on good terms with his colleagues, and whether they ever quarrelled with him about his religion. According to Mrs Smith, Clark didn't hesitate to preach to William Page, warning him he was jeopardizing his immortal soul. If he could do this to Page, then did he subject his fellow-officers to similar lectures? As we know, the teachings of Methodism were fiercely anti-alcohol, yet there seems to have been a culture of heavy drinking within the Dagenham force. The pub crawl indulged in by Parsons and Butfoy just hours before Clark's murder was surely not an isolated incident. The Police Orders show that Rowan and Mayne dismissed huge numbers of officers for drunkenness, so the situation at Dagenham was not untypical.

Clark's previous experience of police life had been at the headquarters of K Division at Arbour Square. In any organization, you would expect a central office to be run along much more rigid lines than far-flung outposts. The senior management are able to keep a close eye on what is going on and ensure that the rule-book is followed. Clark may have found that at Dagenham they made their own rules, and not liked what he saw. Inspector William Richardson, who was in overall charge of the Ilford Division which included Dagenham, was a veteran of the Bow Street Horse Patrol which had been absorbed into the Metropolitan Police in 1836.[17] Dagenham's first sergeant, Samuel Tebenham, was another. It is easy to imagine them galloping along, armed with pistols, left largely to their own devices in the battle against highwaymen. They may have found it difficult to enforce the new, bureaucratic regime of Rowan and Mayne, with its emphasis on matters such as making sure orange peel was moved into the gutter in case people slipped on it.

Against

First of all, police involvement in the murder was specifically rejected at the trial of Parsons in March 1848. The chief prosecutor said that 'there did not appear reason to suppose, although there might have been rumours, that the police of Dagenham were in any degree participating by knowledge, act, or deed, with the fate of the unfortunate man'. We know that when Jonas Stevens first saw the body he cried 'Oh, God', and fainted away, and was still shocked and ill later that evening at Mrs Page's. A killer who reacted like this would deserve an Oscar.

Let's now look at the practicalities. In order to murder Clark the police would have had to get together from their various beats and somehow decoy him into the cornfield. At the same time, they would have stuck to their normal routine as far as they were able throughout the fatal night, ensuring that they were seen by many people in the right place at the right time. It has to be said that if they did combine to commit the murder, they made a very poor job of covering their tracks, and an absolute mess of the inquest.

Also, the murderers would have been covered in blood. A police officer only had one uniform, which was worn even when off duty, and it would have been almost impossible for them to have committed the murder and cleaned themselves up in time for the following day, especially if they were wearing the (optional) summer uniform of white trousers. They would have had to don plain clothes before committing the murder and then somehow get rid of them. No witness in Dagenham came forward to say they saw two or more policemen together that night.

Did Clark's religion really make him exceptional? The Police Orders show that Richard Mayne insisted on Bibles being provided at police stations, and in some forces church attendance was compulsory. PC George Bakewell of the Birmingham police wrote that officers had to march to church with a Bible under the arm, and remembered that 'This exhibition frequently caused a considerable extent of merriment to the idlers and drunkards of the area'.[18] The 1851 religious census shows that Dagenham had a high number of churchgoers of various denominations. It was an opportunity to meet people socially, to mingle before and after the service and catch up with the local gossip. Years later, Clark's colleague John Farnes was to cross the Atlantic and join the Mormon trail to Utah, only to die on the journey. This is evidence that later in life at least, Farnes may have developed strong religious convictions. The other Dagenham policemen may not have had Clark's zeal, but they were not necessarily anti-religious.

Clark has been represented time and time again as standing alone outside the established group of Dagenham police officers. However, he was not the only new boy in Dagenham. He, Hickton and Stevens were drafted in together. Clark is also portrayed as naïve, new to the force, an innocent Bible-bashing boy way out of his depth. In fact, he had had a year's experience of police work in Stepney in the East End, and must have come up against some very demanding and risky situations. Clark would have learned to deal with a range of different types of people. The rookie of the Dagenham force in June 1846 was in fact Jonas Stevens, whose short police career was only just beginning.

Was Sergeant Parsons the killer?

For

There was certainly widespread suspicion of Parsons at the time. As early as 19th July 1846 the *Weekly Dispatch* pointed the finger, writing that 'The suspected party is no other than a member of the police!' We have Henry

Clements' sworn statement that in the Red Lion at Romford Parsons said to himself 'Poor fellow, I wish I had not done it now'. And what about the sergeant's behaviour during the quarrel with his sister Julia at the police station two months after the murder?

She is alleged to have shouted 'You know you are guilty of it', to which his response was to call her a 'bloody bitch'. Under questioning, Julia had always done her best to protect Parsons, so his attitude appears unreasonable to say the least.

As we have seen in Chapter 8, the report of the death of Ralph Page in the *Chelmsford Chronicle* of 3rd September 1847 describes Parsons as having been the prime suspect up until that point: 'In the opinion of many, the sergeant, who still remains in Ilford Gaol, unable to procure bail, has been relieved of much of the suspicion against him'.

We know from Abia Butfoy's evidence that older officers were told to keep certain things from the 'young hands' who had recently joined the force. The Dagenham contingent was certainly under a cloud at the time of Clark's arrival. The shocking sight of the drunken constables Hayes, Oliver and Greaves rampaging through the village waving their cutlasses at all and sundry had occurred just a matter of days before. Did Parsons perhaps think Clark was an Establishment spy? In the *Official encyclopaedia of Scotland Yard*, Martin Fido and Keith Skinner write that 'it was suspected that some Dagenham officers were accepting bribes to cast a blind eye to smuggling. Clark was sent to the station as an incorruptible young officer'.[19]

Another long-standing theory centres on George Clark's supposed close relationship with Maria Parsons. 'Was it the sergeant's wife?' screams the headline of an article by an Inspector Forrest in the Metropolitan Police magazine *District Three*.[20] Clark and Maria had lived under the same roof for six weeks, and the 24 year-old Mrs Parsons was certainly closer in age to Clark than to her husband.

Clark seems to have been cheerful, friendly and sympathetic, and Maria may have found him good company. Was Parsons, on the other hand, difficult to live with? As we have seen, after emigrating to Canada with his second wife Annie, he was regularly brought up before the police court accused of beating her.[21] We have seen that at the Clark inquest, Julia Parsons described how she and Maria met Clark and Parsons shortly after 9pm on the night of the murder. Mrs Parsons seemed to be sharing a joke with Clark, and his action of pretending to lift her up onto the horse has been interpreted as very daring indeed, and a sure sign that something was going on between them.

Against

In defence of William Parsons, it must be said that he was clearly in a fragile mental state at the time of the reported quarrel with Julia. He was crying, and seems to have been close to a complete breakdown. Consider the circumstances: his sick wife Maria had been taken away to her parents' home at Barkingside by this time, and in all likelihood he never saw her again. He was also under 24-hour surveillance, which must be difficult to bear. As for Henry Clements' statement (uncorroborated, it must be remembered) about what he overheard Parsons say in the Red Lion, it could easily be interpreted as merely regretting he did not go on duty that night. Perhaps Parsons was musing on the possibility that he could have captured the killers, or maybe even saved Clark's life, if he had been nearby and on horseback.

A modern reader might well ask why Parsons went to such lengths to pretend he was on duty. Why didn't he just call in sick and be done with it? The whole sorry saga might then all have been avoided. However, it must be remembered that automatic sick pay is a relatively modern phenomenon. In the early days of the police, if an officer missed duty because of illness his pay was reduced or even stopped altogether, although if he had been injured on duty special provision might be made.[22]

Could Clark really have had an affair with Maria Parsons, causing her husband to murder him in a frenzy of jealousy? It is an intriguing and even appealing theory, but there is a lack of solid evidence to support it. The incident with the horse on the evening of Clark's murder may well have been blown up out of all proportion. Maria Parsons had not long given birth to her daughter. She had been below par ever since, and complained of feeling very tired on the evening of the murder. Three months later she would be dead, struck down by typhus. In fact, Clark's light-hearted joking with Maria in the presence of her husband would serve to indicate that the relationship between Clark and Parsons was a good one. A constable would hardly indulge in such banter if he was on bad terms with his sergeant.

If Clark was indeed an Establishment spy, then it has to be said that the Commissioners, Rowan and Mayne, would have been immediately suspicious of Parsons after the murder. Yet as it happened, attention turned to the police only when they were suspected of lying at the inquest. And why would Clark have been such a threat to Parsons that he needed to be killed? Surely not because he was about to report the culture of heavy drinking at Dagenham, which must have been very old news indeed. The reason had to be something far more serious. The question of possible collusion between the police and local criminals will be considered below. In any case, Clark seems an unlikely choice of informant. A spy would surely have been expected to blend in with the group. He would go to the pub with them, pay attention to what they were saying, and hope that after a few drinks they might incriminate themselves. Yet George Clark can hardly be described as 'one of the boys'.

If Parsons really wanted to put Clark away for good, then there were opportunities to do the job more efficiently. Parsons could, for example, have given Clark the Thames-side marsh beat in place of John Farnes, had him ambushed and thrown into the water, and then put the blame on smugglers. Clark was living alongside Parsons at the station, so the sergeant could even have slipped some poison into his food. The Wants stream which went through Dagenham was notoriously unsanitary, and villagers were at risk of intestinal infections even during a cholera-free summer such as 1846. The death certificate of the eight-month old child, Mary Ann Hawkins, who was buried the same day as Clark, shows that she died of dehydration after an attack of diarrhoea. If Clark had expired after a stomach upset, it's possible that it would not have been seen as even remotely suspicious.

Did the police connive with the murderers?

It was certainly believed by many people that the police were involved in some way even if they did not carry out the murder themselves. This is confirmed by the *Times,* which in November 1846 reported that 'the police, who, by the false statements which they made when before the coroner, led to a supposition that they were either directly *or indirectly* implicated in the murder...'[23] We have noted the anonymous letter-writer who claimed that Clark was killed by smugglers, who carried on their trade 'with the connivance of the Police.' Clark had refused to co-operate with this, and 'it was considered by all parties the best plan to put him out of the way.' The smugglers carried out the murder, to which 'the Police were well privy.'

It certainly has to be said that there were very few arrests and convictions for smuggling in Dagenham at that time, although it must have been widespread. As we have seen, the *Official encyclopaedia of Scotland Yard* mentions the suspicion that the Dagenham police were bribed to turn a blind eye. Perhaps they went one step further, and were actively involved. Clark may have been shocked to see smuggled or stolen goods circulated among the officers. He could have been silenced after threatening to reveal what was going on, the police distancing themselves from the murder by getting others to do the job. The local villains may even have called the tune by having some kind of deep-rooted hold over the police. Yet all this must remain pure speculation until concrete evidence is found.

Was Abia Butfoy the prime mover?

As we know, Butfoy was Clark's predecessor on the Eastbrookend beat. Newspapers described him as a 'vigilant officer', but was this really so? Local people told the *Times* reporter that a 'notorious gang' operated in the immediate area of the murder. Yet a search of the Petty Sessions newspaper reports, plus Essex Quarter Sessions records, have failed to turn up a single arrest or prosecution of any Eastbrookend resident, whether it happened to be George Blewitt, William Page, or any of their neighbours. Abia Butfoy had five children to support in 1846, on his constable's wage of only a guinea a week (£1.05), and was very fond of his beer. If Dagenham policemen were indeed being bribed, he is a very likely candidate. It does not take a great leap of the imagination to see Butfoy in the pay of this 'notorious gang' of thieves (or, indeed, smugglers) operating on his beat.

Butfoy was, of course, the first of the Dagenham officers to admit having lied at the Clark inquest. He travelled to Scotland Yard on 15th August to reveal the truth to the Commissioners in person, then stood up at the next hearing to make a clean breast of things to the world. Butfoy portrayed himself then as a rather comical figure, staggering out of the Rose and Crown after the pub crawl on the afternoon of the murder. Parsons, he claimed, saw he was drunk and told him to go home, sleep it off and not to worry about going on duty. Thus Butfoy was able to declare that he was in his own bed, dead to the world in an alcoholic stupor, when Clark was killed. A very effective alibi, especially as the only person in a position to know the truth was Elizabeth Butfoy, and wives were not called to testify against their husbands.

This version of events was denied by Parsons, which is no great surprise. As we have seen, Parsons' tactic was simply to deny everything. Yet Thomas Kimpton also stood up and declared that what Butfoy was saying wasn't true. He, Kimpton, had seen Butfoy with his own eyes at the police station at midnight. Butfoy had approached from the direction of his own house, which was only a few doors away, then called out 'All right, Sergeant' to let Parsons know he was going off duty. Kimpton, like Butfoy, had begun his evidence by announcing there would be no more lies: 'I have nothing further to say than to tell the truth.' Would he then immediately perjure himself again over the relatively trivial matter of whether his colleague had been on duty? Kimpton was in deep trouble, his reputation ruined because he had repeatedly covered up for Parsons. He must have known he would face criminal proceedings at some point. Butfoy, on the other hand, may have profited from the halo effect of being the first to reveal all to the authorities. The pair publicly clashed, and we must consider which one to believe.

If Butfoy did invent the whole story, then he clearly had something to hide.

At the same hearing, on 20th August 1846, Butfoy seemed to want to take control and actively interfere with the proceedings. When Isaac Hickton was taking the oath, Butfoy claimed that he was only pretending to kiss the Bible, and the ritual had to be repeated *three* times. Butfoy was at this point clearly trying to discredit Hickton too.

It's also interesting to note that Butfoy was the least affected by the horror of the murder scene. When Thomas Kimpton hung back from approaching the corpse, Butfoy mocked him by calling him 'a pretty cow-hearted sort of policeman'. Was this because the discovery was no surprise to Butfoy? If he had been honest, he would have warned Clark about the 'notorious gang' on the Eastbrookend beat. Was he perhaps in their pay? Perhaps Butfoy was growing worried about Clark getting close to the truth about what had been going on. Mrs Smith does not mention any police involvement. Were there layers she did not know?

The Coroner clearly had his doubts about Butfoy. In his closing speech before the jury retired to consider their verdict, he reminded them to think carefully about Butfoy's version of events. Could Butfoy, he asked, prove that he had not been on duty that night? The jury, of course, then returned a verdict which did not name the potential murderer or murderers, and Butfoy later escaped being tried for perjury. Yet we have seen in Chapter 10 that when Butfoy was admitted to the lunatic asylum at Colney Hatch, a medical officer wrote: 'He is suspected and reported to have been engaged in the murder of a Policeman some three years since in Essex, since which time his mind has been more or less affected. He was put on trial for the crime, but for want of evidence, acquitted.' This could merely be seen as an example of the way rumours can distort the truth. Yet Butfoy's behaviour in the asylum shows he was obsessed with Clark's death: '...talks incoherently, generally in his soliloquies bringing in the expression Murder...during the night he is frequently restless – Starting in his sleep, crying "Murder, Murder"'.[24] Was Butfoy, like Lady Macbeth in her sleepwalking scene, plagued by a guilty conscience? Or, on the other hand, must he be seen as yet another victim of this whole tragic sequence of events?

Was it a crime of passion?

The theory that Clark had an affair with Maria Parsons and was murdered by her husband in a jealous rage has been considered above. Yet did Clark have other romantic entanglements that could have provoked the killing? In the early weeks of the inquiry, as we have seen, attention was focused on a woman named Susan Perry, whom Clark had met at Arbour Square, where she worked as a domestic. Clark and Susan had been seen together several times in Dagenham during the short time he was stationed there. Susan was separated from her husband James Perry, and detectives were told that he was seen leaving a pub on Beacontree Heath with three companions on the night of Clark's murder. There is no record of James Perry living in Dagenham at the time, so what was he doing there? The Heath is, of course, not far at all from Clark's beat.

One of the saddest aspects of the whole case is that Clark was only a few days away from being married to Elizabeth How. The detectives lost no time in travelling up to Eversholt to interview the bereaved fiancée. Did she, they wondered, have another admirer who would stop at nothing to prevent the wedding? They may have also covertly checked out Elizabeth's own movements over the previous weeks. Such speculations, however, did not bear fruit. The manhunt for James Perry ended when he was tracked down to a Kent cement works. He was subjected to lengthy questioning by at least two detectives, but must have had a cast-iron alibi as he was not detained. Apparently Clark was not involved in the break-up of the Perrys' marriage, a man named James Everett being responsible.

We must admit that there is certainly plenty of evidence of Clark having several friendships with young ladies. There was Mary Ann Jones, for example, the 'friend in youth' who stitched the memorial sampler. In 1858, Mrs Smith was to say in her deposition that William Page actually pitied an unnamed young lady who was very upset about Clark's death: 'It is that poor girl I am thinking about...' Mrs Smith also described her husband as 'so jealous', and was frightened that he would see Clark talking to her. Yet the overriding impression of George Clark is of someone who did his best to live according to the tenets of his religion. He would have had to be a monstrous hypocrite to be able to hand out Methodist tracts every day, while all the time thinking nothing of breaking the Commandments himself. His friendships were surely just that, nothing more. Clark grew up with two sisters, had no brothers, was used to female company, and had the knack of being popular with the opposite sex – but there is absolutely no evidence of a Fatal Attraction-type affair.

What else has been put forward?

Two other local rumours are worth mentioning. One is that Clark was tipped off about an illegal gambling session to be held in a ditch near the Four Wants. He turned up unexpectedly to arrest the participants, and paid with his life. A mixture of local men and outsiders were involved. This story was handed down by the family of Elijah and Sophia Reader, who took over the Merry Fiddlers beerhouse at Beacontree Heath in the late 1850s. The Readers would have been privy to much local gossip, so the theory cannot be discounted out of hand. However, let's consider the circumstances of the attack on PC Coleman in 1858. He was close to the Four Wants when he was beaten and left for dead by a gang who leapt from a ditch. This seems to fit in much better with the gambling den story. After all, the Readers arrived in Dagenham at about the right time, the late 1850s, whereas the attack on Clark had occurred twelve years before.

There were gypsy settlements on the open land at Beacontree Heath (known as 'Nanny Goat Common') and Chadwell Heath. Nelly Reader remembered the gypsies regularly brawling in Green Lane. Rumours arose that a gang of gypsies murdered Clark, yet there has never been any solid evidence to back up this theory. Perhaps it is just an example of human nature's common tendency to put the blame on outsiders.

So, are we any closer to solving the crime?

Conclusion: 'Faithful even unto death'

In this book we have tried to look at the George Clark murder case as logically and dispassionately as possible, using all the surviving original sources. We embarked upon our research without preconceived ideas, not setting out to advance any particular solution. The unsolved killing of George Clark has many echoes of the Jack the Ripper murders, with many theories and suspects being put forward over the years. In May 2005 the Internet bookseller Amazon offered an astonishing 240 titles on the Ripper killings.

In 1846, when Clark met his end, the science of detection had hardly moved on since the days of Brother Cadfael, the medieval detective in the novels of Ellis Peters. The crime scene at Eastbrookend was doubtless full of clues that could not be interpreted at the time. The Metropolitan Police Fingerprint Bureau was not set up until 1901. The Forensic Science Laboratory followed in the 1930s, and DNA profiling was developed in the mid-1980s. George Clark's body itself, the truncheon, his hat thrown into the cornfield, the cutlass stuck into the hedge right up to the hilt – all these would carry some trace of the murderers, such as blood, hair, or fibres of clothing. There is a high probability that had the crime taken place today, Clark's killers would not have escaped justice.

Unfortunately, there is no clinching evidence that would solve the case beyond doubt. Weighing up the balance of probabilities, as outlined in the previous chapter, we feel the most plausible solution is the one put forward by Mary Ann Smith in 1858, when she accused her husband William Page and his fellow corn-stealers. Yet PC Abia Butfoy's behaviour certainly raises suspicions, and his involvement cannot be entirely discounted.

New evidence may yet emerge to provide a conclusive answer to the mystery. Clark's cutlass, truncheon and blood-soaked stock were still in existence in 1858 when Blewitt was charged. The Metropolitan Police Crime Museum (popularly known as the Black Museum) was founded in the mid-1870s using items collected over previous years. Perhaps the Clark artefacts may yet be discovered in storage there, ready to be subjected to modern forensic examination. Other possibilities include the emergence of a diary, letters or a signed confession. Perhaps a notebook of Inspector Jonathan Whicher giving his views and observations on the case will be discovered. Yet the mystery is part and parcel of the attraction of the story – as with Jack the Ripper, some devotees prefer the crime to remain unsolved.

The newly-planted Clark memorial tree in 1996

The presentation by Commander Kendrick

As the 150th anniversary of the murder approached, Barking and Dagenham police officers and local historian Lee Shelden made plans to mark the occasion. Sergeant Peter Stratton and the Community Involvement Team encouraged schoolchildren to try to solve the mystery. The cable TV station Channel One broadcast a programme showing Barking police in 1846 uniforms re-enacting the search for the body at Eastbrookend.

The events culminated on Sunday 30th June 1996. The main focus of attention was Clark's burial place in Dagenham Parish Churchyard. Local officers had spent 18 months raising the £1,600 needed to restore the memorial. A group of invited guests, including members of the Clark family and high-ranking police officers, gathered at the graveside. Mike Reith, the Vicar of Dagenham, rededicated the stone before leading a service inside the church, which included two songs performed by children from Hunters Hall Primary School, situated near Clark's beat.

Guests then travelled to Eastbrookend. Descendants of Clark's sister Mary planted an ash tree close to the site of Thomas Waters Brittain's farm and unveiled a plaque. The next event was a ceremony at nearby Eastbrook Comprehensive School. Commander David Kendrick presented Clark's great-great niece with a framed certificate signed by Metropolitan Police Commissioner Paul Condon. This was followed by the official opening of a travelling exhibition on the murder, accompanied by music from the Metropolitan Police Band.

The momentous day came to a close. Guests said their goodbyes and dispersed. And so we too must return to the churchyard to take our final farewell of Clark. His name now reaches the wider public via the Metropolitan Police Roll of Honour. He is also listed on the National Police Memorial in the Mall, unveiled by the Queen in April 2005. Yet George Clark has never been forgotten by the community which he served. He made a good impression on the people of Dagenham in the brief six weeks he lived amongst them. Dagenham folk have always remembered him (in the words of Refero writing in 1898) as:

'..a brave young Constable, who so long ago, in the performance of his duty, was 'Faithful even unto death.'

The restored memorial, 1996

NOTES ON THE TEXT

CHAPTER 1

1   From a series of newspaper articles 'The diaries of Charles J. Kilby' published in the *Woburn Reporter* in the 1950s. These have been made available to us by his descendant Mrs Angela Knox.

2   *The Chelmsford Chronicle* 25th September 1846. Five months previously, it had promoted the merits of barley: '…workmen employed at the Duncormick limestone quarries gave up the use of potatoes, and used barley-meal for stirabout in the morning and evening, with barley-bread and milk to dinner, and admit they never at any time wrought so well, were so strong, or enjoyed such good health as during the time they substituted barley for potatoes...' (3rd April 1846).

3   This amount had remained the same since the 1820s. See Nigel E. Agar: *The Bedfordshire farm worker in the nineteenth century* (The Bedfordshire Historical Record Society, 1981) pp. 64-67.

4   *Chelmsford Chronicle* 16th July 1858.

5   Agar, *Bedfordshire farm worker in the nineteenth century,* p.137.

6   *Kelly's Directory of Bedfordshire* (1847). Elizabeth had been born in the village of Stevington, also in Bedfordshire, but her parents moved to Eversholt shortly after her birth.

7   *Register of Joiners January 1843 to April 1857, warrant numbers 19889 – 35804.* (The National Archives, MEPO 4/334.) The information given on each new recruit at this time is restricted to his name, date of appointment, warrant number, cause and date of his removal from the force, and the names and addresses of his referees.

8   The Metropolitan Police, in *Quarterly Review* 99, 1856, pp. 164-7, quoted in Andrew Barrett & Christopher Harrison: *Crime and punishment in England, a sourcebook* (Routledge, 1999) pp. 239-241.

9   'As the main need for police protection in those days was at night-time, about twice as many men were on duty during the night as during the day'. From *A brief history of the Metropolitan Police,* c.1969, adapted from a series of articles by F.E. Heron in the Metropolitan Police training school magazine with additional material by A.R. Pike OBE, – issued to mark the 140th anniversary of the Force.

10 Quoted in J.J. Tobias: *Crime and police in England 1700-1900* (Gill & Macmillan, 1979) pp.82-83.

11 Clive Emsley: *The English police: a political and social history* (Longman, 2nd edition, 1996) p. 206.

12 Martin Fido & Keith Skinner: *The official encyclopaedia of Scotland Yard* (Virgin, revised edition 2000) p.19.

13 Emsley, *The English police,* p. 206.

14 Montagu Williams: *Round London* (1894), as quoted on the website http://www.victorianlondon.org.

15 According to Peter Kennison & David Swinden 'This changed in August 1830, having previously read "Police Force". *From Behind the blue lamp – policing North and East London* (Coppermill Press, 2003) p.9.

16 Christopher Pulling: *Mr Punch and the police* (Butterworths, 1964) p.42.

17 Pulling, *Mr Punch and the police,* p.42.

[18]   Adam Hart-Davis: *What the Victorians did for us* (Headline, 2001) p.204.

[19]   Mervyn A. Mitton: *The policeman's lot: antique British police equipment including truncheons and tipstaves* (Quiller Press, 1985) p.115.

[20]   *Police Orders,* 15th September 1845 (The National Archives, MEPO 7/11).

[21]   *The Chelmsford Chronicle,* 25th June 1847.

[22]   *The Essex Standard,* 20th March 1840.

[23]   David Taylor: *Crime, policing and punishment in England,* 1750-1914 (Macmillan, 1998) p.75.

[24]   *Return of the various ways in which the Police are useful to the Community in Addition to their more urgent duties* (The National Archives, HO 73/3).

[25]   *The Daily News,* 13th February 1846.

[26]   *The Daily News,* 25th March 1846.

[27]   *The Morning Chronicle,* 28th June 1845.

[28]   *The Morning Chronicle,* 9th June 1845.

[29]   *Douglas Jerrold's Weekly Newspaper,* 25th July 1846.

CHAPTER 2

[1]   *The Chambers Pocket Dictionary* defines 'sylvan' as 'relating to woods and woodland; wooded'.

[2]   G.A. Hillyar-Ruell: Dagenham – an Essex village cause (from the *Methodist Recorder,* 1912). See also the Ordnance Survey maps *Dagenham 1915, Rush Green 1914, Beacontree Heath & Valence 1914, and Parsloes 1915,* reprinted by Alan Godfrey with commentary by Tony Clifford, which illustrate the rural nature of the area before the building of the Becontree Estate.

[3]   The *Dagenham Post,* 22nd October 1952. See also John McCann: *Clay and cob buildings* (Shire Publications, 2nd edition 1995).

[4]   The Frys first leased the cottages in 1824. Elizabeth's daughters Katharine and Rachel described them as 'surrounded by trees, mostly willows, on an open space of lawn, with beds of reeds behind them and on either side covering the river bank. They are open to the south-west, and are only to be attained by a rough and circuitous cart-road, or by crossing the water in front of the cottages'. From: Elizabeth Fry in Barking and Dagenham, in *Recording the past: a selection of local history articles by James Howson* (London Borough of Barking & Dagenham libraries department, 1996) p.57.

[5]   June Vansittart (editor): *Katharine Fry's book* (Hodder & Stoughton, 1966) pp. 98-99.

[6]   *Kelly's Directory of Essex,* 1845.

[7]   *The Times,* 11th October 1804.

[8]   William Ford is also said to have preferred to travel in a 'tumble-cart' which, having only one seat, meant that he was not obliged to offer anyone a lift. During his lifetime he had constant arguments with Dagenham's vicar, Thomas Lewis Fanshawe, over the amount of tithes to be paid. Carrying this dispute beyond the grave, Ford stipulated in his will that nobody of the name of Fanshawe was to be connected with the school in any way.

[9]   *Kelly's Directory of Essex,* 1845.

[10]   G.A Hillyar-Ruell: Dagenham – an Essex village cause (from the *Methodist Recorder,* 1912).

[11]   Details of the content and distribution of tracts at that time are given in the *Wesleyan-Methodist Magazine,* March & April 1843.

CHAPTER 3

1 J.P. Shawcross: *A history of Dagenham in the county of Essex* (Skeffington & Son, 2nd edition 1908) p.28.

2 H.C. Fanshawe: *History of the Fanshawe family* (Andrew Reid & Co., 1927) p.344.

3 During her visits to Dagenham, Elizabeth Fry attended the Beacontree Heath Methodist Chapel, and also held public meetings in barns in the area. She wrote in 1831 that 'I have felt so strikingly the manner in which the kindness and love of the neighbourhood has been shown to me…The clergyman and his wife almost loading us with kindness, the farmers and their wives very kind and attentive, the poor the same…' From: Elizabeth Fry in Barking and Dagenham, in *Recording the past: a selection of local history articles by James Howson* (London Borough of Barking & Dagenham libraries department, 1996) p.59. As the 1830s wore on, and their children one by one left home, the Frys eventually ceased their Dagenham holidays. Elizabeth Fry died after a stroke on 12th October 1845 at Ramsgate, aged 65. She was laid to rest at the Quaker burial ground in North Street, Barking. The funeral was attended by over a thousand people, probably including many of her acquaintances from nearby Dagenham. Elizabeth's husband Joseph was later buried beside her. The gravestone has now been moved to Wanstead Burial Ground, but the remains of Elizabeth Fry are still at Barking.

4 *County Treasurer's Bills and Vouchers, West Division Midsummer* 1846 Essex Record Office (Q/FAb 111/6).

5 From a talk given at Rectory Library, Dagenham, as reported in the *Dagenham Post* 19th January 1949. Cyril Hart was brought up in Dagenham, and in the 1940s carried out a great deal of research into its history, which he deposited in Valence House Museum.

6 Herbert Hope Lockwood: The Bow Street Mounted Patrol on Essex Highways (in *Essex 'full of profitable thinges': essays presented to Sir John Ruggles-Brise,* edited by Kenneth Neale (Leopard's Head Press, 1996) pp.311-330.

7 In his article *The Stations of J Division, Ilford,* Bryn Elliott writes that 'patrolmen were provided with cottages with stabling attached; a tablet signifying the horse patrol and number was attached to the wall of each cottage. The two Ilford stations were numbers 63 and 64…The rider was to reside with his family at the station house, in an existence which was severely regulated. Unable to keep any animals fed on corn, be they pigs, fowl or any other beast, additionally he was not to stray more than two miles from his station house unless on duty'. Station 63, a cottage on the Ilford High Road near St Mary's Church, was occupied by the officer patrolling Ilford to Stratford. Until 1836-7 this was James Outhen. He resigned in order to become landlord of the nearby Three Rabbits public house, having married the widow of the previous licensee James Wood. Outhen was succeeded by Samuel Tebenham, who moved into the cottage with his wife Mary and their children William (born c1825) Hannah (c1827), Mary Jane (c1829), Samuel (c1831). Their youngest child George was born c1838. On the evidence of census returns, the building was still named Patrole [sic] Cottage well into the 19th century. See Herbert Hope Lockwood: The Bow Street Mounted Patrol on Essex Highways (in *Essex 'full of profitable thinges': essays presented to Sir John Ruggles-Brise,* edited by Kenneth Neale (Leopard's Head Press, 1996) pp.311-330).

8 Pages 62-63 of J. Spencer Curwen's *Old Plaistow* contain a vivid description of the arrival of the first Metropolitan Police officers in Plaistow, singing a popular tune 'In Bun-hill Row there lived a dame' as they marched in. This has been believed, erroneously, to refer to the force's arrival in Dagenham in 1840. It continues: 'And what a comical squad they were, all sorts and sizes, ex-soldiers and men-o'-war's men, broken down tradesmen, and others. One of them, formerly a seaman, old Tom Connor, was about five-foot-six high

and had only one eye, the other he had lost in an engagement. He was at the battle of Trafalgar, from which he returned in the ship which brought home Nelson's body'.

[9] *Ilford in 1840: K division: the places taken in, and the distribution of men, stations etc.* (Photocopy of an original document, the location of which is unknown.)

[10] Countless secondary sources state that the room above the shop at the corner of Crown Street and Bull Street was the first Dagenham police station. These include the Dagenham Digest, January 1956, p.13, and *Residents and Visitors: some Barking and Dagenham personalities,* 1992, pp.12-14. A photograph of the shop in the Valence House archives was labelled some time before 1965 as the first police station. It would be interesting to know why this belief arose. The station used from 1850 was about ten minutes' walk from Dagenham Village. Although the majority of officers took up residence in this new building, the subsequent census returns show that some officers did continue to live in the village. It seems likely, therefore, that policemen did lodge above the corner shop in question at one time. It has the advantage of being in a prime position at the junction of the two most important roads in the village. It may be significant that the occupier of the shop for many years was grocer Thomas Smith, who helped in the search for Clark and whose daughter married a Dagenham police constable named Thomas Spurrier in 1860.

[11] *Dagenham Parish Council Poor Rate and Church Rate books* (Valence House Museum).

[12] Douglas G. Browne: *The Rise of Scotland Yard* (Harrap, 1956) p.83.

[13] The *Chelmsford Chronicle,* 21st February 1840.

[14] *Documents on the Metropolitan Police district extension – various* (The National Archives, MEPO 2/76).

[15] *The Essex Standard,* 10th January 1840.

[16] *The Essex Standard,* 23rd June 1843.

[17] *The Chelmsford Chronicle,* 19th September 1845.

[18] William Parsons' referees were 'Mr G. Hedge, Sidestrand, North Walsham, Norfolk, and others' (The National Archives, MEPO 4/333). Sidestrand is on the north coast of Norfolk, near Cromer. It is quite a distance from the villages of Attleborough and Shropham, to the south-west of Norwich, where Parsons spent his childhood.

[19] *The Daily News,* 17th March 1846.

[20] *The Chelmsford Chronicle,* 15th May 1846.

[21] *Police Orders,* 11th May 1846 (The National Archives, MEPO 7/11).

[22] *Particulars of premises in the occupation of the Metropolitan Police* (The Metropolitan Police Historical Collection, Charlton).

[23] *The Times,* 1st September 1849.

[24] *Chelmsford Chronicle* 3rd January 1840.

[25] *Chelmsford Chronicle* 25th June 1847.

[26] *Chelmsford Chronicle* 21st February1840.

[27] *Chelmsford Chronicle* 21st February 1840.

[28] *The Chelmsford Chronicle,* 3rd January 1840.

[29] *The Chelmsford Chronicle,* 3rd July 1846.

[30] *Chelmsford Chronicle* 21st February 1840.

[31] Richard Harding Newman, gentleman, of Witch Elms (*White's Directory of Essex,* 1848).

32 *The Chelmsford Chronicle,* 31st January 1840.

33 James Stones [sic], farmer, of Goosehays (*White's Directory of Essex,* 1848).

34 *The Chelmsford Chronicle,* 31st January 1840.

35 *The Chelmsford Chronicle,* 26th December 1845.

36 *Minutes of the meetings of the Governors of Ford Endowed School, with accounts, 23rd May 1839-2nd July 1868* (Valence House Museum).

37 Arthur Conan Doyle: *The Copper Beeches* (first published in the *Strand Magazine,* June 1892).

CHAPTER 4

1 One police sergeant and six constables were appointed to the new Dagenham force in 1840. The 1845 *Kelly's Directory of Essex* doesn't give the number of officers, merely declaring that 'a station of the metropolitan police is established here'. The 1848 *White's Directory of Essex* gives the number of constables as seven. It is therefore possible that there was a seventh Dagenham constable in June 1846, not called to testify at the Clark inquest because he was either absent or on day duty at the time of the murder.

2 John G. O'Leary, in *Dagenham place names* (1958) writes that Eastbrook 'is practically the oldest Dagenham place name. It comes from a family named Eastbrook whose name first appears in 1284 and lasted until 1691' (p.33.)

3 *The Times,* Monday 6th July 1846.

4 J.P. Shawcross: *A history of Dagenham in the county of Essex* (Skeffington & Son, 2nd edition 1908) p.24.

5 J.G.O'Leary in *The Book of Dagenham* decided, perhaps wisely, not to attempt to disentangle the various farms at Eastbrookend. The following table summarizes their names over the Victorian and Edwardian periods, indicating the perils that await historians attempting to study this part of Dagenham. Extra confusion is caused by yet another Eastbrook Farm situated in Rainham Road North (formerly Tanyard Lane).

Occupier in 1846	Mrs Mihill	T.W. Brittain	Mrs Stone
Name of property in census returns			
1841 census	Not named	Eastbrookend Hall	Huntings
1851 census	Not named	Eastbrookend Farm	Huntings
1861 census	Not named	Eastbrook End farm	Eastbrookend House
1871 census	Grove Farm	Eastbrook Farm	Not named
1881 census	Not named	Eastbrookend Farm	Eastbrookend Lodge
1891 census	Eastbrook End Farm	Eastbrook End Farm [sic]	Eastbrook End House
1901 census	Eastbrook End Farm	Eastbrook Farm	Not named
Map evidence			
Tithe map & schedule 1844	Not named	Eastbrookend Old Hall	Not named
OS 1844	Myalls	Eastbrook End	Eastbrook House
OS 1864 25inch	Eastbrookgrove House	Eastbrookend Farm	Eastbrookend House
OS 1914	Eastbrookend Farm	Eastbrook Farm	Eastbrookend House

6   People living in the Eastbrookend area refer to the wider area of open land, not just the track, as the Chase.

7   Jack West: *Personal memories of Dagenham Village* (Stockwell, 1993) p.45.

8   The reason Clark's beat ended at Fels Farm was that the boundary between Dagenham and Romford was further south in the 1840s than it is now. Evidence for this is found in contemporary maps. The 1844 1-inch Ordnance Survey, for example, shows the parish boundary following Harvey's Lane (to the east of what is now Dagenham Road) and continuing as the track leading to Thorntons Farm on the western side of the road. Thorntons Farmhouse itself is shown as lying on the Romford side of the boundary. Samuel John Neele's 1797 map of Essex shows a similar line. Maps of early Dagenham in both a *Brief History of Barking and Dagenham* by James Howson and *Becontree and Dagenham: a report made for the Pilgrim Trust* by Terence Young (Becontree Social Survey Committee, 1934) also put the boundary line at Eastbrookend. The first edition 25 inch Ordnance Survey map, drawn up in the 1860s, puts the boundary approximately 400 metres further north. This is the modern boundary, and a coal duty post dated 1861 stands there today, outside nos. 98-100 Dagenham Road.

9   Tony Clifford: *Barking and Dagenham buildings past and present* (London Borough of Barking & Dagenham 1992) p.17.

10   *Clifford, Buildings,* p.40.

11   Shawcross, p.27.

12   Ian Currie, Mark Davison and Bob Ogley: *The Essex weather book* (Froglets, 1992) p.8.

13   *The Marlborough Times,* 3rd February 1893.

14   Shawcross, p.27.

15   It is worth noting that the family themselves always used the surname Parson, not Parsons. As the Dagenham police sergeant was generally referred to as William Parsons, especially in contemporary newspapers, it has been decided to do the same in the main text of this book to avoid confusion.

16   The children of William and Jemima Parson baptized at Attleborough were: George (1818), Caroline (1820), Frederick (1822), Fitz Henry (1824), Julia (1826), Harriet (1827), Amelia (1829). Arthur was baptized at Shropham in 1830. (The International Genealogical Index, as consulted on the Internet site www.familysearch.org).

17   The death and subsequent inquest was reported in The Morning Chronicle 12th January 1846. See also *Guy's Hospital Register of Admissions and Discharges 3 Jan 1844 - 27 Dec 1848* (London Metropolitan Archives). According to his death certificate, Fitz Henry injured his right foot in the fall. *The Kentish Mercury* of 24th January 1846 reported Fitz Henry Parsons' funeral thus: 'The unfortunate police constable, who died from a melancholy accident in her Majesty's dockyard, in St George's Hospital, was removed to the station house, Woolwich Dockyard, and on Saturday last his remains were interred in St Mary's Churchyard, Woolwich, followed not only by the police sergeants and constables of his own division, but a great many others from the various other districts, as a mark of respect to one who bore a most exemplary character in the force. The mournful procession consisted of upwards of an hundred members of the force. The Commissioners have defrayed all expenses attending the funeral'. The probate indexes at First Avenue House, Holborn, London, show that Fitz Henry's mother Jemima waited until 9th July 1859 before applying for a grant of administration of his estate, valued at under £20. Jemima herself was to die aged 71 three months after this, in October 1859.

18   George Bakewell: *The Observations on the Construction of a New Police Force* (1842). This is quoted on the West Midlands Police Museum website (http://www.westmidlandspolicemuseum.co.uk).

¹⁹ Shawcross, p.275. It is interesting to read in the 1937 obituary of PC William James Rawson that: 'PC Rawson came to Dagenham in 1898 and was made the constable at Beacontree Heath two years later. No-one wanted the job, for the heath was notorious for its lawless characters and the Macedonian gypsies who camped there'. (*Dagenham Post,* 13th August 1937).

²⁰ *The Chelmsford Chronicle,* 21st August 1840.

²¹ *Murder of PC George Clark at Dagenham* (The National Archives, MEPO 3/53). This is abbreviated subsequently in these notes to *Clark Murder File.* This is the major source for the study of this case. It consists chiefly of correspondence, expenses claims and memos. There are also witness statements from the inquest into the death of Clark. These appear at first glance to be original, but closer inspection reveals that some of the dates were first entered as 1856 and then changed to 1846. This would suggest that the statements are copies made in the 1850s, possibly at the time of the prosecution of George Blewitt in 1858.

²² *Clark Murder File* (MEPO 3/53).

²³ *Clark Murder File* (MEPO 3/53). Unfortunately we do not have Levy's first name or the exact location of his home, but he evidently lived very close to Miller's Corner.

²⁴ *Clark Murder File* (MEPO 3/53).

²⁵ *Clark Murder File* (MEPO 3/53).

²⁶ Personal communication (letter) from Bob Jeffries, Hon. Curator, Thames River Police Museum 11th April 2003.

²⁷ The fatalities were: PC John Barton, drowned in 1838 when he fell in the River Lea from an unprotected towpath; PC Peter Beadle, accidentally drowned in 1840 when he fell in London Docks; PC John Husbands, drowned in 1840 in the Grosvenor Canal after having fallen from an unprotected bank; PC Thomas Everett, drowned in London Docks in 1842 having fallen from the unprotected quayside; and PC Charles Reynolds, drowned in 1842 in the London Docks having accidentally fallen in. They all died while on night duty. From the Metropolitan *Police Book of Remembrance 1829-1889* (http://www.met.police.uk/history/remembrance2.htm)

CHAPTER 5

¹ James Payen: *A tangled yarn* (Charles H. Kelly, 1891) pp.12-13.

² *The Essex Standard,* 10th July 1846.

³ The field name information is from the *Dagenham Tithe Schedule and Tithe Map,* 1844 (Valence House Museum).

⁴ Clark Murder File (MEPO 3/53). *The Times* of 4th July quotes Kimpton as saying that the staff was found in a ditch.

⁵ *Clark Murder File* (MEPO 3/53).

⁶ *The Essex Standard,* 2nd July 1858.

⁷ *Assizes: Home, Norfolk and South-Eastern Circuit: Depositions* (National Archives, ASSI 36/9). This is subsequently abbreviated in these notes to Depositions.

⁸ *Clark Murder File* (MEPO 3/53).

⁹ *The Essex Standard,* 2nd July 1858.

¹⁰ *Clark Murder File* (MEPO 3/53).

11   *The Times,* 24th August 1846.

12   *The Morning Chronicle,* 6th July 1846.

13   *The Times,* 6th July 1846.

14   *Depositions* (National Archives, ASSI 36/9).

15   *The Morning Chronicle,* 6th July 1846.

16   *The Times,* 6th July 1846.

17   Simon Dell writes that 'Rattles were carried in the breast pocket over the heart in order to protect against knife attacks. In several recorded incidents the life of a Peeler was saved when the rattle deflected a blade'. From *The Victorian Policeman* (Shire, 2004) p.21.

18   *Depositions* (National Archives, ASSI 36/9).

19   'COLLIN, Joseph, Romford, Essex – Gen.Pract.; MRCS 1836; LSA 1835'. (*Provincial Medical Directory, 1847*).

20   *Clark Murder File* (MEPO 3/53).

21   *Depositions* (National Archives, ASSI 36/9).

22   *Depositions* (National Archives, ASSI 36/9).

23   *The Times,* 7th July 1846.

24   *Police: Murder of Constable Clarke [sic] at Dagenham* (The National Archives, HO 45/1551).

25   *The Morning Chronicle,* 24th July 1846.

26   *County Treasurer's Bills and Vouchers, West Division, Epiphany 1847* (Essex Record Office, Q/FAb 112/2).

27   *Clark Murder File* (MEPO 3/53).

28   The Times reporter incorrectly names the Walker brothers as Amos and Moses. Several later writers on the Clark case have relied on the *Times* reports and have perpetuated the error.

29   Charles Dickens: *Sketches by Boz* (1836) chapter XXI, 'Brokers' and marine-store shops'.

30   *The Times,* 6th July 1846.

31   Joan Lock: *Dreadful deeds and awful murders – Scotland Yard's first detectives* (Barn Owl Books, 1990) pp.75-76.

32   From Henry Worsley: Juvenile depravity (1849), quoted in J.J. Tobias: *Nineteenth-century crime: prevention and punishment* (David & Charles 1972) p.17.

33   An 1846 Romford rate book in the collection of Havering Local Studies Library gives the owner as Thomas Woodfine, whose brewery was situated on Church Hill, Hornchurch.

34   It is worth mentioning that *The Essex Standard* of 10th July 1846 gives his name as Thomas Palmer, not Joseph. The newspaper also declares that Clark's hat was found on Sunday evening, not morning. These statements are incorrect. The report of the inquest on Palmer, and the burial entry in the registers of Dagenham Parish Church, both give his name as Joseph.

35   *The Essex Standard* 10th July 1846.

36   A peck is a measure of capacity for dry goods, amounting to 2 gallons.

[37] Judith Flanders writes that 'Whether women attended [funerals] or not was a vexed question. Many manuals said absolutely not, as women could not contain their emotions and would be overcome. Other books accepted that women did go...' From *The Victorian House* (HarperCollins 2003) p.333. When George Hollest, the murdered Perpetual Curate of Frimley, Surrey, was buried in October 1850 it was a decidedly all-male affair. The *Times* reported that the sons and brothers of the deceased were the only family mourners. Hollest's widow Caroline did not attend.

[38] A Thomas George Young 'late of the parish of Romford, labourer' was later to plead guilty to larceny at the Essex Quarter Sessions of January 1848, and was sentenced to twelve calendar months hard labour in the Ilford House of Correction. *Conviction Book 1846-1850* (Essex Record Office, Q/RSc 1/8).

[39] *The Morning Chronicle,* 22nd July 1846.

[40] *The Times,* 28th July 1846.

[41] This still exists as the Golden Lion, situated at the junction of the High Street and North Street. 'Of those in the town only the Golden Lion, formerly known as the Lion or the Red Lion, still functions in its ancient buildings...' *Hornchurch and Romford, extract from volume VII of the Victoria History of Essex,* edited by W.R. Powell (Institute of Historical Research 1978, reprinted by the London Borough of Havering 1988) p.62.

[42] *The Morning Chronicle,* 22nd July 1846.

CHAPTER 6

[1] *The Times,* 15th July 1846.

[2] *County Treasurer's Bills and Vouchers, West Division, Epiphany 1847* (Essex Record Office, Q/FAb 112/2).

[3] *The Times,* 15th July 1846.

[4] *The Times,* 15th July 1846.

[5] A Vestry meeting a month previous to Clark's arrival had elected two churchwardens. They were Henry Fanshawe, brother of the vicar, and Thomas Waters Brittain. The Dagenham Vestry Minutes are held at the Essex Record Office (D/P 69/8/1), and a typescript of the minutes for 1789-1848 is held by Valence House Museum at E1(352).

[6] *The Morning Chronicle,* 22nd July 1846.

[7] *The Morning Chronicle,* 23rd July 1846.

[8] *The Morning Chronicle,* 23rd July 1846.

[9] *The Times,* 24th July 1846.

[10] *The Times,* 24th July 1846.

[11] *Clark Murder File* (MEPO 3/53).

[12] *Clark Murder File* (MEPO 3/53).

[13] *Clark Murder File* (MEPO 3/53).

[14] *The News of the World,* 26th July 1846.

[15] *Clark Murder File* (MEPO 3/53).

[16] *The News of the World,* 26th July 1846.

17   *The Chelmsford Chronicle,* 21st August 1846. This is, incidentally, further evidence in support of Clark's beat not stretching to Wheel Farm where James Parfey Collier lived.

18   *Clark Murder File* (MEPO 3/53).

19   *The Morning Chronicle,* 24th July 1846.

20   According to Maeve E. Doggett, 'Until well into the nineteenth century there was a general common-law rule that spouses were incompetent to testify for or against one other. This incompetence applied to both criminal and civil proceedings; it applied to events occurring before as well as well as during the marriage and it endured after the marriage had ended'. *From Marriage, wife-beating and the law in Victorian England* (University of South Carolina Press, 1993) p.46.

21   *Clark Murder File* (MEPO 3/53).

22   *The Morning Chronicle,* 24th July 1846.

23   *Chambers Pocket Dictionary* defines the word 'fustian' as 'a kind of coarse twilled cotton fabric with a nap'.

24   *The Morning Chronicle,* 24th July 1846.

25   *The News of the World* 26th July 1846.

26   His name is variously given as Walsh, Welsh or Welch. This book uses the spelling used in the documents found in the *Clark Murder File* (MEPO 3/53).

27   *The Times,* 12th August 1846.

28   *The Times,* 12th August 1846.

29   *The Chelmsford Chronicle,* 14th August 1846.

30   *The Essex Standard*, 14th August 1846.

31   *Douglas Jerrold's Weekly Newspaper,* 22nd August 1846.

32   *The Observer,* 16th August 1846.

CHAPTER 7

1   *Clark Murder File* (MEPO 3/53).

2   It was not until April 1847, nine months after the beginning of the Clark investigation, that the detectives submitted their expenses claims to the Commissioners. The total bill amounted to nearly £50. It would be even longer before the detectives received payment, as the Commissioners referred the claims to the Home Secretary for his approval. *Clark Murder File* (MEPO 3/53).

3   *The Times,* 21st August 1846.

4   From Known to the Police (1908), quoted in Andrew Barrett & Christopher Harrison (eds): *Crime and Punishment in England: a sourcebook* (Routledge 1999) pp. 288-289.

5   *The Morning Chronicle,* 21st August 1846.

6   *Clark Murder File* (MEPO 3/53).

7   *The Weekly Dispatch,* 23rd August 1846.

8   *The Observer,* 23rd August 1846.

9   *The Times,* 21st August 1846.

[10] *The Weekly Dispatch,* 23rd August.

[11] *The Times,* 24th August 1846.

[12] *Douglas Jerrold's Weekly Newspaper,* 29th August 1846.

[13] *Chambers Pocket Dictionary* defines the word 'suborn' as 'to persuade someone to commit perjury, a crime or other wrongful act, e.g. by bribing them'.

[14] *Clark Murder File* (MEPO 3/53).

[15] *The Globe,* 14th September 1846.

[16] *The Weekly Dispatch,* 13th September 1846.

[17] The Dagenham electoral roll for the time of Clark's death includes George and John Sammel [sic], both of Triptons Farm near Beacontree Heath. It is likely that one of these men was the juror who fell sick. *Electoral register for Southern Division 1845-46* (Essex Record Office, Q/RPr 1/4).

[18] *Douglas Jerrold's Weekly Newspaper,* 19th September 1846.

[19] 'Rawlings, Benjamin William, Romford House' (from list of Romford attorneys in *White's Directory of Essex,* 1848).

[20] *The Bedford Mercury,* 19th September 1846.

[21] The 1841 census shows James and Susan Perry living in Blue House Lane, Corbets Tey. They are both recorded as aged 20, but it must be borne in mind that adults' ages were rounded down to the nearest 5 years in that particular census. James is described as an agricultural labourer.

[22] *The Chelmsford Chronicle,* 25th September 1846.

[23] *The Essex Standard,* 25th September 1846.

[24] *Douglas Jerrold's Weekly Newspaper,* 26th September 1846.

[25] Coincidentally, George Corbin had been returning from Fairlop Fair with PC George Hall when the latter was thrown from his horse and killed. This occurred during the night of Friday 4th July, just hours after George Clark's body had been found (see Chapter 5).

[26] *Clark Murder File* (MEPO 3/53).

[27] *The Bedford Mercury,* 26th September 1846.

[28] *The Illustrated London News,* 3rd October 1846.

[29] *The Bedford Mercury,* 3rd October 1846.

[30] *Clark Murder File* (MEPO 3/53).

[31] *The Times,* 10th October 1846.

[32] *Police Orders* 8th October 1846 (The National Archives, MEPO 7/12).

[33] *The Times,* 22nd September 1846.

[34] Jonathan Wild, described as 'the greatest criminal mastermind of the eighteenth century', was both a receiver of stolen goods and a thief-taker. He was hanged at Tyburn in 1725. See Andrea McKenzie, 'Wild, Jonathan (*bap.* 1683, d. 1725)', *Oxford Dictionary of National Biography,* Oxford University Press, 2004. [http://www.oxforddnb.com/view/article/29394]

[35] *The Times,* 25th September 1846.

[36]   *The Morning Chronicle,* 24th September 1846.

[37]   *An account of prisoners committed to and subsisted in this Gaol from the 1st day of April 1845 to the 31st day of March 1846 both days inclusive for offences committed within the liberty of Havering Atte-Bower* (Essex Record Office, Q/FAb 111/6).

[38]   *Clark Murder File* (MEPO 3/53).

[39]   *Police Orders,* September 1846-June 1848 (The National Archives, MEPO 7/12).

[40]   *The Times,* 12th November 1846.

[41]   Letter dated 24th October 1846 (*Clark Murder File, MEPO 3/53).

[42]   *Clark Murder File* (MEPO 3/53).

[43]   John Julian's police career lasted thirty-five years. He remained a sergeant and retired in May 1865 on a pension of £48 10s 8d per annum. *Metropolitan Police: Records of Police Pensioners* (The National Archives, MEPO 21/7).

CHAPTER 8

[1]   *Clark Murder File* (MEPO 3/53).

[2]   The *Times* gives 10th March, but the date on the indictments themselves is 9th March. *1847 Essex Lent Sessions* (National Archives ASSI 94/2483).

[3]   *The Times,* 16th March 1847.

[4]   *The Times,* 16th March 1847.

[5]   As we have seen, the death of Fitz Henry in 1846 had left William Parsons with three surviving brothers – George (baptized 1818), Frederick (1822) and Arthur (1830). It would be interesting to know which of these was the Home Secretary's coachman. Arthur is surely too young, and Frederick's subsequent history is unknown. In the 1881 census George is listed as landlord of the Yorkshire Grey Inn in King Street, Cambridge. He died in September 1885 at Addenbrook's Hospital, Cambridge, aged 66.

[6]   *County Treasurer's Bills and Vouchers, West Division Epiphany 1846* (Essex Record Office, Q/FAb 111/2).

[7]   Tony Clifford & Herbert Hope Lockwood: *Mr Frogley's Barking, a first selection* (The London Borough of Barking & Dagenham, 2002) pp. 26-27.

[8]   *The Essex Standard,* 3rd January 1851.

[9]   *The Essex Standard,* 12th June 1835, reporting evidence given by Luke Miller, Keeper of the House of Correction, to the House of Lords Select Committee on Gaols and Houses of Correction.

[10]   *The Essex Times,* 2nd October 1880.

[11]   David Occomore: *Curiosities of Essex: being glimpses of Essex history as seen from broadside ballads* (Ian Henry, 1984).

[12]   *Clark Murder File* (MEPO 3/53).

[13]   Oddly enough, in April 1853 a George Allison was promoted from Sergeant to Inspector, in K Division. *Strength and establishment of Metropolitan Police 1830-1872* (National Archives, MEPO 2/26).

[14]   *The Times,* 8th April 1847.

[15]   *The Times,* 8th July 1847.

[16] *The Times*, 3rd July 1847.

[17] Shawcross, p.117.

[18] Geoffrey Taylor: Who murdered Police Constable 313 K Clark? (article in the *Metropolitan Police History Society Newsletter*, 1993).

[19] From the chapter on Battlesden parish churchyard in *Ye Old Mortality: Bedfordshire Monumental Inscriptions* (copy in the collection of the Society of Genealogists).

[20] *County Treasurer's Bills and Vouchers, West Division Michaelmas 1847* (Essex Record Office, Q/FAb 112/8).

[21] *The Times*, 28th February 1868.

[22] *The Essex Herald*, 20th July 1847.

[23] Henry Mayhew & John Binny: *The criminal prisons of London and scenes of prison life* (C. Griffin, 1862), p. 102.

[24] Anonymous: *Five years' penal servitude, by one who has endured it* (Richard Bentley & Son, new edition 1878) p.53.

[25] *The Essex Herald*, 28th December 1847.

[26] J.G. Torry: *Chelmsford Prison* (East Anglian Magazine Ltd 1980), p.44.

[27] *Five years' penal servitude*, p.23.

[28] *The Globe*, 19th September 1846.

[29] *The Essex Herald*, 3rd August 1847.

[30] *The Lincoln and Lincolnshire Standard*, 28th July 1847.

[31] *Clark Murder File* (MEPO 3/53).

CHAPTER 9

[1] The change of administration in June 1846, when Robert Peel's government fell, had been carried out without a general election being held.

[2] *The Essex Herald*, 10th August 1847.

[3] *The Chelmsford Chronicle*, 3rd September 1847.

[4] *Minutes of the meetings of the Governors of Ford Endowed School, with accounts, 23rd May 1839-2nd July 1868* (Valence House Museum). That the Page family was in difficult circumstances in the mid-1840s is also proved by an entry in the records of Dagenham's Uphill Charity. It shows that in October 1845 £15 was given for Ralph Page junior, aged 14, to be bound apprentice to a wheelwright 'due to the misfortune of his parents'. A transcript of the Uphill records is held at Valence House Museum.

[5] A rod is a pre-decimal unit of length equivalent to 5.5 yards (5.03 metres).

[6] Charles Dickens gives an amusing description of a prison van in chapter 12 of *Sketches by Boz* (1836). 'The covered vehicle, in which prisoners are conveyed from the police-offices to the different prisons, was coming along at full speed. It then occurred to us, for the first time, that Her Majesty's carriage was merely another name for the prisoners' van, conferred upon it, not only by reason of the superior gentility of the term, but because the aforesaid van is maintained at Her Majesty's expense: having been originally started for the exclusive accommodation of ladies and gentlemen under the necessity of visiting the various houses of call known by the general denomination of "Her Majesty's Gaols"'.

The vans are also mentioned in *Police Orders* of 17th December 1841: 'The prison vans of C and K Divisions and the Horses belonging to them will be transferred to G Division on Monday morning next, the Forage from the above Divisons will be sent to G Division on Sunday next, as well as all the Utensils belonging to the Vans and Horses'. (The National Archives, MEPO 7/7).

[7] *Five years' penal servitude,* p. 30.

[8] David Taylor: *Crime, policing and punishment in England, 1750-1914* (Macmillan 1998) p.149.

[9] Hepworth Dixon: *The London prisons* (1850, reprinted by Garland, 1985) pp.132-146.

[10] *The Times,* 30th January 1847.

[11] *The Essex Herald,* 10th August 1847.

[12] *Mayhew & Binny,* p.248.

[13] *Five years' penal servitude,* p.35.

[14] *Millbank Prison Admissions register* (The National Archives, PCOM 2/27).

[15] *Mayhew & Binny,* p.239.

[16] *Five years' penal servitude,* p.54.

[17] *Mayhew & Binny,* p.146.

[18] *Five years' penal servitude,* p.48.

[19] *Five years' penal servitude,* p.45.

[20] Simon Thurley: *The lost buildings of Britain (Viking, 2004)* pp.166-167.

[21] *Mayhew & Binny,* p.242.

[22] Hepworth Dixon: *The London prisons* (1850) pp.132-146.

[23] *Clark Murder File* (MEPO 3/53).

[24] *Clark Murder File* (MEPO 3/53).

[25] *The Times,* 23rd July 1847

[26] From John Wade: A treatise on the police and crimes of the Metropolis (1829) quoted in J.J. Tobias: *Nineteenth-century crime: prevention and punishment* (David & Charles 1972) p.141.

[27] *The Times,* 30th January 1847.

[28] *The Times,* 2nd September 1848.

[29] *Northampton Gaol register, 1848-55* (The National Archives, HO 23/8).

CHAPTER 10

[1] *The Chelmsford Chronicle,* 10th March 1848; The Essex Standard, same date.

[2] *Essex Lent Sessions 1848* (The National Archives, ASSI 94/2509).

[3] *The Essex Standard,* 10th March 1848.

[4] *The Times,* 1st March 1850.

[5] David T. Hawkings: *Criminal Ancestors* (Sutton, revised edition 1996) pp. 204-205.

6   Sarah Wise gives several interesting anecdotes concerning Theodore Williams. He went to Newgate to interview the body-snatchers turned murderers in the notorious Italian Boy case of 1831. In 1836 Williams himself was involved in 'an infamous brawl in the vestry of St Marys'. From *The Italian boy: murder and grave-robbery in 1830s London* (Cape, 2004) pages 123 & 255.

7   *Criminal petitions series II, 1839-54* (The National Archives, HO 18/230/7).

8   *Mayhew & Binny*, p.224.

9   Reg Rigden: *The floating prisons of Woolwich and Deptford* (pamphlet, London Borough of Greenwich, 1976).

10 *The Times*, 8th January 1849.

11 *Five years' penal servitude*, pp 52-53.

12 *Mayhew & Binny*, p.213.

13 *Mayhew & Binny*, p.200.

14 David T. Hawkings: *Criminal Ancestors* (Sutton, revised edition 1996) p.17.

15 *Hulk registers and letter books, 1847-49* (The National Archives, HO 9/16).

CHAPTER 11

1   *Criminal petitions series II, 1839-54* (The National Archives, HO 18/230/7).

2   *Northampton Gaol register, 1848-55* (The National Archives, HO 23/8).

3   *The Times*, 12th April 1849.

4   *The Times*, 16th June 1849.

5   On 30th January 1847, the *Times* reported that the Warrior held 484 inmates.

6   *Hulks returns September 1848* (The National Archives, HO 8/97).

7   *The Times* 18th July 1849.

8   *Criminal petitions series II, 1839-54* (The National Archives, HO 18/230/7).

9   *Correspondence and warrants 1849 Oct 11 - 1849 Dec 31* (The National Archives, HO 13/98). Thomas Kimpton's petitions are to be found in *Criminal petitions series II, 1839-54* (The National Archives, HO 18/233/7).

10 There is a remote possibility that the William and Annie Parsons who took ship to British Columbia on the Norman Morison were not the couple in question. However, our ex-police sergeant was a miller by trade; had a wife named Anne; and does not appear on the 1851 British census. All available evidence does therefore point to him being the Canadian settler. The passenger list (men only) can be seen at: http://www.fortlangley.ca/nmorison.html

11 Joan Lock: *Blue murder? Policemen under suspicion* (Hale, 1986) p.86.

12 The departure of the ship was announced in the Times 19th October 1849: 'Norman Morison, about 600 tons, purchased by the Hudson's Bay Company, sailed today, 70 emigrants, terms: guarantee of £17 a year, with lodging and maintenance, under 5 year contract'. More details on the early settlement of this part of British Columbia can be found in *History and Heritage of Colwood, Vancouver Island, BC,* on the website http://www.vancouverisland.com together with the section on the Mill Hill National Park at http://www.crd.bc.ca/parks/brochures/cultural_history.pdf

[13] Over the years this road has also been known as Dagenham High Street and Romford Road. It is now Rainham Road South.

[14] *Particulars of Premises in the Occupation of the Metropolitan Police* (Metropolitan Police Historical Collection, Charlton).

[15] *The Essex Standard,* 6th August 1852.

[16] *The Times,* 24th July 1852.

[17] Hector Gavin: *Sanitary ramblings, being sketches and illustrations of Bethnal Green* (1848, reprinted by Frank Cass & Co in 1971) p.34.

[18] The building has now been converted into a gated community of luxury apartments called Princess Park Manor.

[19] *The Times,* 2nd July 1851.

[20] *The Colney Hatch Asylum committee minutes and reports, accounts, letter and visitor books, patient and staff records,* and miscellaneous records (London Metropolitan Archives, H12/CH). The report on Butfoy may have been written by W.C. Hood, Medical Superintendent of the male department of the asylum.

[21] 2,696 inmates were buried there from 1851 until its closure in 1873. From Richard Hunter & Ida MacAlpine: *Psychiatry for the poor* (Dawsons of Pall Mall, 1974) p.69.

[22] H.C. Fanshawe: *The history of the Fanshawe family* (Andrew Reid & Co. Ltd, 1927) p.341.

[23] *The Essex Standard,* 19th March 1858.

CHAPTER 12

[1] Martin Fido & Keith Skinner: *The official encyclopaedia of Scotland Yard* (Virgin, revised edition, 2000) p.476.

[2] The Ilford magistrates no longer used a room at the Angel Inn. According to the 1862 *Kelly's Directory of Essex,* 'Petty Sessions are held at the gaol every Saturday at eleven o'clock'.

[3] *The Essex Standard* 2nd July 1858.

[4] Blewitt had been baptized in January 1798 at St Andrew's, Hornchurch, the tenth child and fourth son of Joseph and Mary Blewitt.

[5] Blewitt's choice of a faded blue smock frock accords with the definition of his surname as 'nickname for a habitual wearer of blue clothes or for someone with blue eyes'. From Patrick Hanks & Flavia Hodges: *Dictionary of surnames* (Oxford University Press 1988) p.57.

[6] *Assizes: Home, Norfolk and South-Eastern Circuit: Depositions* (The National Archives, ASSI 36/9).

[7] In the 1862 *Kellys Directory of Essex* he is listed as a stationer of the High Street Brentwood.

[8] *The Essex Standard,* 5th August 1853.

[9] *Minutes of the meetings of the Governors of Ford Endowed School, with accounts, 23rd May 1839-2nd July 1868* (16th June, 1842) (Valence House Museum).

[10] *The Essex Standard,* 9th July 1858.

[11] *The Essex Standard,* 9th July 1858.

[12] *The Essex Standard,* 9th July 1858.

13 *Murder of Francis Saville Kent, aged 4 years, by Constance Emilie Kent* (The National Archives, MEPO 3/61).

14 The 1851 census of Rush Green lists George Blewitt and Edward (Ned) Wilcox on the same page, separated by only one other household (HO 107/1772 folio 21).

15 42 year-old barrister John Humffreys Parry was known for his theatrical style. Twenty years later, in 1878, he represented the artist James McNeill Whistler in the libel case brought by John Ruskin.

16 *The Times,* 26th July 1858.

17 5th August 1858 saw the first transatlantic telegraph message. Cables had been laid by the ship *Agamemnon.* The first telegraph link from Britain to Australia was not established until 1872.

18 According to page 9 of *Police in Victoria, 1836-1980* (Victoria Police Management Services Bureau), in 1853 alone 54 Metropolitan Police officers travelled to Australia to work for the Victorian force.

CHAPTER 13

1 *The Times,* 18th October 1858.

2 There is no confirmation of this theft and conviction in the local newspapers. *The Chelmsford Chronicle,* 8th October 1858, reports that 'Henry Prail, of Dagenham, labourer, was convicted in a fine of 10s and costs 8s 6d for stealing turnips growing in a field, the property of Mr T.W. Harris, farmer, Romford, on the 20th ult'. Since the death of Ralph Page, Thorntons Farm had been occupied by a William Harris. It is possible, therefore, that it was PC Coleman who arrested the turnip-stealers, but that after the time of the attack on him the press claimed the incident involved corn.

3 See the article 'Unsolved Victorian crimes' by Christine Wagg (*Chadwell Heath Historical Society Newsletter,* November 2002, p.6), which acknowledges information supplied by Neal Shelden.

4 The Winmill family occupied Beacontree Heath Farm in the early 19th century and were also associated with Valence House and Valence Farm. The name is commemorated in Winmill Road in Dagenham.

5 Farnes family biographical information supplied by Geri Zollinger and Ken Monson at http://euler.me.berkeley.edu/~kmonson/famhist.html#LTF

6 Robert Melrose came to Canada on the second voyage of the Norman Morison in 1852/53. Extracts from his diary can be read at http://www.joansjoy.ca/NMAnn.html

7 In 2005 the Six Mile Pub celebrated its 150th anniversary, culminating with a day of festivities on 9th July when its guests were invited to 'Party like it's 1855'. Further information on the pub and its history can be found at http://www.sixmilepub.com

8 Sir Richard Mayne's will was proved 19th January 1869. A grand obelisk was later erected over his grave, in direct opposition to his wish for a plain tombstone.

9 *The Times,* 31st December 1868.

10 Clive Emsley: 'Mayne, Sir Richard (1796-1868)', *Oxford Dictionary of National Biography,* Oxford University Press, 2004 [http://www.oxforddnb.com/view/article/18444]

11 Joan Lock: *Dreadful deeds and awful murders – Scotland Yard's first detectives* (Barn Owl Books, 1990) p.118.

[12] Lock, *Dreadful deeds and awful murders,* p.116.

[13] Nicholas Pearce's final home, the 300 year-old Mount View Cottage in the village of Gerrans, was demolished in February 2002 in spite of much local opposition.

[14] Douglas Browne, *The Rise of Scotland Yard* (Harrap, 1956), p.159.

[15] Lock, *Dreadful deeds and awful murders,* pp.162-163.

[16] Browne, *The rise of Scotland Yard,* p.160. John Dickson Carr used Jonathan Whicher as a character in *Scandal at High Chimneys,* a crime novel set in 1865. He has Whicher declare that "I arrested Constance Kent before I'd got enough evidence; and it finished me. The King [i.e. Mayne] might have backed me up, and stood by me...He didn't stand by me, and that's that". (Corgi paperback edition 1970, p.71).

[17] *Kelly's Directory of Essex,* 1886, lists Frederick Stratford as 'registrar of births and deaths and school attendance officer for Hornchurch, Rainham and Great Warley'.

[18] *The Essex Times,* 23rd October 1878.

[19] John W. Laskin, *Fireside talks about Brentwood* (typescript, produced by the Brentwood Secretarial Academy, 1920).

[20] Personal communication (letter) from Jeremy West, April 2003.

[21] It will be noted that the spelling of the place-name had by this time changed to 'Wantz', whereas the earlier usage had been 'Wants' or 'Wonts'.

[22] *The Dagenham Post,* 19th January 1949.

[23] The Book of Remembrance can be consulted online at http://www.met.police.uk/history/remembrance2.htm.

[24] *The Times,* 17th September 1852.

[25] The baptism of Annie Amelia is listed in the *Lamplough name index,* compiled by Denis Strangman (http://home.vicnet.net.au/~adhs/Lamplough.html).

[26] Denis Strangman: *The gold rush to Lamplough, near Avoca in Victoria, Australia, 1859-1860.* (http://home.vicnet.au/~adhs/Article.html)

CHAPTER 14

[1] Shawcross, preface, p.vi.

[2] A standing building survey made by the Passmore Edwards Museum at 2-16 Church Street recorded a 14th century timber framed building. See Museum of London: *Church St/Church Lane, Dagenham RM10: an archaeological post-excavation assessment and updated project design* (Museum of London 2000) p.4.

[3] Jack West: *Personal Memories of Dagenham Village* (Stockwell, 1993) p.80.

[4] *The Dagenham Post,* 7th December 1983.

[5] *The Essex Times,* 23rd October 1878.

[6] Valence House Museum, Becontree Avenue, Dagenham RM8 3HT (for opening times, see http://www.barking-dagenham.gov.uk)

[7] The Dagenham Parish Church burial registers can be seen on microfilm at the Local Studies Centre, Valence House Museum. It also holds a list of monumental inscriptions in the churchyard, compiled in 1984.

8   In 1901 the land was sold to the Morris Aiming Tube and Ammunition Company, which went into liquidation in 1909. The site was then bought by the Sterling Telephone and Electric Company. Among the products manufactured by Sterling over the next three decades were radio receivers, headphones, loudspeakers, and lighting apparatus. During World War II the company was chosen to manufacture small arms, and from then until its closure in the mid-1980s it produced the Lanchester, Patchett and Sterling series of sub-machine guns. See Peter Laidler & David Howroyd: *The guns of Dagenham* (Collector Grade Publications Inc., 1995).

9   *The Barking Advertiser* 29th July 1983.

10   Mary Gay, quoted in Tony Clifford: *Dagenham Pubs Past & Present,* p.13. For more information about the Gay family, particularly the brothers Cecil, Ernest, Bert and Fred who fought in the First World War, see: http://www.pals.org.uk/cdgay.htm

11   Hooks Hall Farm now owned by the London Borough of Barking & Dagenham and run as Eastminster Riding School. Vehicle access is from Upper Rainham Road in Hornchurch, although pedestrians can still reach it from Eastbrookend via the Chase.

12   Bob Chisholm: Dagenham's Dead Dog River (article in *Essex Countryside*, October 1984, p.37).

13   Jack West: *Jack West funeral director* (Stockwell, 1988 pp.84-87. It was known for many years as Becontree Cemetery.

14   George Currie was a Dagenham churchwarden for many years, and a founder member of the Barking and Dagenham Labourers' Friend Society in 1875.

15   After Mrs Stone's time the property became known as Eastbrookend House. A building named the Bell House stood in Rush Green Road near Beacontree Heath. It was demolished some time after 1938 and the Ford sports ground now stands on the site. The bell which had been on its roof was then transferred to Eastbrookend House, which then assumed the name of the Bell House.

16   One extremely large memorial in Dagenham parish churchyard, close to the church entrance, records the names of the Stone, Ford and Sutton families. They were evidently closely connected.

17   Personal communication (letter) from Julian Litten (author of the *English way of death*) dated 28th January 1991: 'I think we can safely say that the possibility of PC Clark having been buried upright is an exaggeration, delicately embroidered in its telling over the last one hundred and fifty years'.

18   *The Daily Mail,* 18th January 2005.

19   *The Essex Times,* 7th February 1931.

20   *The Evening Standard* 9th January 1939.

21   *The Evening News,* 25th February 1939.

22   *The Dagenham Post,* 26th March 1975 and 2nd April 1975.

23   Geoffrey Taylor: Who murdered Police Constable 313 K Clark? (article in the *Metropolitan Police History Society newsletter,* 1993).

24   Personal communication (letter) from Inspector Mark Clarkson, dated 17th January 2005, confirmed that new Dagenham officers are no longer taken to Clark's grave.

25   *The Essex Times,* 24th January 1885.

26   *The Essex Times,* 21st January 1885.

27   John Woodgate: *The Essex Police* (Terence Dalton, 1985) pp.53-58.

CHAPTER 15

[1] *The Times,* 22nd November 1839.

[2] *The Times,* 14th July 1846.

[3] Fred Brand: *A Barking Rose: a waterside story of the last century* (privately published, 1923) p.20.

[4] *Clark Murder File* (MEPO 3/53).

[5] *The Police Review and Parade Gossip,* 2nd December 1898.

[6] *The Morning Chronicle,* 6th July 1846.

[7] *The Weekly Dispatch,* 20th September 1846.

[8] Notes taken from interviews with Nellie Reader can be seen at Valence House Museum (*Beacontree Heath documents,* E1(900)).

[9] *The Essex Herald,* 7th September 1858.

[10] Ronald Pearsall: *The table-rappers: the Victorians and the occult,* (Sutton 2004, reprint of 1972 edition) pp. 29 & 36.

[11] Martin Fido & Keith Skinner: *The official encyclopaedia of Scotland Yard* (Virgin) revised edition, 2000, pp.475-478.

[12] *Archdeaconry of Essex marriage licences, bonds and allegations 1827* (Essex Record Office, D/AEL 1827).

[13] This section draws on unpublished research by Mark Shelden into the life of Mary Ann Smith. The couple's financial situation was clearly not good, as they appear many times in the records of Dagenham charities. They received, for example, countless coats, blankets and items of flannel and calico from the William Ford fund, the archives of which can be seen at Valence House Museum.

[14] According to an article in *the Times* 19th March 2005, images 'which appear at the moment when sleep recedes and which momentarily persist into waking life' are called 'hypnopompic visions'.

[15] From unpublished notes made by Lee Shelden from interviews with Bill Potter in the late 1980s.

[16] *The Essex Countryside* August 1966 vol 14 no 115 pp 754-55.

[17] Fido & Skinner, *Official encyclopaedia,* p.43.

[18] George Bakewell: *The Observations on the Construction of a New Police Force* (1842). This is quoted on the West Midlands Police Museum website (http://www.westmidlandspolicemuseum.co.uk).

[19] Fido & Skinner, *Official encyclopaedia,* pp. 73-74.

[20] Article by Inspector Forrest in the magazine *District Three: the magazine of No.3 District,* Metropolitan Police (Winter 1958).

[21] Information supplied from Pam Gaudio from material at the British Columbia Archives.

[22] *Police Orders* 9th April 1845 (MEPO 7/11).

[23] *The Times,* 12th November 1846.

[24] *The Colney Hatch Asylum committee minutes and reports, accounts, letter and visitor books, patient and staff records, and miscellaneous records* (London Metropolitan Archives, H12/CH).

Post-mortem reports on George Clark

1/ Given to the inquest hearing on 4th July 1846

Joseph Collin of Romford surgeon on oath says:

I was called to deceased at half past eight last evening. Found him in Mr Collier's field where it was stated he had been found. I then examined his head and found a large opening in the skull six or eight inches in circumference. The scalp was cut off and laying by the side of the head. This wound was likely to have been occasioned by some blunt instrument. The truncheon produced might have caused such a wound. This wound of itself would and must have caused death within three or four minutes. The portion of bone broken in could not last night be discovered. I then had him removed to where he now lies where I further examined him. I then discovered at the back part of his neck a wound an inch and a half in depth extending down to the spine. There was also on the top of the head where the scalp had been taken off a deep cut in the bone and extending very nearly through the bone caused no doubt by a cutlass or some such sharp instrument. The leather stock which he wore was cut through, and on removing that another deep wound was seen extending down to the vertebrae right through the oesophagus and windpipe, then under the right ear there was a wound extending horizontally coming out nearly to the opposite side. This last wound had the appearance of having been occasioned by a double edged knife. Either of these last wounds which I have described would have caused almost instant death. The face appeared to have been a good deal bruised, the chest was also bruised and there was a superficial cut over the left shoulder. The left hand forefinger was nearly cut through. The wound on the back of the head, the fracture of the skull would have caused death, or the wound in the throat through the windpipe, or the horizontal wound at the side of the neck under the right ear - either would cause death almost instantly. This morning I have been shown by Sergeant Parsons some pieces of bone. They are doubtless portions of deceased's skull.

2/ Given to a later inquest hearing on 23rd July 1846, after Clark's body had been exhumed

Joseph Collin re-examined on oath says:

I this morning examined again the body of deceased in company with Mr Butler surgeon of Romford. It was not a great deal more decomposed than when I last saw it. The wounds presented rather a different appearance looking larger owing to the integuments shrinking. My attention was directed [more?] particularly to the large opening in the skull with a view of ascertaining if a pistol ball had been discharged into the head. On examining the opposite side of the head there was no corresponding opening. I then examined the wound under the ear. This was situate about 2 inches under the ear. A cutlass belonging to the police was produced and I fitted it into the wound. It was the cutlass deceased had the night he was murdered. It would pass up an inch and a half. I feel certain this wound could not have been produced but by some sharp instrument or knife. I am positive it was not occasioned by a ball of any description. The cutlass might have produced it but I am of opinion it was not sharp enough to have done so. I found another fracture of the skull extending from the large wound downwards towards the neck. This was a defined wound and must have been occasioned by some blunt instrument and may have been done at the same time as the large wound. I have nothing further to state but that my former evidence is now confirmed by the result of this examination today. Either of the wounds about the head or neck was of itself sufficient to cause death. I feel satisfied the cutlass could not have cut through the stock and inflicted the wound in front of the neck. That on the back of the neck might have been done by a cutlass. My opinion is the two wounds on the throat – I mean the one through the stock and that under the right ear – were caused after deceased was on the ground and before he was dead. I came to that conclusion from a quantity of blood being found on the right shoulder and only a small spot in front of his shirt. The blood might flow 2 or 3 minutes after death.'

Charles Butler of Romford surgeon on oath says:

I was present today the 23rd inst. with Mr Collin and with him examined deceased. My attention was particularly directed to wounds with a view to ascertain if there had been any pistol ball or shot. We examined very minutely every part and there was no wound corresponding with that which would be found if a bullet had done it. There was no trace of a ball or shot to be found. I have heard the evidence given by Mr Collin and I coincide with him in every point.

3/ Evidence given at the prosecution of George Blewitt in 1858

Joseph Collin on his oath saith:

I am now residing at Elmsden in Essex I am now in Holy Orders. In the month of June 1846 I was practising as a Surgeon at Romford. On the evening of the 3rd of July 1846 I recollect being sent for to attend at Dagenham to see the body of a policeman. I attended and was shewn into a field of standing corn in the occupation of Mr Collier. I there saw the body of a policeman. The first thing I observed was about one half of the scalp cut off and laid under the deceased's head. There was a great quantity of blood. The body was afterwards removed to a house belonging to Mrs Gray called Hunters Hall and I there more minutely examined the body. The first wound was about 4 inches in length extending across the head from right to left deeply penetrating into the substance of the bone such a wound as might be produced by a cutlass. The second wound was a large hole on the left side of the head from 3 to 4 inches across and about 8 inches in circumference sufficiently large to admit my hand, it was jagged and there was a fracture of the bone extending from the lower edge of this large opening to the base of the skull. There was a third wound in front of the throat dividing all the soft parts through the gullet and windpipe completely down to the vertebrae corresponding exactly with the cut in the stock now produced. There was a fourth wound on the back of the neck, dividing the vessels, so as the head was nearly severed from the body.

There was a fifth wound just under the left ear communicating with the large wound in front, it appeared to be caused by a 2 edged knife or a dagger.

I think a pitchfork would not cause such a wound. The little finger of the left hand was nearly cut off and a small cut on the left shoulder. The chest appeared to have been very much bruised as if knocked about. The wounds were quite sufficient to cause almost immediate death. I attended the Inquest before Mr Lewis at the time at the Cross Keys, Dagenham.

Source: Clark murder file, National Archives (MEPO 3/53). Some punctuation has been added to the above transcriptions

POLICE OFFICERS KNOWN TO HAVE SERVED IN DAGENHAM IN THE 1840s (IN ORDER OF JOINING THE FORCE)

NAME	APPROX YEAR OF BIRTH	PLACE OF BIRTH	DATE OF JOINING	HEIGHT & FORMER OCCUPATION (IF KNOWN)	COLLAR NUMBER	WARRANT NUMBER	SERVICE DETAILS
Thomas **NORTON**	N/K	N/K	N/K		276K	N/K	N/K
John Burnside **FARNES**	1807	Southwark, Surrey	c.1831	Bookbinder	325K	7042	Dismissed 10 Nov 1846
James **HALL**	1795	Swaffham, Norfolk	5 Sept 1834	5' 9"	336K	9828	Transferred to Bow St Horse Patrol 4th Division 2 Jan 1837 (this later absorbed into Met) Retired on pension 29 November 1854 due to ill health
George **HARVEY**	1806	Brandeston, Suffolk	13 July 1835	5' 8"	165K	10681	Retired on pension 3 Aug 1858
Sgt Thomas **PEARSON**	1815	Barking, Essex	24 Nov 1836		32K	12213	Promoted Sergeant 13 Jan 1840 Died in service 23 Aug 1849
Abia **BUTFOY**	1810	Bethnal Green, Middlesex	23 Apr 1837	Weaver, Also Army 8 yrs	140K	12654	Dismissed 10 Nov 1846
Sgt Samuel **TEBENHAM**	1798	Framlingham, Suffolk	20 Nov 1837	5' 11" Butcher	36K	15536	Served in Bow St Horse Patrol 4th Div Promoted Sergeant 13 Jan 1840 Died in service 17 Sep 1845
Sgt William Richard **PARSONS**	1817	Norwich, Norfolk	30 Dec 1839	5' 7" Miller	36K	15787	Dismissed 9 Mar 1848
William Edward **HENNEM**	1820	Finsbury, Middlesex	13 Jan 1840			15967	Removed from K Division 8 April 1841 Resigned 2 Aug 1841
Thomas **KIMPTON**	1815	Hendon, Middlesex	13 Jan 1840	Saddler & harness maker	340K	16138	Dismissed 16 July 1847
Timothy **DREW**	1815	Kanturk, Cork, Ireland	14 May 1840	5' 10" Labourer	387K	17044	Resigned 24 July 1861
Joseph **POOLE**	1818	Barking, Essex	14 Apr 1841	6' 1"	374K	18198	Promoted Sergeant 30 Oct 1852 Retired on pension 20 May 1865
Sgt James **LEWIS**	1821	St Brides, Middlesex	12 Sep 1842	5' 9" Printer	4K	19661	Promoted Sergeant 2 Jan 1847 Acting Inspector 14 years Retired on pension 8 Dec 1864
Acting Sgt George **CORBIN**	1818	Northbourn, Sussex	24 Oct 1842	6' Labourer Also Army 6 years	43K	19743	Promoted Sergeant 16 August 1848 Retired on pension 24 September 1859
Timothy **HAYES**	N/K	N/K (Gave referees from Paddington & Marylebone, Middlesex)	24 Oct 1842			19744	Dismissed 11 May 1846
Isaac **HICKTON**	1813	Derby	12 Dec 1842	5' 9" Currier	85K	19850	Dismissed 16 July 1847
James **OLIVER**	N/K	N/K (Gave referees from Ticehurst, Sussex)	20 May 1844			21203	Dismissed 11 May 1846
Robert **GREAVES**	N/K	N/K (Gave referees from Leicester Square, London/Middlesex)	6 Jan 1845			21772	Dismissed 11 May 1846
George **CLARK**	1826	Battlesden, Bedfordshire	2 Jun 1845	Agricultural labourer	313K	22098	Murdered on duty 29/30 June 1846
Jonas **STEVENS**	N/K	N/K (Gave referees from Long Acre & Leather Lane, London)	18 May 1846		73K	23215	Dismissed 10 Nov 1846
George **DUNNING**	N/K	N/K (Gave referees from Clerkenwell, Middlesex)	6 July 1846		397K	23390	Transferred to Dagenham 17 August 1846 Resigned 26 Sep 1846

POLICE OFFICERS KNOWN TO HAVE SERVED IN DAGENHAM, 1850s & 1860s *(IN ORDER OF JOINING THE FORCE)*

NAME	APPROX YEAR OF BIRTH	PLACE OF BIRTH	HEIGHT	PREVIOUS OCCUPATION	DATE OF JOINING	COLLAR NUMBER	WARRANT NUMBER	SERVICE DETAILS
Frederick **STRATFORD**	1821	Blackfriars, Surrey	5' 7"	N/K	21 Nov 1842	K33	19820	Promoted to Sergeant & transferred to Dagenham 10 Jul 1847 Retired on pension 21 Jul 1876
William **MILES**	1823	Epsom, Surrey	N/K	N/K	23 Dec 1843	K76	20898	Resigned 6 Sep 1852
Edward **GRAY**	1824	Market Weighton, Yorks	5' 10"	Labourer	20 May 1844	K59	21202	Died in service 3 May 1863
Joshua **HITCHMAN**	1824	Bloxham, Oxon	5' 7"	Labourer	3 Aug 1846	N/K	23487	Dismissed 7 Aug 1865 ("Absent from duty with out leave and found drunk")
John Henry Beard **NICHOLLS**	1826	Cheltenham, Gloucs	N/K	N/K	7 Sep 1846	K348	23590	Resigned 5 May 1852
William **PEARSON**	1820	Linton, Kent	N/K	N/K	7 Dec 1846	N/K	23883	Resigned 20 July 1851on pension £25 per annum "having become disabled due to injuries received during the execution of his duty"
Charles **HONEYBOURN**	1826	Harefield, Middlesex	5' 9"	N/K	1 Nov 1847	K166	24894	Died in service 25 Sep 1864
James **BLAIN**	1823	Sandy, Beds	5' 8"	Groom	22 Nov 1847	K268	24958	Resigned 5 Dec 1867
Henry **GAYLER**	1822	Ayot St Peter, Herts	5' 8"	Labourer	24 July 1848	K429	25600	Dismissed 14 Sep 1864 ("Drunk while on duty")
George Champ **DEW**	1829	Bridport, Dorset	5' 7"	Ropemaker	16 July 1849	N/K	26920	Resigned 24 May 1876
Harry **SUGG**	1831	Appleshaw, Hants	N/K	N/K	15 Apr 1850	N/K	27547	Dismissed 31 Mar 1851
Samuel Henry **BROWN**	1826	Shepperton, Middlesex	5' 7"	Labourer	11 Nov 1850	K337	27983	Retired on pension 5 Apr 1867
John **RICHARDSON**	1828	Ross, Herefordshire	5' 9"	Labourer	14 Apr 1851	K176	29128	Dismissed 25 May 1861 ("Inside a public house 7 hours while on duty and brought away from tap room drunk")
Francis **RUSHTON**	1829	Longton, Staffs	5' 8"	Gamekeeper	17 Oct 1853	K113	31818	Died in service 3 Mar 1868
Thomas **SPURRIER**	1833	Epsom, Surrey	5' 11"	Butcher	30 Oct 1854	K358	33061	Resigned 20 Jan 1866
Edward Benjamin **KIDDLE**	1836	Forncett, Norfolk	5' 8"	Butcher	18 Dec 1854	K480	33161	Resigned 16 Oct 1872
Frederick **BAKER**	1834	Willingale, Essex	5' 9"	Labourer	21 May 1855	K239	33663	Promoted & transferred to R Division 19 May 1871
Stephen **BROOKER**	1834	Ditchling, Sussex	5' 7"	N/K	8 Oct 1855	K75	34083	Dismissed 12 Dec 1867 "Drunk when paraded for duty"
Henry J. **BADDERLY**	1837	Pimlico, Middlesex	5' 9"	Engraver	12 Apr 1858	K408	36946	Resigned 3 Jun 1861
Robert **WARD**	1837	Lingwood, Norfolk	5' 9"	N/K	7 Jun 1858	K368	37097	Transferred to Chatham 3 Dec 1860
John **ROWLAND**	1827	Church Taunton, Devon	5' 10"	N/K	13 Jun 1859	K344	38068	Transferred to S Division 28 Dec 1861
Thomas **AMES**	1835	Maidstone, Kent	5' 8"	Bricklayer	16 July 1860 Army 4 years	K430	39130	Dismissed 27 Nov 1862 ("Lying asleep in a manger while on duty")

The following served at Dagenham, but only limited information is available:
Joseph **HORWOOD** (K43), Police Constable **COLEMAN**, William **COOPER**

Select Bibliography

ANONYMOUS: *Five years penal servitude,* by one who endured it (Richard Bentley & Son, new edition, 1878)

ASCOLI, David: *The Queen's Peace* (Hamish Hamilton, 1979)

BARRETT, Andrew & HARRISON, Christopher (editors): *Crime and punishment in England: a sourcebook* (Routledge, 1999)

BRANCH-JOHNSON, William: *The English prison hulks* (Johnson, 1957)

BROWNE, Douglas G: *The rise of Scotland Yard* (Harrap, 1956)

CAMPBELL, Charles: *The intolerable hulks: British shipboard confinement 1776-1857* (Heritage Books, 1994)

CLIFFORD, Tony: *Barking & Dagenham buildings past & present* (London Borough of Barking & Dagenham Libraries, 1992)

CLIFFORD, Tony: *Dagenham pubs past & present* (London Borough of Barking & Dagenham Libraries, 1996)

COBB, Belton: *The first detectives* (Faber, 1957)

COBB, Belton: *Murdered on duty* (W.H. Allen, 1961)

DELL, Simon: *The Victorian policeman* (Shire, 2004)

DICKENS, Charles: *Selected journalism 1850-1870* (Penguin, 1997)

EMSLEY, Clive: *Crime and society in England 1750-1900* (Longman, 2nd edition 1996)

EMSLEY, Clive: *The English police: a political and social history* (Longman, 2nd edition 1996)

FIDO, Martin & SKINNER, Keith: *The official encyclopaedia of Scotland Yard* (Virgin, revised edition 2000)

JARVIS, Stan: *Essex murder casebook* (Countryside Books, 1994)

KENNISON, Peter & SWINDEN, David: *Behind the blue lamp: policing North and East London* (Coppermill Press, 2003)

LOCK, Joan: *Dreadful deeds and awful murders: Scotland Yard's first detectives* (Barn Owl Books, 1990)

LOCK, Joan: *Blue murder? Policemen under suspicion* (Hale, 1986)

MASON, Gary: *The official history of the Metropolitan Police* (Carlton, 2004)

MAYHEW, Henry & BINNY, John: *The criminal prisons of London and scenes of prison life* (C. Griffin, 1862)

O'LEARY, John G: *The book of Dagenham: a history* (Dagenham Public Libraries, 3rd edition 1964)

PULLING, Christopher: *Mr Punch and the police* (Butterworth, 1964)

RIGDEN, Reg: *The floating prisons of Woolwich and Deptford* (London Borough of Greenwich, 1976)

SHAWCROSS, J.P: *A history of Dagenham in the County of Essex* (Skeffington & Son, 2nd edition 1908)

STRATMANN, Linda: *Essex murders* (Sutton, 2004)

THOMAS, Donald: *The Victorian underworld* (John Murray, revised paperback edition 2003)

THURLEY, Simon: *Lost buildings of Britain* (Viking, 2004)

WHITMORE, Richard: *Victorian and Edwardian crime and punishment from old photographs* (Batsford, 1978)

Picture Credits

We would like to thank copyright holders for granting permission to use the following:

The Metropolitan Police Historical Collection for the illustrations on pages 10,12,36,93,106,114,148 and colour plates 3&4; Surrey Police Museum, p.23; Essex Police Museum, p.160; South Wales Police Museum, pp.111&140 plus the back cover image of the police officer; National Portrait Gallery, p.176; *Punch* magazine, p.18; Michael Gilham, p.134; Essex Record Office, p.224; Bedfordshire & Luton Archives & Record Service p.6 (top & bottom) and colour plate 1; London Borough of Havering Local Studies Library pp.123 & 162; London Borough of Redbridge Local Studies Library, p.41; London Borough of Barnet Local Studies Library, p.198; Greenwich Heritage Centre, p.180; *The Barking & Dagenham Post,* p.286 (bottom). The sampler pictured in colour plate 6 and the photographs on pages 231,234,236 & 242 are from private collections. The illustrations on pages 4,28,144,154, 250 (top & bottom), 254,255,257,258,264,286 (top),288, plus the endpaper map are either copyright of the authors or from the authors' private collections. The cartoon on p.113 is from the *Comic Almanack* 1843; the illustrations on pp.168,186 & 190 are from Mayhew & Binny's *Criminal prisons of London* (1862). Despite our best efforts we have currently been unable to trace the copyright holders of the illustrations on pages 38,40,84,91 & 128, and will be happy to rectify this in future editions. The remaining illustrations are courtesy of Valence House Museum, London Borough of Barking & Dagenham.

Acknowledgements

We are grateful for the assistance given to us by descendants of those involved in the case, particularly Margaret Wicks and George Hollingsworth; Valerie Butfoy; Doreen Maguire; Geri Zollinger and Ken Monson.

We are also indebted to the following for information and advice relating to police history: Ray Seal and Steve Earle, Val Sng, Maggie Bird and Chris Pilgrim, former and current staff of the Metropolitan Police Historical Collection, Charlton; Fred Feather and Sarah Ward, former and present curators of the Essex Police Museum; the late Bert Lockwood for sharing his knowledge of the Bow Street Horse Patrol and Ilford Gaol; Julia Mason of the South Wales Police Museum; Robin Gillis; Bernie Brown; Geoffrey Taylor; Bernie Barrell and Ronald Smith.

Heartfelt thanks are extended to the following, who were kind enough to share their memories of old Dagenham: the late Bill Potter; Rosemary Rogers; Phyllis Weatherhead; the late Jack West; Don and Jeremy West; Colin Wood. We would like to thank Mark Gentry and Barbara Barton for help with Holy Trinity Church, Barkingside.

We are also indebted to the following:

In **Bedfordshire:** Angela Knox; Mr & Mrs John Harris of Milton Bryant; Richard Ireland and Wendy Featherstone of Eversholt; Sue Edwards and the staff of Bedfordshire & Luton Archives & Record Service.

In **Elmdon, Essex:** Dr D.A. Melford OBE; the Reverend Mike Warren; Rector John Simmonds; Patricia Hunter; Marjorie Morgan.

In **Australia:** Wendy Baker; Val Date; Sue McBeth; Christine Morrison.

In **Canada:** Carol Hale; Pam Gaudio; David Wong.

Grateful acknowledgements are also due to: Carol Bailey; Jennifer M. Boyd-Cropley; Michael Farnham; Janet Green; Kate Henderson; Trudie Jackson; Paul Morton; Sharon Palmer; Alan Pearce; Sophie Pigott; Mike Stallion; Pam Woolcombe.

Finally, we would like to thank: Joyce A Shelden; Mark Shelden; Neal Stubbings; the staff of the Essex Record Office; Tony Clifford; the staff at Valence House Museum.

Notes on the authors

Linda Rhodes was baptized at Dagenham parish church, and brought up in Eastbrook Drive, just a stone's throw from the scene of George Clark's murder. In 2002 she gave a series of talks on the case, which eventually led to the writing of this book. Linda is currently Local Studies Librarian for Barking & Dagenham.

Lee Shelden also lived near Clark's beat as a child. He has long been regarded as the authority on the George Clark case, and acknowledged as such in the *Official Encyclopaedia of Scotland Yard*. Lee was also the driving force behind the events commemorating the 150th anniversary of the murder in 1996.

Kathryn Abnett is the daughter of a police officer. Her family have lived in Dagenham for over 200 years. Kathryn has contributed to several publications on the history of the borough, including *On the Home Front: Barking & Dagenham in World War 2,* and *Residents & Visitors: some Barking & Dagenham personalities.*